THE STATES AND THE NATION SERIES, of which this volume is part, is designed to assist the American people in a serious look at the ideals they have espoused and the experiences they have undergone in the history of the nation. The content of every volume represents the scholarship, experience, and opinions of its author. The costs of writing and editing were met mainly by grants from the National Endowment for the Humanities, a federal agency. The project was administered by the American Association for State and Local History, a nonprofit learned society, working with an Editorial Board of distinguished editors, authors, and historians, whose names are listed below.

EDITORIAL ADVISORY BOARD

James Morton Smith, General Editor
Director, State Historical Society
of Wisconsin

William T. Alderson, Director
American Association for
State and Local History

Roscoe C. Born
Vice-Editor
The National Observer

Vernon Carstensen
Professor of History
University of Washington

Michael Kammen, Professor of
American History and Culture
Cornell University

Louis L. Tucker
President (1972–1974)
American Association for
State and Local History

Joan Paterson Kerr
Consulting Editor
American Heritage

Richard M. Ketchum
Editor and Author
Dorset, Vermont

A. Russell Mortensen
Assistant Director
National Park Service

Lawrence W. Towner
Director and Librarian
The Newberry Library

Richmond D. Williams
President (1974–1976)
American Association for
State and Local History

MANAGING EDITOR

Gerald George
American Association for
State and Local History

Hawaii

A History

Ruth Tabrah

**With a Historical Guide
prepared by the editors of
the American Association for
State and Local History**

W. W. Norton & Company
New York · London

American Association for State and Local History
Nashville

Copyright © 1984, 1980
American Association for State and Local History

All rights reserved

First Edition

Published and distributed by W. W. Norton & Company, Inc.
500 Fifth Avenue
New York, New York 10110

Library of Congress Cataloguing-in-Publication Data

Tabrah, Ruth M
  Hawaii, a history.

  (The States and the Nation series)
  Bibliography: p.
  Includes index.
  1. Hawaii—History. I. Title. II. Series:
States and the Nation series.
DU625.T24   996.9   80-11671
ISBN 0-393-30220-2

Printed in the United States of America

3 4 5 6 7 8 9 0

There are so many who, knowingly and unknowingly, helped me in the writing of this bicentennial history of Hawaii. To all of them my deepest gratitude: State Archivist Agnes Conrad; Takao Ito; University of Hawaii Hamilton Library Hawaiian-Pacific Collection Curator David Kittelson; Connie Fukumoto; Kiyo Masuda; Joseph K. Mossman; Sung Dai Seu; former Speaker of the House Tadao Beppu; Bishop Yoshiaki Fujitani; Mr. and Mrs. Kinji Kanazawa; Tom McCabe; State Senator Neil Abercrombie; David K. Trask, Jr.; Chief Justice William Richardson; the late David Thompson of ILWU; the family of the late Koji Ariyoshi; Chad Taniguchi; Yasuki Arakaki; Philip Hooton; Duane and Sheila Black and the Florentino Hera family of Lanai; that superb writer of Hawaiiana, Alfons Korn; Hawaii State Librarian Ruth Itamura; the Reverend Darrow K. Aiona; Cecilia Lindho; Aluliki's Winona Rubin; Judge William Laube of Monterey, California; Gerald George of the American Association for State and Local History; and all the tremendous reference librarians of Hawaii State Library's Hawaii and Pacific Room, and the Hilo Public Library. Mahalo nui loa.

Contents

	Historical Guide to Hawaii	ix
	Invitation to the Reader	xxv
1	The Turning Point	3
2	Hawaiian Roots	11
3	The Great Kohala Chief	23
4	The Reign of Hiram Bingham	34
5	The Advent of Democracy	49
6	The Last of the Kamehamehas	66
7	The Beginning of the End	78
8	The "Reform Party"	94
9	*Aloha Oe:* Farewell to Thee	99
10	Territoriality	108
11	The Rise of Labor	125
12	The Roaring Twenties	135
13	Social Process	145
14	The Bitter Test of War	154
15	Victory: Overseas and at Home	176
16	Statehood	191
17	*Aloha Aina:* A Love for the Land	203
	Suggestions for Further Reading	225
	Index	227

Original Maps by Jean Tremblay
   Hawaii: Contemporary Map Keyed to Text   Facing page xxii
   Hawaii: Migration to the Hawaiian Islands   Facing page 208

Historical Guide

TO HAWAII

prepared by the editors of the
American Association for State and Local History

Introduction

The following pages offer the reader a guide to places in this state through which its history still lives.

This section lists and describes museums with collections of valuable artifacts, historic houses where prominent people once lived, and historic sites where events of importance took place. In addition, we have singled out for detailed description a few places that illustrate especially well major developments in this state's history or major themes running through it, as identified in the text that follows. The reader can visit these places to experience what life was like in earlier times and learn more about the state's rich and exciting heritage.

James B. Gardner and Timothy C. Jacobson, professional historians on the staff of the American Association for State and Local History, prepared this supplementary material, and the association's editors take sole responsibility for the selection of sites and their descriptions. Nonetheless, thanks are owed to many individuals and historical organizations, including those listed, for graciously providing information and advice. Our thanks also go to the National Endowment for the Humanities, which granted support for the writing and editing of this supplement, as it did for the main text itself.   —*The Editors*

Pu'uhonua o Hōnaunau

Hōnaunau

★ The royal line of *alii* or chiefs and the sacred laws of *kapu* dominated Hawaiian culture before the arrival of foreign settlers and missionaries in the early nineteenth century. As representatives of the gods, the *alii* presided over the elaborately detailed *kapu* system that regulated everyday life and buttressed the ancient Hawaiian religion. The punishment for

Restored temple house of Hale-O-Keawe

breaking *kapu* was death, unless the violator could reach a refuge sanctified by the *mana* or spiritual power of deified chiefs. The most sacred and best preserved such asylum is Pu'uhonua o Hōnaunau on the island of Hawaii. Now maintained as the Pu'uhonua o Hōnaunau National Historical Park, this place of refuge and the adjoining ancestral home of the Hawaiian royal family together constitute an impressive reminder of the way life used to be in Hawaii.

The *kapu* system formed the structure of Hawaiian life for perhaps a thousand years. This ancient code prescribed the proper conduct for everything from land ownership to sexual relations. Dietary prohibitions were particularly strict, extending to what foods women could eat and dictating separate food preparation and dining by the sexes. Because these laws were believed to be divinely given, violation was an offense to the gods and thus required punishment by death lest an offended god take his revenge out on everyone. No matter what the circumstances or how minor the violation, breaking *kapu* brought a sentence of death, unless the offender escaped to a place of refuge like that at Pu'uhonua o Hōnaunau.

The concept of a refuge or asylum hinged on the Hawaiians' reverence for *mana,* the special spiritual power of the high chiefs. The chiefs' *mana* pervaded not just their persons but their possessions and

x

even the ground they walked on. Respect for *mana* prohibited commoners from walking in a chief's footsteps, touching his possessions,
or letting their shadows fall on the palace grounds. As with other *kapu,*
violation would lead to death. Yet the sanctity of *mana* also provided
the basis for the *pu'uhonua* or place of refuge. *Mana* remained in the
bones of dead chiefs and hence sanctified the mausoleum temple or
heiau in which these bones were placed. Protected by the dead chiefs'
mana, these temples came to be regarded as sanctuaries or refuges for
breakers of *kapu.* After a ceremony of absolution performed by the
priest or *kahuna,* the violator could then return home safely, free from
danger. Others who sought refuge included defeated warriors awaiting
the outcome of battle and noncombatants—the aged, the young, those
unable to protect themselves during the fierce island wars.

Pu'uhonua o Hōnaunau was one of six such refuges on the island
of Hawaii. The sanctuary adjoined the ancestral home of the royal
lineage that produced Kamehameha, the great Kohala chief who united
all the islands in the early nineteenth century. The palace grounds
included a collection of thatched buildings, royal fish ponds, and a
royal canoe landing, all forbidden to commoners and protected by
warriors. Separating the palace grounds from the refuge was a massive
stone wall approximately one thousand feet long, ten feet high, and
seventeen feet wide. This wall was erected about 1550, perhaps as a
monument to Keawe-ku-i-ke-ka'ai, the ruling chief at the time. After
his death, a *heiau* was erected to house his remains. Since his *mana*
remained in his bones, this mausoleum temple sanctified the area. The
sacredness of the Hale o Keawe *heiau* increased further with the burial
of at least twenty-two more Kona chiefs over the next two and a half
centuries, ending with the deification of a son of Kamehameha in the
early nineteenth century.

According to legend, Kaahumanu, the favorite wife of Kamehameha, took refuge at the Pu'uhonua o Hōnaunau after a quarrel with
the great chief. Her pet dog revealed her hiding place, however, and
she and Kamehameha reconciled. At his death in 1819, she became
kuhina nui—a sort of executive officer, with more power than a prime
minister—to his heir and exerted enormous influence over the affairs
of the kingdom. In particular, she instigated the break with *kapu* later
that same year. At her encouragement, Kamehameha II defied the sacred laws of *kapu* and deliberately committed taboos long forbidden

by the old religion. This defiance of the power of the gods marked the end of *kapu* and signalled a basic change in Hawaiian culture. Their perspectives broadened by decades of foreign contact, the Hawaiians refused to submit any longer to the religious tyranny of their ancestors. In the wake of this development, *pu'uhonau* ceased to function as well, and *heiau* were dismantled throughout the islands. The *heiau* at Pu'uhonau o Hōnaunau survived because of continued veneration of the remains of Kamehameha's ancestors, but after the bones were removed in 1829, this temple was also demolished.

The Hawaiian royal family retained ownership of the palace and temple grounds until the late nineteenth century. In the 1890s Charles R. Bishop purchased the property and added it to his estate. In 1961, the 180-acre site became a national historical park under the administration of the National Park Service. Now restored to its appearance in the late eighteenth century, the Pu'uhonua o Hōnanau National Historical Park is open to visitors daily.

The focus of the park is the palace-refuge complex. The palace grounds include several examples of early housing construction, a special stone on which the chiefs played the game of *kōnane,* the *keone' ele* or royal canoe landing, and a royal fish pond or *he-lei-pālalu.* The massive L-shaped stone wall that separates the palace from the *pu'uhonua* has survived virtually intact for over four centuries, although it was repaired in 1902 and again in 1963–1964. At its north end stands the reconstructed Hale o Keawe *heiau.* An 1823 sketch by the Reverend William Ellis, an American missionary, made possible an accurate reconstruction of the structure on the original stone platform. The remnants of two earlier *heiau* also remain in the refuge, as well as a *kōnane* stone and the Keoua stone, according to legend the favorite resting place of a Kona chief. The Kaahumanu stone marks the location where Kaahumanu hid during her flight from Kamehameha. Elsewhere in the park are other temple foundations, a village site, burial caves, petroglyphs, and sledding tracks used for recreation by the chiefs. Park programs include orientation talks by park interpreters, a self-guided tour of the refuge and palace grounds, and a living-history program of traditional Hawaiian crafts and skills.

The Pu'uhonua o Hōnaunau National Historical Park preserves the most historically significant remnant of the traditional society that reigned in Hawaii prior to the arrival of outsiders at the close of the eighteenth century. It offers a rich opportunity to learn about and experience that ancient island culture.

Mission Houses Museum

Honolulu

★ When Hiram Bingham and his fellow missionaries journeyed from New England to Hawaii in 1819 and 1820, not even the most optimistic anticipated the profound impact their work was to have on the island kingdom. While they were sent principally to bring the Christian religion to the native residents, over the forty years that followed their

Missionaries' frame house

influence extended to politics and government, the economy, education, and social customs. The missionaries filled the void created by the crumbling of the traditional island culture and provided direction and purpose essential to the emergence of modern Hawaii. The three structures that served as the mission's headquarters have been preserved as the Mission Houses Museum, a fitting monument to these men and women and their pivotal roles in shaping nineteenth-century Hawaiian society.

In 1819, the American Board of Commissioners for Foreign Missions, a Congregational organization, dispatched Bingham and his associates to establish the Sandwich Islands Mission. The Pioneer Company included seven married couples, five children, and three young Hawaiians who had been educated at the Foreign Mission School in Connecticut. After a six-month voyage aboard the *Thaddeus,* the group arrived in the Hawaiian islands in April 1820 and shortly thereafter established the first mission station—four grass houses just outside Honolulu. These temporary structures not only provided shelter for the missionary families but also served as a focus for mission activities

during the first year and a half. Although a prefabricated house arrived
by ship from Boston on Christmas day, 1820, it was August of the
following year before the first family moved into it. The residence was
not the island's first frame structure, but it was certainly the largest
and required the king's permission to construct. Once King Liholiho
consented, the missionaries erected the four-bedroom structure, sup-
plementing the pre-cut lumber with salvaged ship timbers and native
materials. When completed, the simple frame house stood as an oasis
of New England culture within the foreign land.

In addition to providing much-needed residential space, the new
structure served as a center for mission programs. Principal among
these was Christianizing the Hawaiians. During their first couple of
years, the Americans made little headway, but the conversion of Kaahumanu, the new young king's chief advisor (and his late father's
favorite wife), in 1823 won broader acceptance for their teachings.
Under the influence of Bingham, the mission's leader, the island kingdom became a virtual theocracy; New England Protestantism took the
place of the old *kapu* system in ordering the lives of the Hawaiians.
The missionaries' influence soon extended as well to the nation's diplomatic relations, political development, and economic direction. The
symbol of the mission's central role in Hawaiian life was Kawaiahao
Church, a massive stone New England-style church designed by
Bingham and constructed between 1839 and 1842. Adjoining the mission station, the new structure dominated the city long after the mission closed.

Another major goal of the Sandwich Islands Mission was to bring
literacy to the islands. The Hawaiian language had never been committed to writing, so the missionaries faced an unenviable task. Although it took years of work to establish a phonetic standard, the first
spelling sheet in Hawaiian was printed in 1822, when the mission
press first began operations. The missionaries had brought the small
second-hand Ramage press with them on board the *Thaddeus,* but other
duties prevented printer Elisha Loomis from setting up shop until January 1822. In the years that followed, the press turned out volumes of
printed material in the Hawaiian language, ranging from a translation
of the Bible to textbooks and handbills. The press thus became the
cornerstone of the mission's education program, providing the materials for a network of schools extending to every district in the islands.

By the mid-1840s, Hawaii had one of the highest literacy rates in the world.

The establishment of a network of seventeen mission stations testified to the expansion of activities in the mission's first two decades. To staff these, the ABCFM dispatched twelve more companies of missionaries, including ministers, doctors, printers, teachers, and business agents. The size of the mission operations complicated the work of the Honolulu headquarters. For example, someone had to coordinate the distribution of food, clothing, furniture, and other supplies required by the Americans. When grass huts proved unsuitable as warehouses, Levi Chamberlain, the mission's business agent, began construction of a more permanent facility in 1830. The two-story coral-block structure, not completed until December 1831, provided space for a business office, storage, and living quarters for the Chamberlain family. Between it and the frame house, the mission in 1841 erected a bedroom wing—thus completing the present-day complex of mission houses.

The Sandwich Islands Mission proved enormously successful in its work, and the ABCFM began in the late 1840s to encourage the independence of the Hawaiian churches. Finally in 1863 the board withdrew its financial support and closed the mission. Some of the missionaries returned to the United States; but others stayed on, continuing the mission's work or taking active roles in island politics and business. The mission property remained in private hands until the early twentieth century, when the three main buildings became the property of the Hawaiian Mission Children's Society, a genealogical society made up of the missionaries' descendants.

The Mission Houses Museum now stands as the oldest and most significant symbol of the role of Protestant missionaries in nineteenth-century Hawaii. The restored frame house erected in 1821, open to visitors, includes parlors, bedrooms, kitchens, and cellar and reflects the missionaries' New England roots and their communal living arrangements during the early years. Furnishings include items imported from the United States, China, and elsewhere, a variety of native crafts, and even some pieces hand-made by the missionaries—a mixed collection that illustrates the various cultural influences in Hawaiian society. On the other side of the museum complex stands the Chamberlain house. Of particular interest are the dutch doors and block-and-tackle, which recall the structure's earlier function as a storehouse.

Between the two buildings is the bedroom wing to the frame house. Erected about 1841, the small coral building now houses the museum's printing exhibits.

In addition to tours of the historic properties in the complex, the museum sponsors formal exhibits, school programs, and research facilities. It also provides a walking tour of historic sites in downtown Honolulu, including Kawaiahao Church and Iolani Palace. Although the city has many sites associated with the history of Hawaii in the nineteenth and early twentieth centuries, none surpass the Mission Houses Museum in illuminating the forces that shaped the Hawaiian nation in the mid-nineteenth century.

U.S.S. *Arizona* Memorial

Pearl Harbor

★ Few events in recent history rival in significance the Japanese attack on the United States naval base at Pearl Harbor on December 7, 1941. The immediate consequence was the United States' entry into World War II, but perhaps more significant in the long term was how that event altered the course of American

Memorial at Pearl Harbor

social, economic, and political life and influenced the structure of international relations. What is often ignored, however, is the impact of the event on Hawaiian history. In the wake of the attack, the American territory underwent a controversial period of tight military rule that had enormous impact on the shaping of contemporary Hawaii. The U.S.S. *Arizona* Memorial commemorates this pivotal event and honors the thousands who lost their lives there.

Pearl Harbor comprises a series of natural locks on the south coast of Oahu near Honolulu. Named for the pearl oysters that grew in the water there, the harbor went undeveloped until the late nineteenth century. In 1884 the United States obtained exclusive rights to establish a fuel and supply base there, but it was 1902 before dredging operations removed part of a coral bar that limited full access by deep-draft ships. With that obstacle out of the way, the United States proceeded with plans to develop the harbor as a strategic base for American naval operations in the Pacific. In 1916 Pearl Harbor was made the head-quarters of the Fourteenth Naval District.

Over the next twenty-five years, the United States invested considerable sums of money in building up the installation. By 1941 the base included a battleship dock, a floating drydock, a large repair basin, a fuel depot, a submarine base, a section base, the district headquarters, and the Naval Air Station on Ford Island. The installation's facilities and strategic location gained significance for the United States in 1940 and 1941, when deteriorating relations with Japan threatened American interests in the Pacific. Recognizing that the Hawaii-based Pacific Fleet was the key to United States military strength in the region, the Japanese government apparently began making plans to attack the Pearl Harbor installation as early as December 1940. Negotiations with the United States continued into November 1941, but by mid-October the Japanese Navy General Staff had approved attack plans, expecting a quick decisive victory that would cripple the United States. On November 26, the Japanese navy began moving into place, and by December 7 the warships had arrived at the planned launch position 275 miles north of Oahu. At 6:00 a.m. the first wave of fighters, bombers, and torpedo planes headed for their target.

Despite cautionary alerts from Washington and defense preparations by local civilian officials, the naval base at Pearl Harbor was not prepared for the Japanese attack, which first hit at 7:55 a.m. In two waves of bombing that lasted until about 9:45 a.m., the Japanese either sank or seriously damaged eighteen American warships, including six Pacific Fleet battleships moored on "Battleship Row," and destroyed or damaged nearly two hundred fifty aircraft. Deaths totaled 2,403, including Navy, Army and Marine personnel and sixty-eight civilians, and over a thousand more were wounded. The Navy lost in the one attack three times as many men as in the Spanish-American War and World War I combined. In contrast to the devastating American losses, their assailants had only 164 casualties and lost only twenty-nine planes, five midget submarines, and one I-Class sub.

Over half the American fatalities came from the bombing of the U.S.S. *Arizona*. Launched in 1915 and modernized in 1929, the thirty-one-thousand-ton battleship was one of the six units in the Pacific Fleet Battle Force moored on the southeast shore of Ford Island. The *Arizona* was one of the first targets of the Japanese: only fifteen minutes into the attack a 1,600 pound armor-piercing bomb ripped into the vessel and set off a massive explosion in the powder magazine. Within nine minutes, the ship broke in half and sank to the bottom of the harbor. Of the 1,550 men on board, only 289 survived. After the attack ended, only about 150 bodies could be pulled from the wreckage, leaving the bodies of approximately 1,100 Navy and Marine personnel entombed there.

Luckily for the United States, its aircraft carriers were not in port and escaped damage. Of the battleships, only the *Arizona,* the *Utah,* and the *Oklahoma* were not salvaged. The shipyards, fuel storage areas, and submarine base suffered only slight damage. While certainly crippling American military strength in the Pacific, the Pearl Harbor attack did not knock the United States out of the picture. On December 8, the United States declared war on Japan, thereby entering World War II. The details of the war and its impact on American life and world order are familiar to many, but few understand the problems Hawaii endured during the course of the war. Military rule severely abridged civilian rights, and the injustices of that era had significant repercussions for Hawaiian politics and society in the postwar era.

The *Arizona* remains today at the bottom of Pearl Harbor as a tomb for those interred in its hull and as a memorial to the 1941 tragedy. In 1962, a white concrete memorial was erected over the sunken battleship. Resting on pilings driven deep into the coral rock harbor floor, the memorial includes a bell room housing the ship's bell, a semi-open room for ceremonies and observation, and a shrine room, where the names of the 1177 sailors and Marines killed on the ship have been engraved on a white marble wall. A flagpole affixed to the mainmast of the *Arizona* still flies the American flag, a privilege extended by the Navy to no other inactive ship. On the shoreline overlooking the harbor is a visitor center erected in 1980. This structure provides a variety of support facilities, including a theater where visitors can view a documentary film on Pearl Harbor and a museum that provides exhibits on the *Arizona* and the Japanese assault. All are located within the boundaries of the Pearl Harbor Naval Base, which still remains the headquarters of the United States Pacific Fleet.

Visitors to present-day Hawaii are usually most intrigued by the state's exotic Polynesian heritage and its luxury resort atmosphere. They often fail to realize that this island paradise has had its own share of the social, economic, and political problems that vacationers think they have left behind. The U.S.S. *Arizona* dramatically calls attention to one tragic event and the obstacles and challenges it posed for twentieth-century Hawaii.

Other Places of Interest

*The following suggest other places of
historical interest to visit. We recommend that
you check hours of operation in advance.*

ALA MOANA HOTEL, *2365 Kalakaua Avenue, Honolulu, Oahu.* The oldest
hotel in Waikiki, built 1901.

ALOHA TOWER, *Pier 9, Honolulu Harbor, Honolulu, Oahu.* Ten-story
building constructed in 1926 and symbolic of early tourism industry; used
by the military in World War II.

BERNICE P. BISHOP MUSEUM, *1355 Kalhiki Street, Honolulu, Oahu.*
Natural and human history, with rare examples of canoes, shields, head-
dresses, ceremonial objects, featherwork, and other artifacts from Hawaiian
life pre-contact to modern era.

CHINATOWN HISTORIC DISTRICT, *bounded approximately by Beretania
Street, Nuuanu Stream, Nuuanu Avenue, and Honolulu Harbor, Honolulu,
Oahu.* Center of Chinese life, with early-twentieth-century buildings and
Hawaii Chinese History Center at 111 N. King Street.

COOK LANDING SITE, *two miles southwest of state 50, southwest section
of Waimea Bay, Kauai.* Where Capt. James Cook, the first Western visitor
to the islands, disembarked in 1778.

FALLS OF CLYDE, Pier 5, Honolulu Harbor, Honolulu, Oahu. An 1878
four-masted sailing ship used as a freighter, passenger ship, oil tanker, and
now a floating museum taking passengers on rides in Mamala Bay.

GROVE FARM HOMESTEAD MUSEUM, state 58 one mile southeast of
Lihue, Kauai. Sugar complex begun in 1854 and in use until 1978.

HALE HOIKEIKE (OLD BAILEY HOUSE), *Iao Valley Road, Wailuku, Maui.*
Example of architecture of early missionary houses, begun in 1833 and built
of lava rock and stucco; includes a museum.

HANALEI MUSEUM, *Hanalei, Kauai.* Rice implements and furniture of different ethnic groups living on the island, in an 1880s plantation-style house.

HAWAII VOLCANOES NATIONAL PARK, *Hawaii.* Fossil footprints of
men, women, children, and hogs left after a 1790 eruption of Kiluanea
volcano; visitor center.

HONOLULU ACADEMY OF ARTS, *900 S. Beretania Street, Honolulu,
Oahu.* Traditional arts of Oceania, collection of Japanese prints, Asian art

(including bronzes and furniture), and traditional and contemporary Western art.

HULIHEE PALACE, *Alii Drive, Kailua-Kona, Hawaii.* Restored lava and stucco house begun in 1838, with later alterations; built for early island governor and later owned by King Kalakaua. Museum with exhibits of tapa and featherwork.

IOLANI PALACE, *364 S. King Street, Honolulu, Oahu.* Elegant seat of Hawaiian government after 1893, with ornate carved woods and plaster cornices; occupied by King Kalakaua and Queen Liliuokalani and later the territorial capitol.

KALAUPAPA NATIONAL HISTORIC PARK, *Molokai.* Located on peninsula where Father Damien De Veuster, a Belgian priest, gave his life caring for victims of Hansen's disease (leprosy) in the late nineteenth century.

KAMAKAHONU, *northwest edge of Kailua Bay north and west of Kailua Wharf, Kailua-Kona, Hawaii.* Temple remains, stone walls, and royal platform from last residence of King Kamehameha in early nineteenth century.

KAUAI MUSEUM, *4428 Rice Street, Lihue, Kauai.* Exhibits of items from Hawaii, with emphasis on Kauai, and ethnic displays.

KEIAWA HEIAU, *Aeia Heights Drive, Aeia, Oahu.* Small prehistoric structure surrounded by low walls, used as temple of healing.

LAHAINA HISTORIC DISTRICT, *west side of Maui on state 30.* Seaport that was center of whaling industry in 1800s and capital of Maui. Includes Baldwin House, 1835; Hale Paahao Prison, 1851; Lahainaluna missionary school, founded 1831; and Hale Pa'i Printing House.

LYMAN HOUSE MEMORIAL MUSEUM, *276 Haili Street, Hilo, Hawaii.* Restored Lyman house, built in 1839 for missionaries; adjacent modern natural-history museum with Hawaiiana, missionary, and ethnic collections.

MOOKINI HEIAU, *northern tip of Hawaii one mile west of Upolu Point Airport, near Hawi, Hawaii.* Remains of sacrificial temple, with twenty-foot stone walls and birthstone of Kamehameha I.

OLD RUSSIAN FORT, *state 50, 200 yards southwest of Waimea River bridge, Kauai.* Remains of outer walls and foundations of Russian fort built 1816–1817.

PUU-KOHOLA HEIAU NATIONAL HISTORIC SITE, *north end of Hawaii off state 26, about one mile southeast of Kawaihae, Hawaii.* Stone temple and wall built by Kamehameha I and center of his effort to unify the islands.

PUU O MAHUKA HEIAU, *state 83, four miles northeast of Haleiwa, Oahu.* Built before contact with Westerners: largest temple on island and reputed to be where Vancouver's men were sacrificed.

QUEEN EMMA SUMMER PALACE, *2913 Pali Highway, Honolulu, Oahu.* Restored home of Emma and Kamehameha IV, with furnishings and memorabilia of family, including tapa, featherwork, and quilts; built 1847.

ROYAL MAUSOLEUM, *2261 Nuuanu Avenue, Honolulu, Oahu.* Completed in 1865, chapel added 1922; where Kamehameha family members and ancient chiefs are interred.

ULA PO HEIAU, *off Kailua Road, Kailua, Oahu.* Prehistoric terrace temple with small enclosures and stone mounds.

U.S. ARMY MUSEUM, *Battery Randolph, Kalia Road, Fort DeRussy, Honolulu, Oahu.* Military exhibits related to activity of U.S. Army in the Pacific; in a pre-World War I coast artillery defense bastion.

WAIOLI MISSION DISTRICT, *off state 56, Hanalei, Kauai.* Complex of church, community hall, mission house, and other structures related to missionary activity begun in the 1830s; an early restoration effort in 1921 with unusual mixture of Western and Polynesian styles of architecture.

WASHINGTON PLACE, *320 S. Beretania Street, Honolulu, Oahu.* Built about 1846; where Hawaiian governors have lived since 1921.

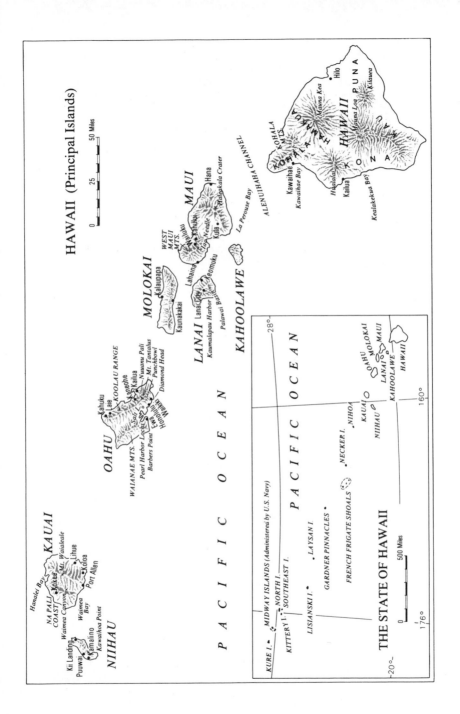

HAWAII (Principal Islands)

50 Miles
25
0

KAUAI

Hanalei Bay
NA PALI COAST
Mokee
Lihue
Waimea Canyon
Mt. Waialeale
Waimea Bay
Koloa
Port Allen
Kii Landing
Puuwai
Kamalino
Kawaihoa Point

NIIHAU

P A C I F I C   O C E A N

OAHU

Kahuku
Laie
KOOLAU RANGE
Kailua
Kaneohe
Nuuanu Pali
Mt. Tantalus
Punchbowl
Diamond Head
Schofield
Wahiawa
Ewa
Honolulu
WAIANAE MTS.
Pearl Harbor Locks
Barbers Point

MOLOKAI

Kalaupapa
Kaunakakai

LANAI

Lanai City
Kaumalapau Harbor
Palawai Basin

MAUI

Hana
Haleakala Crater
Kahului
WEST MAUI MTS.
Wailuku
Waiehu
Lahaina
Kula
Honokau
Maalaea
La Perouse Bay

KAHOOLAWE

ALENUIHAHA CHANNEL

HAWAII

Hilo
Mauna Kea
Mauna Loa
Kilauea
KOHALA MTS.
Kawaihae
Kawaihae Bay
Hilalala
Kailua
Kealakekua Bay

K O H A L A
H A M A K U A
P U N A
K A U
K O N A

P A C I F I C   O C E A N

THE STATE OF HAWAII

28°

KURE I.
MIDWAY ISLANDS (Administered by U.S. Navy)
KITTERY I.
NORTH I.
SOUTHEAST I.
LISIANSKI I.
LAYSAN I.
GARDNER PINNACLES
FRENCH FRIGATE SHOALS
NECKER I.
NIHOA
KAUAI
NIIHAU
OAHU
MOLOKAI
LANAI
MAUI
KAHOOLAWE
HAWAII

500 Miles
0

176°
160°
20°

Invitation to the Reader

IN 1807, former President John Adams argued that a complete history of the American Revolution could not be written until the history of change in each state was known, because the principles of the Revolution were as various as the states that went through it. Two hundred years after the Declaration of Independence, the American nation has spread over a continent and beyond. The states have grown in number from thirteen to fifty. And democratic principles have been interpreted differently in every one of them.

We therefore invite you to consider that the history of your state may have more to do with the bicentennial review of the American Revolution than does the story of Bunker Hill or Valley Forge. The Revolution has continued as Americans extended liberty and democracy over a vast territory. John Adams was right: the states are part of that story, and the story is incomplete without an account of their diversity.

The Declaration of Independence stressed life, liberty, and the pursuit of happiness; accordingly, it shattered the notion of holding new territories in the subordinate status of colonies. The Northwest Ordinance of 1787 set forth a procedure for new states to enter the Union on an equal footing with the old. The Federal Constitution shortly confirmed this novel means of building a nation out of equal states. The step-by-step process through which territories have achieved self-government and national representation is among the most important of the Founding Fathers' legacies.

The method of state-making reconciled the ancient conflict between liberty and empire, resulting in what Thomas Jefferson called an empire for liberty. The system has worked and remains unaltered, despite enormous changes that have taken

place in the nation. The country's extent and variety now surpass anything the patriots of '76 could likely have imagined.
The United States has changed from an agrarian republic into a
highly industrial and urban democracy, from a fledgling nation
into a major world power. As Oliver Wendell Holmes remarked
in 1920, the creators of the nation could not have seen completely how it and its constitution and its states would develop.
Any meaningful review in the bicentennial era must consider
what the country has become, as well as what it was.

The new nation of equal states took as its motto *E Pluribus
Unum*—"out of many, one." But just as many peoples have
become Americans without complete loss of ethnic and cultural
identities, so have the states retained differences of character.
Some have been superficial, expressed in stereotyped images—
big, boastful Texas, "sophisticated" New York, "hillbilly"
Arkansas. Other differences have been more real, sometimes instructively, sometimes amusingly; democracy has embraced
Huey Long's Louisiana, bilingual New Mexico, unicameral Ne-
braska, and a Texas that once taxed fortunetellers and spawned
politicians called "Woodpecker Republicans" and "Skunk
Democrats." Some differences have been profound, as when
South Carolina secessionists led other states out of the Union in
opposition to abolitionists in Massachusetts and Ohio. The result was a bitter Civil War.

The Revolution's first shots may have sounded in Lexington
and Concord; but fights over what democracy should mean and
who should have independence have erupted from Pennsylvania's Gettysburg to the "Bleeding Kansas" of John Brown,
from the Alamo in Texas to the Indian battles at Montana's
Little Bighorn. Utah Mormons have known the strain of isolation; Hawaiians at Pearl Harbor, the terror of attack; Georgians
during Sherman's march, the sadness of defeat and devastation.
Each state's experience differs instructively; each adds understanding to the whole.

The purpose of this series of books is to make that kind of understanding accessible, in a way that will last in value far
beyond the bicentennial fireworks. The series offers a volume
on every state, plus the District of Columbia—fifty-one, in all.

We have asked authors not for comprehensive chronicles, nor for research monographs or new data for scholars. Bibliographies and footnotes are minimal. We have asked each author for a summing up—interpretive, sensitive, thoughtful, individual, even personal—of what seems significant about his or her state's history. What distinguishes it? What has mattered about it, to its own people and to the rest of the nation? What has it come to now?

To interpret the states in all their variety, we have sought a variety of backgrounds in authors themselves and have encouraged variety in the approaches they take. They have in common only these things: historical knowledge, writing skill, and strong personal feelings about a particular state. Each has wide latitude for the use of the short space. And if each succeeds, it will be by offering you, in your capacity as a *citizen* of a state *and* of a nation, stimulating insights to test against your own.

James Morton Smith
General Editor

Hawaii

A History

1

The Turning Point

IN 1898, the end of Hawaii's political independence signaled a strange turn in American policy, a turn by which
Hawaii was to pose sixty years of challenge to the practice of the federal government's democratic ideals. After more
than twenty years of statehood, that challenge continues.

To be Hawaiian, whether by blood, residence, or cultural allegiance, is in contemporary Hawaii a highly emotional choice.
Disharmony, ardent and occasionally violent protest, the clash
of ideals and values, the struggle for political and economic
advantage, are dominant strands of past history and present experience.

In 1978–1979, islanders celebrated the bicentennial of the
first Hawaiian contact with western ideas and technology in the
accidental visit of the British expedition of Captain James Cook.
Since 1778–1779, when the population of these islands was totally Hawaiian, an increasing stream of visitors, immigration
from every part of the world, and intermarriage have now produced as cosmopolitan a community as any on this planet. Yet
the Hawaiian-ness of this eight-island American state and its
vast archipelago of islets, reefs, and shoals has not been lost in
a people whose blood, lifestyle, speech patterns, values, and
cuisine blend East and West—Polynesian, Asian, Malay,
Hispanic, and Caucasian.

No one single element in the multicultural population of mod-

ern Hawaii is a majority. No one single culture dominates as
does that of Hawaiian, which less than a century ago seemed
doomed to extinction. The special identity of modern Hawaii is
this Hawaiian-ness, and yet Hawaiians, whose values and culture and, to an amazing extent, language give these islands their
unique character, wish now to win legal status as "native Americans." This is one of the paradoxes that gives this fiftieth state
its special character.

More than a thousand years ago, the Polynesian ancestors of
contemporary Hawaiians settled these islands, bringing with
them the focal value of *aloha aina,* with its meaning of deep
love for the land of the islands and for the seas that surround
them, of respect for all the life that land and sea sustain. It was
a value that carried a natural ethic of conservation and resource
protection. Were I to choose a subtitle for this bicentennial history, it would be *"Aloha Aina:* the making of modern Hawaii,"
for it is this spirit that has sustained islanders through the bitter
tests of loyalties and identity in a turbulent labor history,
through the difficult aftermath of Pearl Harbor and the army's
rule of Hawaii in World War II, a spirit and slogan with which
Hawaiian activists of the 1970s identified themselves. Paradox:
the very decade in which a resurgence of *aloha aina* was heard
was the decade in which high rises mushroomed in Honolulu
and on Maui, freeways paved miles of Honolulu's small densely
populated island, Oahu, and the rate of crimes against people
and property rose alarmingly.

Until 1893, these islands that stretch between nineteen and
twenty-two degrees of latitude north of the equator, some two
thousand miles west of the Pacific coast of the United States,
were an independent Polynesian kingdom. In January 1893, a
small group of American residents—many of them Hawaiian-
born missionary sons—staged a short, successful, and nearly
bloodless revolution in which they overthrew the Hawaiian
monarchy and deposed Liliuokalani, Hawaii's queen. The sole
aim of these men was to accomplish the annexation of Hawaii to
the United States, and for five years, until their ambitions were
satisfied, they governed the islands as an oligarchy under the
name Republic of Hawaii.

The entire spectrum of two hundred years of Hawaiian history, and the background of American interest in and influence on the Hawaiian Kingdom is best understood by starting with the experience of Annexation Day, and the ceremony that marked the Republic of Hawaii's successful conclusion, August 12, 1898. That date and that event mark a turning point in both Hawaiian and American history.

Few Hawaiians were in the crowd waiting for the walking gates to Iolani Palace to open that humid August morning in Honolulu, the capital, the largest town, and the center of commerce of the island chain. In 1898, Hawaiians had become a minority in the population of their islands. For them Annexation Day was a day of lamentation and despair. In vain, thirty-seven thousand of them—nearly every man, woman, and child of Hawaiian ancestry—had signed a petition to the United States Congress and to the American president protesting:

> We particularly resent the presumption of being transferred like a flock of sheep, or bartered like a horde of savages, by an unprincipled minority of aliens who have no right, no legal power, no influence over us, not even a claim of conquest by fair-handed warfare, and we cannot believe our friends of the great and just American nation could tolerate annexation by force against the wishes of the majority of the population.[1]

In vain, for the past five years, they had sought aid in restoring the monarchy from the United States government and from Americans who had long been their closest and best friends. Throughout his four-year term, President Grover Cleveland had reinforced Hawaiian hopes for redress and restoration of their queen by his careful investigations and his refusal to condone annexation. Sympathy for Hawaiians and their cause came from such vocal Americans as popular journalist Charles Nordhoff

---

1. Nancy Jane Morris, *Ka Loea Kalaiaina, 1898: A study of a Hawaiian-language newspaper as a historical reference source* (Honolulu: University of Hawaii. Typescript thesis for the degree of Master of Arts, no. 1196: Pacific Island Studies, 1975), p. 12. Ms. Morris footnoted her source for quote as U.S. Congress, Senate, Foreign Relations, Hawaiian Islands, Report with Testimony before Subcommittee Dec. 27, 1893–Feb. 13, 1894 (Washington: 1894), p. 1737.

who did his best to convince his countrymen that Liliuokalani had been wrongfully removed from her throne.

Events far removed from Hawaii and the concerns of the Hawaiians decided the issue. In May of 1898, the blowing up of the battleship *Maine* in Havana harbor began what enthusiasts like Colonel Theodore Roosevelt called "a splendid little war." Admiral Thomas Dewey led American battleships into the Pacific to confront Spain—and the Filipinos who were fighting for their independence from Spain—in the Philippines. Captain Glass of the U.S.S. *Charleston* took Guam almost by accident on the way. For a number of years Honolulu's protected lochs, Pearl Harbor, had been intermittently used as a concession in return for Hawaiian relief from a 30 percent American sugar tariff. With the Spanish-American War, the navy needed Pearl Harbor as a permanent, full-time, American-governed mid-Pacific coaling station. The navy's demands and the expansionist pressure of Congress and the press forced mild, peaceably inclined President William McKinley to approve the annexation that became a reality with the ceremonial changing of the flags at Iolani Palace that morning of August 12, 1898.

At ten o'clock, when the palace gates opened to admit a waiting crowd, the Hawaiian flag flew from the stone balconies of the building that the leaders of the Republic of Hawaii had seen fit to rename the Executive Building. To most of those waiting at the walking gates, it was still the Palace, and they so referred to it as they stood, the dust from King Street's traffic of horse trams, dray wagons, and buggies settling on them, and the morning sun burning down. Those elite who had tickets to the choice reserved seats on the palace lanais waited on the shady grounds of the Hawaiian Hotel, a block away on the corner of Richards and Hotel streets.

Hawaiian directions are not north, south, east, west, but instead are given in terms of *mauka* ("toward the mountains"), *makai* ("toward the sea"), or the names of places in either direction along the shore. A block *mauka* of the palace, on Beretania Street, there was no sign of life that morning and no sound from the stately white-columned mansion, Washington Place, now the home of Hawaii's governors, then the private residence of Liliuokalani, Hawaii's last queen. A block toward Waikiki from the palace, on the *makai* side of King Street, the great coral stone structure of Kawaiahao Church slowly filled with Hawaiian women who knew the ancient mourning chants.

By half-past ten, the leaders of the "Reform Party" and of the "Reform Party's" Republic of Hawaii, their supporters, and friends who held tickets to the reserved seats on the palace lanais were in their places. They were, most of them, *haole*—a term common to island vocabularies, a Hawaiian word whose original meaning was "white-skinned foreigners." For these ticket holders the morning was an occasion for jubilation. They and their planter colleagues on Kauai, Maui, Molokai and the big island of Hawaii were sincerely convinced that if they had not moved to take over the Hawaiian government in 1893, Great Britain was ready to step in and Queen Liliuokalani equally ready to offer her islands as a British protectorate.

The 1896 census counted 45,000 *haole* (including Portuguese and "other Caucasians"), but of these a substantial number had remained loyal to the queen and her cause. Though commonly thought of as one class of people in Hawaii, *haole* residents then as now varied in kinds and classes of individuals from professional men and executives to common laborers and unemployed ne'er-do-wells. Among them was as wide a range of political persuasion as of economic status. In the public seats set out on either side of the palace drive for general spectators were many *haole* men and women for whom that Annexation Day was as painful as for Hawaiians themselves or for those ardently royalist one-fifth of the islands' population, the Chinese.

For more than a century, Chinese had been prominent in the Kingdom of Hawaii. They had enjoyed rights, privilege, and a franchise which would be terminated after today by America's Chinese Exclusion laws. Few Japanese were present on the palace grounds that Annexation Day morning. They were a recent addition to the kingdom's population, contract labor most of them, tied to the plantations in such a binding fashion that those who tried to run away from their contract were caught by the police and imprisoned. For those thirty thousand Japanese in Hawaii on Annexation Day, America's Chinese Exclusion laws would also mean a denial of equal rights, privilege, and franchise.

Many of the Chinese in the public seats on Iolani Palace grounds had walked miles to be present at the ceremony. They sat watching and listening, with deep concern in their eyes. There was no doubt whatever in their minds about the virtues of democracy, for their countryman, Sun Yat-sen, was about to export that idea of government from Hawaii to China itself, and they had pledged energy and funds to support him.

It was exactly 11:15 A.M. when a parade of 25 Hawaiian policemen, the National Guard (mostly Americans), and 319 marines and sailors from the American naval vessels in Honolulu harbor marched up the palace drive between the rows of spectators. With every eye on them, they took up guard posts around the flags on the palace lanais, both first and upper story, and around the raised platform built for the program at the foot of the palace steps. Those flags were the flags still of the Kingdom of Hawaii, their eight red, white, and blue stripes symbolic of the eight islands of the kingdom united in 1796 by Kamehameha the Great. In the corner of the flag, a Union Jack testified to Kamehameha's friendship with the country that, in Hawaiian, was known as *Beretania*. At half-past eleven Sanford Ballard Dole, president of the five-year Republic of Hawaii, took his place on the platform. He was Honolulu-born, the son of American missionary parents, a lawyer and much respected judge who had served under the queen. His cousin, young Jim Dole, would not arrive in the islands until the following year, 1899, to develop pineapple as a large-scale commercial crop. In 1898 (as it had been for forty years previously and was to continue to be for the next seventy years), sugar was Hawaii's economic base, the real power behind island government, the real reason behind the thrust for annexation, which would insure that never again would Hawaiian sugar profits be eroded by American import tariffs, traditionally 30 percent.

The speeches that began at 11:35 did not mention this, nor did they dwell on the "manifest destiny" impetus of those Americans who saw the possession of Hawaii as a logical step in expansion across a wide new frontier for the United States:

the entire Pacific. When the speeches were done, the band
began to play the Hawaiian national anthem. At this point
twenty-two of the twenty-five Hawaiian policemen could no
longer bear to stay. Quietly, many of them weeping, they hurried to the rear of the palace where they would not have to see
their beloved flag fall.

At 11:57 the bugle sounded its sad notes signaling the Hawaiian flag's final slow descent. From the harbor, American naval
vessels fired a 21-gun salute. While the guns were still resound-
ing, the flag collapsed into the foreign hands standing ready to
fold it. At that instant, piercing the echoes of the cannon, piercing the awful stillness that descended on the palace and its
grounds, there sounded the voices of Hawaiian women raised in
the high keening wail of a mourning chant. The voices came
from a block away, from the great mission church of Kawaiahao, but the terrible grieving seemed to fill the atmosphere, to
dominate the ceremony.

The lament continued while once again the bugle blared, and
exactly at noon the new flag was run up in the old one's place.
A sudden gust of wind unfurled Old Glory as it reached the top
of the staff. Cheers resounded from the reserved seats. A few
cheers were raised from the spectators on the lawn, but in most
of the public seats men and women sat in silence, eyes brimming with tears that spilled over and ran down their cheeks.

For the Hawaiians and for those who identified with their
cause there was nothing left to do but to live on. A forty-sixth
star had been sewn into the flag raised that morning. It was not
the usual American flag but one symbolic of a promise made in
the annexation of these islands, a hope held out for the Hawaiians whose longest previous subjection to a foreign power had
been five months under the provisional government of a British
commander in 1843. There were in 1898 still only forty-five
stars in the American flag, only forty-five states in the American
Union. The promise and hope made implicit in the special flag
used in the August 12, 1898, ceremony was that Hawaii could
become the forty-sixth state. When that happened, through the
power of their vote, Hawaiians could again play a key role in
making the decisions affecting their beloved *aina,* the land of

islands that had been theirs for more than a thousand years.

It was a bitter end to their independence as a nation. These islands that during the course of the nineteenth century had three times almost become French or British, had once in some locations flown the Russian flag, were now the first overseas possessions of the United States. Paradox: Americans who had proclaimed independence as a goal for all free men had now acquired their first overseas dependency. To many islanders the acquisition of Hawaii by annexation marked a shift from democratic ideals that a century of Americans had exported to the Kingdom of Hawaii.

How all this happened, and why, is a story that begins two years after the original thirteen American colonies declared their independence from Great Britain in 1776.

2

Hawaiian Roots

*T*HE first Americans to see these islands were seven colonists who were not yet aware their fellow countrymen had revolted and were becoming a new free confederation. They had left England in July 1776 as crew on the two ships of Captain James Cook's third expedition to the Pacific, before the news of the American Revolution could be sailed across the Atlantic Ocean. On January 18, 1778, sailing north from Tahiti, they sighted Oahu and then Kauai. Late on the afternoon of January 20 they dropped anchor in Kauai's Waimea Bay.

The impact of their sudden appearance on the people there was exactly what the impact might be on contemporary islanders if an extragalactic space ship suddenly landed in the middle of Honolulu's Ala Moana Shopping Center parking lot. Astonishment. Fear. Awe. Curiosity. Then, in the absence of any apparent danger, the extending of homage and honors and an attempt at communication with visitors from a different world.

No one aboard the *Resolution* or *Discovery* had any idea such islands as these existed. No trace of them appeared on any known charts of mariners. Only in legends did memories of these islands remain in Tahiti and the Marquesas, home islands from which Polynesian voyagers had pioneered here to the twentieth parallel north of the equator. To the largest and most southerly of these mid-Pacific islands that sprawl across the

11

ocean some two thousand miles west of the North American continent these ancient voyagers gave the name *Havaiki*. In the distant past, when they ventured out from southern India or south China through the straits and into the Pacific, the Polynesians had originally come from a homeland called by that name, a homeland whose location was obscured in the legends of these Vikings of the Pacific. Over the centuries, they settled island groups in an oceanic triangle bounded by Hawaii on the north, New Zealand on the southwest, and Easter Island on the southeast. Early European explorers gave them the Greek name Polynesians ("people of the many islands"), but in their own closely related languages these ancient island peoples simply called themselves "The Men." *Ka poe kahiko*, the people of the past, is the way Hawaiians refer to their Polynesian ancestors.

Expert navigators, the Polynesians roamed thousands of miles in great mat-sailed double canoes. With them when they arrived in Hawaii and Kauai about 700 A.D. were pigs, dogs, fowl, and the starts of their basic food plants: coconut, taro, breadfruit, and bananas. In the shelters on these twin-hulled vessels was also the *ti*, whose long, broad leaves were used in a variety of ways including religious ceremonies, and two shrubs, *mamake* and *wauke*, a mulberry and a fig whose pliant bark made excellent tapa cloth. Chiefs, commoners, and the *kahunas*, who were the priests and expert professionals of every art and skill, were the passengers on those colonizing voyages. Theirs was a theocratic society. Important as the plants and animals was the spiritual freight carried by those in the canoes. With them were the images of their gods, and permeating them was a deep reverence for *mana*, the basic spiritual essence which they believed was shared in varying degrees by all living things—that, indeed, was innate in the very land itself. This precious sacred quality was possessed in graduated abundance by the chiefs, the *alii*, who were the representatives of the gods in ruling over the land, all that it produced, and all those who produced from it. The *mana* of the chiefs was nurtured by careful intermarriage, often between brother and sister of high rank. Ritual and taboo protected this *mana*. Rooted in it was a value system based on aloha, *kokua*, and *aloha aina*. Aloha was once a concept that extended only to a person's kinship group. By 1778 and the stupendous event of foreign contact, aloha had evolved to become a greeting and an attitude that that greeting expressed: a feeling that ranged from receptivity to the deepest affection. Aloha could embrace the stranger, one's family, one's beloved, one's friend.

Kokua, which Hawaiian-English dictionaries define as "help" or "aid," implied helpfulness of a special emotional range and quality. It was aid freely given for the asking, without any thought of reward or expectation of return of the favor. The third value, *aloha aina,* was the keystone of both aloha and *kokua. Aloha aina* was the central focus, the ideal that expressed the land's meaning to *ka poe kahiko* and insured the preservation, the conservation, and the balance of life-giving resources of land and sea.

A rich mnemonic literature of chants had been handed down from generation to generation in these northern islands: chants to accompany the ritual of selecting and cutting down a tree for a canoe, chants to accompany the ritual of sliding the finished canoe into the water, chants that sang of the way to follow the stars and read the signs of wave and wind and current and sea birds to guide the way back to Tahiti and Raiatea. The long voyages back and forth, north and south across the equator, were continued until the 1500s. Then, for reasons that are no longer clear, they abruptly ceased. From that time until January 1778, the peoples of these northern islands lived in the isolation of their own offshore waters. Over the centuries there had been occasional accidental visitors—castaways who were "white skinned foreigners" and whose appearance was striking enough for a word with that meaning, *haole,* to become part of the Hawaiian vocabulary.

Even though they were all one people, with a common language, ancestry, and religion, warfare was a routine part of island life. Young chiefs learned the arts of war—spear throwing and dodging, the use of the wooden dagger they called *pahoa,* skill with sling and stone, and the tricks of hand-to-hand combat—with the same total intensity as the young knights of Europe learned the art of using swords and lance. Each year the

waging of war was suspended for a three or four months' period
between November and February. This session of peace was
makahiki, sacred to the god Lono. It was a time when chiefs
went from district to district with Lono's white tapa banners flying from their canoes, a time when the usual capriciousness of
life was leavened by the diversions of *makahiki:* games, dancing, boxing, wrestling. It was also a time when tribute was
collected from the *makaainana,* the commoners who were liter-
ally tied to the land and whose lives and livelihood depended on
the whims, the fortunes, and the alliances of their chiefs much
as the fate of a European serf depended on the arbitrariness of
his lord. By chance it was at this celebratory and sacred season
that the two ships of Captain James Cook's British expedition
sailed into island waters.

At this period in their history, the eight islands were governed
as four separate independent chiefdoms. The lush northern island of Kauai and its small semiarid neighbor, Niihau, were
under one ruling chief. Ninety miles to the south across a rough
stretch of ocean lay the central island of Oahu, which together
with its thirteen-mile distant neighbor Molokai was a second
chiefdom. The ruler of Oahu generally preferred to reside on
Molokai, with its abundantly stocked fishponds and its *kahunas*
skilled in the art of poisoning one's enemies. Oahu in the days
of *ka poe kahiko* had not yet fulfilled the promise of its name,
which in one interpretation meant "the gathering place." Its
village of *Honoruru* was small and unimportant. A few miles
away, a wind-tousled fringe of coconut palms marked the surfing beach of Waikiki.

The third chiefdom included three islands stretching south
along the ocean bottom rift from which the entire chain erupted
as volcanoes building up over thousands of years to soar high
above the surface of the sea. Lanai and sparsely populated Kahoolawe were ruled by Maui, second largest of all the islands.
The powerful ruling chief of this third chiefdom was often at
war with his southerly neighbor, the fourth chiefdom, a big
island whose original name *Havaiki* had elided with the passing
centuries to Hawaii.

That fourth and largest chiefdom resembled a mini-continent. Its abrupt windward cliffs were interspersed with idyllic green valleys through which waterfalls plunged to the sea and streams could be diverted for irrigation. Its lee coast, low, flat, dry, was edged with black, green, or white sand beaches and the tongues of lava flows. Great stark wastes of lava were everywhere souvenirs of that island's five volcanoes, and as varied as its terrain were its microclimates, from the nearly fourteen-thousand-foot elevations of Mauna Kea and Mauna Loa where it snowed in winter to a Kohala valley where it rained five hundred inches a year to a lee beach where day after day it remained dependably hot and dry. From the days of its first Polynesian settlers, the Big Island's seven districts were sometimes ruled autonomously, sometimes allied in two or more districts under one ruling chief, and sometimes (as in 1778) joined under one individual rule, that of Kalaniopuu, who also controlled the Hana district of Maui. Legends of Hawaii island told of *haole* people landing and settling in Hilo in past centuries and of a shipwreck at Keei in south Kona from which a red-haired *haole* man and woman had made their way to shore. The famous *ehu* strain of red-headed Hawaiians was thought to originate from them.

As the youngest island of the group, Hawaii island was believed to be the home of Pele, the volcano goddess whose image could be seen in the curtain of flames thundering at frequent intervals from Halemaumau, the firepit of Kilauea, the island's most active volcano. It was at the far northern end of the island chain, three hundred miles from the red glow of Pele's firepit, that the British ships *Resolution* and *Discovery* made the first recorded foreign sighting of this uncharted archipelago, in late January 1778.

On two previous Pacific voyages, Cook had visited Tahiti, charted the North and South islands of New Zealand, and been the first to explore the Antarctic Ocean and predict the existence of the continent of Antarctica. He had explored the coasts of Australia and threaded his way up through the scattered atolls and islands of Oceania, "discovering" many Polynesian groups. On this third voyage he was sailing north to the Bering

Sea in search of the Northwest Passage that, should it exist, had the lure of offering a quick trade route from Europe into the Pacific.

It was James Cook's supposition, on sighting land in this supposedly empty part of the ocean, that he was about to make contact with a previously unknown island racial group. Cook's story has been told countless times from the *haole* "discoverer's" point of view. What matters in understanding the background of modern Hawaii, however, is that event put in the perspective of the islanders who stood watching the foreign vessels sail toward their shores.

Samuel Kamakau, a Hawaiian scholar who heard the story from someone who had personal knowledge of the event, put it down from this perspective in his *Ruling Chiefs of Hawaii,* which first appeared in segments in mid-nineteenth-century Hawaiian-language newspapers and was published in English in 1961 by the Kamehameha Schools Press. Kamakau describes how the first to see Cook's two ships were two Kauai fishermen out in the night in their canoe. Startled to see them loom up out of the darkness, they made the immediate surmise that these were the two floating islands on which the god Lono had promised that he would one day reappear. To the fishermen, the tall masts were the trunks and branches of leafless trees, and the sails the white tapa banners of Lono. Strange sounds and smells drifted across the water. Strange lights glowed from the two vessels. Awed and terrified the fishermen fled home to Waimea Bay to tell what they had seen.

By dawn, the bayshore was lined with people. As the two strange ships approached, the valley echoed with shouts of excitement and, from some, cries of fear. Like the fishermen, the people of Waimea and their chiefs marveled at the branching masts of the two "floating islands" and at the sails shaped like giant sting rays. A few ventured out in canoes to take a closer look at the strangers aboard and returned to report in amazement that these were no ordinary beings. They had wrinkled skins with holes in the sides of their bodies into which they could thrust their hands and keep things, and some had heads with queer three-cornered shapes. How else to describe the first sight of European clothing, of pockets, and of three-cornered hats?

"Haole!" said older people who remembered the tales of previous centuries, of white-skinned foreigners wrecked at Hilo, and at Keei in Kona, and later off Lanai. The younger people were, like the fishermen, convinced differently. Who else could this be except the god Lono and his entourage, returning in this season consecrated to him? A priest and a chief went out in a canoe to take Lono a red tapa and perform the ritual essential to the welcome of such a visitor. They pronounced the lifting of the taboo that, by his nature as a god, would have made Lono unapproachable for them.

On board his ship, as this ritual was performed and he heard and recognized the Polynesian words of their language, James Cook realized that these were not an entirely new people, but a group closely related to the Tahitians whose culture and language had become somewhat familiar to him. He corrected his original assessment of them in his journal, but he did nothing to correct their misimpression of his identity, allowing himself to be addressed and treated as their god.

The only hostility during this initial brief visit came from his own men, who gave the people of Kauai their first experience of the sound, sight, and effect of firearms. Lono's ships were abundantly fitted with iron, which to the Hawaiians was a rare and much-coveted material found only in occasional pieces of driftwood. The temptation of so much iron was too great for one Waimean whose audacity was such that he tried to rip a piece off the ship's gunwales. The British, used to thwarting thievery by immediate punishment, put a stop to any further pilfering by shooting the man dead before he completed his try. "Exploding water" the islanders called the strange thing that had killed their comrade. They described to those on shore how a gush of fire had leaped like a freshet of water out of the iron stick carried by a long-tailed god, which was their way of describing Cook's officers. Retribution for what had happened never entered their minds. Was this not Lono and his companions? Punishment by death was equally swift and sure in their own culture when anyone broke a *kapu*. For Polynesians, to offend the gods by behavior that was taboo was most serious, and the assumption in

this Kauai incident was not that the dead man had been pun-
ished for trying to steal, but that he had in some way broken a
kapu of Lono.

Cook's crew, 144 British, Scotch, several Americans, and a
few German seamen, were delighted by the welcome they were
given by the women and girls of Kauai. As had the women of
Tahiti, these *wahines* swam out and swarmed onto the decks of
the ships, offering themselves joyously to their sacred visitors.
Cook worried about the spread of venereal disease from his infected crew to people who showed no evidence of having had
prior contact with syphilis or gonorrhea, but he could control
neither his men's appetites nor the Kauai women's desires to
please the companions of Lono. The foreigners paid little attention to the women's alarmed refusal of food. When they themselves began to eat, they could not understand why the women
jumped overboard and swam ashore.

Captain Cook only vaguely understood the taboos of this society as contrasted to those of his own. For these islanders, the
strict prohibitions laid upon both men and women (but with more
severity on women) were dietary. Men and women were forbidden to eat together, and each household had a separate men's
eating house and a women's eating house. Men prepared and
cooked the food, which women were forbidden to do. Women
could not eat pork, bananas, or coconut except on such rare oc-
casions as mourning at the death of a beloved chief when all
normal behavior was suspended to show the extent to which
their grief led them to abandon the ordinary course of their
lives. Personal and temporary restrictions on eating certain
foods were placed on individuals, including chiefs and chiefesses, by the *kahunas*—the priests who were the arbiters of ritual, political, and social life, the experts, the healers, and the
soothsayers. The punishment for breaking the eating *kapu* was
the same as for breaking the prohibition that warned a commoner not to let his shadow touch that of a chief. *Mu,* the dread
secret police and executioners, were—or seemed to be—
everywhere. A woman who ate a banana, or a boy who failed to
prostrate himself at the approach of a high-ranking chiefess,

died swiftly and immediately from the blow of a club or the throttle of a garrote.

When Cook's two ships sailed on their way, the Kauai chiefs sent messengers by canoe to all the other chiefdoms to tell of the visit of Lono, of the "exploding water," of how smoke came from the mouths of Lono's companions, how their speech sounded like the twittering of lali birds, how their appetite for women was not like that of gods, but of men. For the ten months of Cook's absence, the peoples of the four chiefdoms talked of little else but the events of that visit, of the new things they had observed on his ships, of the cannons from whose mouths came thunder, of the wealth of iron aboard. In November, again at *makahiki* season, when the British returned from their voyage north, they took time to cruise leisurely through these islands, sailing clockwise as Lono would have done. On Maui, the highest ranking chiefs came to visit aboard, and among them was the nephew of the ruling chief of Hawaii, young Kamehameha, whose size and strength and keen intellect made enough of an impression on Captain Cook to be recorded in his journal.

As he sailed through the islands on this second visit, Cook wrote down the names of each island as his British ears heard them. "Oneehow" and then again "Eneeheeow" were his version of Niihau, where he remarked on the excellent quality of the yams, the good water, and the generosity of the women and girls with the favors of their persons to his officers and crew. "Atoui" and "Towai" were Cook's two spellings of Kauai. He recorded Molokai as "Morotai," Lanai as "Ranai" and "O'Ranai," Maui as "Mowee," and Hawaii as "Owhyhee." His junior officer, William Bligh, who would make his own contribution to history as commanding officer of H.M.S. *Bounty,* recorded the name of the island of Oahu as "Woahoo."

Since there existed no collective name for the archipelago, Cook supplied one, christening the group the Sandwich Islands after his patron, the First Lord of the British Admiralty, the Earl of Sandwich. The expedition spent five weeks, the major portion of its stay here, in circumnavigating the big island of Hawaii. Near Mahukona, in Kamehameha's home district of Kohala, people lined the clifftops to watch Cook's ships pass. On the lee side of the island, fifty miles south of Kohala in the Kona district's deep sheltered bay of Kealakekua, Captain Cook found the anchorage he had been seeking. He needed to take on water, to reprovision for the voyage south, and to make certain repairs.

At Kealakekua, the two ships were welcomed by thousands lining the shore, many swimming out to greet Lono and his companions. The ruling chief, Kalaniopuu, hurried to the bay to host his sacred visitors and to try to accommodate all their demands. The British were taken on shore excursions up into the mountains to the huts of bird catchers who plucked the gold and red feathers from which the magnificent cloaks and helmets of the chiefs were made. In the forests, the visitors saw canoes adzed into shape. Aboard the *Resolution* and *Discovery* a reciprocal hospitality prevailed. Hawaiians watched the blacksmiths on the two ships work iron on their forges, and at Cook's order numbers of daggers—*pahoa*—were made as gifts for the chiefs.

It was the British preoccupation with sex that roused Chief Kalaniopuu's suspicions. When he put a *kapu* on women visiting the two ships, the companions of Lono thronged ashore and took women and girls in the villages. On February 4, as Cook finally made ready to leave, the strain on supplies and tempers ashore was close to a breaking point. The British had asked for and received the wooden fence of a *heiau,* a temple, for firewood. Provisions in the district of Kona had been exhausted. Entertaining such a guest for so long was a heavy emotional and ritual burden as well, and it was with relief that the Hawaiians said farewell to their visitors. It was with dismay they saw the ships returning on February 11, only one week later. A severe storm had been encountered off the Kohala coast, and Cook decided they must go back to Kealakekua to make repairs.

Their presence now was an imposition, and others shared Kalaniopuu's suspicions that the British were men, not gods, for *makahiki* was ended, and Cook had returned in a counterclockwise direction. On February 14, after Hawaiian theft of one of his longboats, Cook determined to go ashore personally to take Kalaniopuu hostage against the longboat's return. The tragedy described in most histories as the murder of Captain Cook occurred when he tried to do just this and a warrior protecting his chief struck Cook a heavy blow. As Cook reeled and cried out in pain the Hawaiians shouted that if he could be hurt, he must not be a god. They struck him with more blows, and Captain James Cook, mortal as he was, fell into the shallows at the rocky edge of the bay, dead. Four marines died in the scuffle. The surviving British shot and killed several Hawaiians before swimming to the safety of their ships.

In the tense days that followed, while Cook's remains were given the highest honors of an *alii* by the *kahunas* and the chiefs, his crew took their revenge. They came ashore, burned and sacked a village, cut off the heads of two Hawaiians, stuck them on pike poles, and with these grisly tokens propped in the prow of their longboats, rowed across the bay and back to their two ships.

With this, strangely enough, the tension seemed to lessen. Some of Cook's bones were returned to the British, who gave them a Christian sea burial. Friendly relations with the Hawaiians were re-established so that repairs proceeded and women again went to lie with the visitors whom they now accepted not as the companions of Lono, but as *haole*, quite ordinary men who were white-skinned foreigners. The chiefs had been fond of Cook and continued to refer to him as Lono. They much liked Lieutenant King and tried to persuade Cook's successor, Captain Clerke, to let King remain in Hawaii and become a chief.

On February 22 the *Resolution* and *Discovery*, with all surviving officers and crew, readied for departure. From the Big Island, they sailed to Oahu and anchored at that island's Waimea Bay for a few hours while Captain Clerke and a few officers made a brief visit ashore. They then proceeded on to Waimea Bay, Kauai, and to Niihau where they were urged to take sides in a civil war being waged there. The British were careful to remain neutral during their two weeks on Niihau where they took on water and provisions and, as they had everywhere in the chain, left behind them venereal disease.

Finally, on March 15, 1779, the expedition left island waters.

They left not as gods, but as white-skinned foreigners whose offspring the islanders labeled with contempt as *opala haole* ("foreign rubbish"), yet whose technology was much admired. Guns, cannon, the working of iron and the extension of its uses, the rigging of the foreign ships, the tobacco, the rum, and the free eating of the *haole* visitors made an indelible impact, and it was this introduction to totally new things and new ideas that made Hawaiians ready, when the next *haole* visitors appeared in 1786, to accept with alacrity both most of the items the *haole* offered for trade and the *haole* himself whenever he wished to jump ship and stay.

In turn, the islands had made an equally indelible impression on Cook's men. They described the climate, the scenery, the hula, and the frank ardor of the Hawaiian *wahine* as nothing less than paradise.

3

The Great Kohala Chief

*T*HE strength, the acumen, and the ambition of Hawaii island's great Kohala chief, Kamehameha, came at an opportune time in island history. Alone, each of the chiefdoms now stood vulnerable to the colonial aspirations of the foreign powers who came to look at Cook's "discovery" with covetous eyes. The British were the first to return, Captains Portlock and Dixon in 1786. In that same year, LaPérouse and his two French ships also visited the islands. The late eighteenth century was an era in which independence and self-government for such peoples as the Hawaiians was not an alternative considered by such ambitious colonial empires as Great Britain, France, Spain, the Netherlands, or Russia. The thirteen newly independent American colonies forming a Confederation in 1786 were considered an anomaly.

In 1789, the first ship of American registry, Captain Robert Gray's *Columbia*, appeared in Hawaiian waters. A host of Yankee skippers soon followed. Theirs was an interest protective of the autonomy and independence of the islands, an interest based not so much on political conviction as on the practical matter of keeping the four chiefdoms free and open to American trade. One ruling chief being easier to deal with than were four, they applauded Kamehameha's success in 1796 in uniting Oahu, Maui, and his own Hawaii under his rule. In his youth, Kamehameha had been the first and only chief ever to lift Hilo's Naha

Stone, a huge bench-shaped boulder that today rests on the lawn of the Hilo Public Library. Legend was that whoever should lift that stone would become the one to unite all the islands under his rule, a prophecy remembered in 1782 on the death of Kamehameha's uncle, Kalaniopuu, ruling chief of Hawaii, who bequeathed his nephew the powerful stone and feather talisman of the war god Kukailimoku. Through his belief in these omens, through intrigue, ritual murder, and civil war, Kamehameha made himself ruling chief of the island and then pushed out in a series of devastating attacks to conquer Maui, Lanai, and Molokai. However, he was forced to abandon his conquests in order to consolidate his rule over his own island, and in 1786, when Portlock and Dixon arrived, the four chiefdoms were in a temporary, and exhausted, interval of peace. Lanai was once again under the rule of Maui. Molokai was under the ruling chief of Oahu.

The *haole* ship visitors were rarely regarded as adversaries by the chiefs. Neutrality in island political matters was usually the course followed by these early foreigners. Hawaiian tempers flared when shoddy trade goods were offered them in return for provisions of good quality, or when a high-ranking chief was insulted by a *haole,* but the incidence of violence and assault between Hawaiians and these visitors was minimal. There were instances in these early years of *haole* captains forcibly kidnapping Sandwich Islanders to serve as seamen, but these were as rare as were the few instances of ruling chiefs forcibly detaining *haole* seamen to enter their service.

In general, islanders were eager to sign on a foreign ship and adventure into the world. Their identification of themselves as *kane,* men, became their label: *kanaka.* They were natural seamen, whose loyalty was such that a captain suspecting mutiny among his *haole* crew signed on as many Sandwich Islanders as he could.

One such islander to leave on a foreign ship was not a *kane* but a *wahine*—a young woman who swam out to Captain Charles Barkley's *Imperial Eagle* when he anchored off Oahu for a few hours one May afternoon in 1787. Barkley signed her on as "Wynee" (probably his phonetic spelling of *wahine*), and she stayed aboard to serve as companion and maid to his wife. Several months later, "Wynee" was found stranded in Canton by Chief Kaiana, a Kauai *alii* who sailed that same year as one of the islands' first tourists, a passenger invited to see the Pacific Northwest and the wonders of the Celestial Empire of China by Captain John Meares. Kaiana was a stunning sight in Canton, clad in his magnificent red and gold feather cape and helmet, with a white tapa malo wound around his loins. Chinese street vendors were indignant when he tried to bargain for a bag of oranges by offering them a few nails. Kaiana's British hosts were amused by his concern for the poor boat people of Canton, who pressed hungry faces to the ports of the ship's dining salon, watching the officers and their *alii* guest eat from an abundantly stocked table. When the meal was over, Kaiana took the leftover food up on deck and distributed it to the boat people with what was described as an expression of great pleasure. On his return, in 1788, Kaiana joined the retinue of Kamehameha rather than return to his home chiefdom, for the powerful ruling chief of Hawaii was mustering an army to launch his conquests a second time.

In 1790, Thomas Metcalf of the *Fair American* and four of his crew were murdered off the north Kona coast by a chief who had been insulted by another *haole* captain. The fifth crew member, severely wounded British seaman Isaac Davis, was ordered saved by Kamehameha who had, at this same time, detained John Young of the *Elenora,* a brig captained by Thomas Metcalf's father, Simon, the American who summarily massacred hundreds of Hawaiians at Olowalu, Maui. Kamehameha offered Young and Davis the status of chiefs if they would serve as his advisers in the use of the guns, cannon, and swords he was acquiring from every trader who came by.

A year later, when Captain George Vancouver (a veteran of Cook's expedition) paid the second of his four visits to Hawaii, Davis and Young had become loyal *haole* chiefs with lands, wives, and such conviction of Kamehameha's ability and destiny that they refused Vancouver's offer to take them back home. They were only two among numerous foreigners now residing in the islands. Because of its fine harbor, *Honoruru* on the island of Oahu was rapidly becoming a foreigner's town. By 1789, Oahu had its first Chinese resident, probably from Captain Meares's Chinese crew. Several Chinese spent months on Maui. Others were observed in residence at Kealakekua Bay by Vancouver, whom Kamehameha informed that he had had Chinese carpenters fit his war canoes with swivel platforms for cannon. The islands' new foreign population came from Europe and America as well as from Asia. Don Francisco Paulo de Marin, who became Kamehameha's court interpreter, was an Andalusian gentleman farming on Oahu where he planted the first guava and oranges in the islands, introduced cotton and tobacco, and cultivated a large vineyard in the location of the busy Honolulu arterial roadway that now bears that name, Vineyard Street.

Kamehameha had no illusions about the colonial ambitions of the governments of some of these foreigners. Captain Meares had announced his conviction that Divine Providence intended these islands to become British. Vancouver assumed he had persuaded Kamehameha to sign over his island as a British protectorate, and Kamehameha equally assumed that he had agreed only to protect British seamen in his chiefdom from hunger in return for a promise of aid from British ships against any other foreigners who might try to take his island. Spain was overburdened with colonial administration, although she had sent Lieutenant Manuel Quimper to assess the commercial potential of the Sandwich Islands in 1791. It was Great Britain and France who were most eager for Pacific colonies. Kamehameha was well aware of this. It was as individuals that he accepted their citizens as his close friends, and as equal allies that he chose to regard these governments.

By 1796 he made his final successful conquests of Maui, Lanai, Molokai, and Oahu. Only Kauai and Niihau were not yet under his rule. He kept himself mobile, moving from his capital of Kailua, Kona, to his favorite fishing camp on Lanai, to the fast-growing port of *Honoruru*. In 1800, with a fleet of hundreds of war canoes, thousands of warriors, several foreign vessels he had purchased, and numerous foreign advisers including his loyal *haole* chiefs, Kamehameha set out to conquer that last northern chiefdom of Kauai. In the ninety-mile channel of rough and treacherous ocean that separates Oahu and Kauai, a sudden storm threatened to swamp his fleet. Kamehameha was forced to turn back. A year later, as he readied for a second try, one of the new foreign diseases swept Oahu, a "squatting disease"—*mai okuu*—probably cholera. Hundreds of Kamehameha's men succumbed, and for a time he lay dangerously ill himself. For the next ten years, he contemplated conquest but never launched another expedition. He chose instead to try negotiation of an agreement with Kaumualii, ruling chief of Kauai, to accept Kamehameha as his sovereign but to continue to rule his two islands during his lifetime. American captains Nathan and Jonathan Winship were among those who helped persuade Kaumualii to come to Oahu to make this agreement in 1810.

As a reward, Kamehameha offered a ten-year monopoly in the export of sandalwood and cotton to the Winship brothers and their partner, another American, William Heath Davis. No longer were *alii* so naive in trade as had been Chief Kaiana in China. The use of money was now common and so too was the use of resources other than provisions. The economic base of Kamehameha's kingdom was fast becoming the new trade in sandalwood, for which the market in China was so avid that Hawaii was known there by the name *Tan Heung Shan,* the "fragrant mountains." In their fervor to secure sandalwood cargoes to take to China, American captains began to deliver goods to the chiefs in return for promissory notes against the future cutting of sandalwood from the high chill of mountain forests. It was a trade, an exploitation of a natural resource, that represented a strong break with the *aloha aina* of the past, when the cutting of a tree had been performed with chants and ritual in respect to its *mana.*

The Winships signed their sandalwood monopoly agreement with Kamehameha in July 1812, but the War of 1812 so disrupted American shipping in the Pacific that their privilege could not be exercised. By the time that war was over, every ship calling at island ports was picking up a cargo of sandalwood and every chief who controlled forested lands was sending his commoners into the dank high chill of those mountain forests to spend weeks at a time cutting sandalwood. There was no way for the *makaainana* to refuse this hated labor, but they made sure no new sandalwood would grow again by uprooting every seedling tree as they cut the mature wood.

It was during the height of the sandalwood boom that a German adventurer, Georg Anton Scheffer, apparently decided to take it upon himself to plant the Russian flag in Hawaii, on behalf of his employer, Baranov's Russian American Trading Company of Alaska. Scheffer, who arrived in *Honoruru* in October 1815, posed as a heart specialist, treated the ailing Kamehameha, and was rewarded with a gift of choice lands along the water front. There Scheffer supervised the laying of the foundations of a fort, but when he hoisted the Russian flag over his construction, Kamehameha promptly took his gift of lands back. The Russian flag was hauled down, the new Hawaiian flag was raised in its place, and John Young continued supervision of the fort for Kamehameha's own use. Scheffer was not easily discouraged. He had learned that Kauai's Kaumualii was eager to become independent again, and so he sailed to that island to offer Kaumualii the assistance of the czar. Not only did he promise Kauai independence, but assured Kaumualii that the czar would aid him in overthrowing Kamehameha from his rule of all the other islands, after which Kaumualii and the czar would divide the kingdom between them.

The Kauai chief was delighted. He gave Scheffer lands in several areas, including the beautiful valley of Hanalei, and thirty Hawaiian commoners. Two ships arrived with supplies from Baranov and a number of Aleuts whom Scheffer put to work building forts over which, once again, he hoisted the Russian flag. American skippers off Kauai were threatening to shoot them down unless they were taken down when word reached Kaumualii that Otto von Kotzebue, commander of the Russian naval ship *Rurick* had arrived in Honolulu, denounced Scheffer as an imposter, and assured Kamehameha of the czar's desire for peace and friendship. Immediately, Scheffer was banished from Kauai in a leaky small vessel, and assurance sent to Kamehameha that Kaumualii remained loyal to him.

A Russian who arrived two years after Scheffer's misadventures recorded in his journal the most vivid picture of Kamehameha the Great, a description of his kingdom and its remarkable advances into the labyrinths of civilization, and a prophecy for Hawaii's future. Captain Vassily Golovnin of the *Kamchatka* sailed into Kailua-Kona in 1818 to pay his respects to this ruling chief who insisted his domains be known not as the Sandwich Islands but as the Kingdom of the Ruler of Hawaii. Kamehameha was then in his sixties, and in Ella Wiswell's fine original translation of Golovnin's journal (once available in manuscript in the Hawaii State Archives) the aging Kohala chief was described as "an unusual man gifted by nature with a great mind, a broad vision, and an unusually firm character." [1] Golovnin noted the Hawaiian king's "light green velvet trousers, white shirt, silk kerchief around his neck, coffee brown silk vest, white stockings, shoes, round soft felt hat." Around him, the king's bodyguard was such that Golovnin wrote "a stranger looking army could hardly be imagined." Many of the warriors were naked except for a loincloth. Some wore nothing but a white linen shirt. Some had only a pair of pants. Some were clad only in a vest. A few wore sailors' red woolen jerseys. They were armed with either drawn swords or rusted bayonets. Few of Hawaii's traditional polished wooden spears were in evidence.

Kamehameha greeted his visitor in English, "How do you do?" and then repeated in Hawaiian, *"Aroha!"* He received Golovnin in a large structure that to the Russian resembled a tent. The floor was half covered with finely woven pandanus mats. There were several pieces of European furniture, including a handsome mahogany sideboard holding decanters of wine and rum. Fifty chiefs were present, sitting on the floor in strict observance of the *kapu* that prohibited any chief of lesser rank from sitting at the level of the king. Liholiho, Kamehameha's

1. Ella Lury Wiswell, original typescript translation of Golovnin's journal of his 1818 visit to Hawaii, available until 1977 in the Hawaii State Archives but missing since that date. A revised and somewhat different translation appears in the recently published *Around the World on the Kamchatka*, by V. Golovnin, translated from the Russian by Ella Lury Wiswell (Honolulu: University Press of Hawaii, 1979).

son by his "sacred" high-ranking chiefess, Keopuolani, was a higher rank than his father and so sat discreetly outside the building, which his entering would have made *kapu* to everyone, including the king.

In an interview that he interrupted to change to a British dress officer's uniform, Kamehameha advised Golovnin to proceed on to *Honoruru* where supplies and stores of fresh water would be plentiful. When the Russian did sail into that port, he seemed unaware that the fort he so admired at the harbor entrance was the one started by Scheffer, over which only three years earlier there had flown the Russian flag. Golovnin mentions only that he was impressed by the Hawaiian flag flying over the fort and, in general, by the amazing development of Kamehameha's kingdom.

"We could not help but marvel at the degree of their enlightenment which they owe to their trade with the Americans. Frankly, I was ashamed when I recalled that the eastern shores of Siberia and Kamchatka present no such sight!" Golovnin thought the large plain behind Honolulu harbor an "ideal town site" and "should the national policy of some European power find it necessary to establish a colony in the Sandwich Islands, a better place than the harbor of Honolulu can hardly be found in the entire group." He was pleased to see that on Oahu "for the protection of Europeans there is a police force which sees to it they are not molested by natives," but he was critical of Kamehameha because of this. "If Kamehameha would only take even half the same care of the interests of his subjects as he does of the interests of the Europeans living with him, he would greatly relieve the miserable condition of the common people whose life and property are entirely at the mercy of the chiefs."

Golovnin was impressed by the skill with which chiefs dining aboard his *Kamchatka* used European tableware and at their casual adoption of foreign luxuries and goods. He eluded the intentions of a chiefess who wanted to spend the night with him—she had come aboard with two of her husbands, remained on deck while the men ate, but joined them for wine drinking of which she did more than her share. Golovnin wryly observed that her behavior differed from noblewomen he knew in Europe only in her degree of openness and candor.

Hawaiian strictures on diet were much remarked by Golovnin. In 1816, his fellow Russian, von Kotzebue, had seen the body of a woman floating in Honolulu harbor and been told it was that of someone who had broken the eating *kapu*. On Golovnin's ship one night, a chief who was his guest quickly jumped overboard into a canoe when chicken was served, for that was *kapu* to him. It seemed to Golovnin that their ancient taboos were possibly the Hawaiians' only obstacle to rapid development of their kingdom, and he made the observation that once the Christian faith and the arts of reading and writing should be taken up by Hawaiians, they would within one century reach "a state of civilization unparalleled in history."

He had no way of knowing that a number of Hawaiians overseas had already converted to Christianity or that others, like Kaumualii's eldest son, "George Sandwich," were receiving an education in America. At the very moment of Golovnin's visit to the Hawaiian Kingdom, a young Konan, Opukahaia (Henry Obookaiah), was preaching from New England pulpits, pleading for missionaries to take the message of the gospel to his home islands.

Such a change would not be possible in Kamehameha's lifetime. He was clear eyed about just which new foreign habits and customs intrigued him, which techniques were useful to adopt, and what his people must retain of their own ancient tradition. He approved the foreigners guns, cannons, swords, and sailing ships. He sometimes enjoyed dressing foreign style and sometimes preferred the comfort of a *malo*. He never catered to foreigners, nor felt them in any way superior. Foreigners became his friends, as did Vancouver; his loyal subjects, as did Isaac Davis and John Young; his frustrated employees, as Don Marin, his court interpreter, who lamented Kamehameha's royal prerogative of giving lands as reward for services but then taking them back whenever he was displeased. During these early years of the nineteenth century, the observance of *kapu* was as strict as it had been before the days of foreign contact. Many Hawaiians chafed under the ancient restrictiveness, among them the huge and beautiful Kaahumanu, Kamehameha's favorite wife, a chiefess born the year of Cook's visit. Vancouver, on his visit to the Big Island in 1794, admired Kaahumanu, who was then a handsome sixteen-year-old. Of his more than twenty wives, this headstrong chiefess caused Kamehameha both the most problems and yet gave him the greatest pleasure. He himself, born in the time of *ka poe kahiko* and raised to manhood before the coming of the foreigners, had an outlook quite different from hers. Kaahumanu, more than six feet tall, carrying her weight of more than two hundred pounds with imperious dignity, was a new Hawaiian for she could not remember those days before the foreigners and foreign things brought change to Hawaii *nei.*

As Kamehameha lay on his deathbed in May 1819 in Kailua-Kona, those changes remained superficial, a visible veneer but only a veneer. Scarcely a bay on any island had not held a foreign ship visitor. French, Italians, Portuguese, British, Spanish, Scotch, Americans, and Chinese were residents of the kingdom, mainly in *Honoruru,* one of whose earliest foreign residents was a black freedman from New York state, Anthony Allen, who farmed in Kalihi Valley. In the nearly quarter century of Kamehameha's reign, the fauna of the islands had been altered by the introduction of cattle, sheep, goats, all of which had gone wild and flourished under the protection of a royal *kapu.* The horse, introduced through the Big Island port of Kawaihae by Captain Cleveland in 1803, was fast becoming a popular mode of transportation and, particularly, of recreation and sport. Such foreign vegetables as pumpkins were being grown for the provisioning of ships. On Lanai, in 1801, an enterprising Chinese had harvested a crop of wild sugar cane and boiled it to make the first bricks of raw sugar exported from the islands. The wealth of *alii* was no longer counted in feather cloaks and fine tapa, and although they still relished *poi* dipped with the fingers from a wooden bowl, many of them dined on crystal and fine china. Yet, for them, for the Hawaiian commoner, for the foreigner in the king's service, the basic tyranny of the old gods and their *kapu,* that arbitrary, fearsome sway over life and death, remained unchanged beneath all the veneer of new appearances.

Paradox: it was not the *kapu* and its pall over everyday life that was the world's romantic image of Kamehameha's kingdom, either from foreign visitors or from increasing numbers of Hawaiians migrating overseas. Hawaiian seamen were on every ocean and in most ports of the world. On the Oregon coast, one hundred Hawaiian commoners and their chiefs helped build the trading post of Astoria under a labor contract arranged by Kamehameha with Hudson's Bay Company. In the forests of Idaho, Hawaiians tended trap lines that yielded valuable beaver pelts. Owhyhee River in southern Idaho and Oregon memorializes in its name the murder there of a Hawaiian trapper by an Indian in 1819. The location of the Sandwich Islands was on every sea chart and in the geography books of America and Europe. In print, and by word of mouth, their reputation was that taken home forty years earlier by Cook's expedition. In climate, in scenic beauty and variety, in the ease and pleasantness of life, and in the aloha of the people, the islands ruled by the great chief from Kohala were an earthly paradise.

4

The Reign of Hiram Bingham

WHETHER by chance or design, Kaahumanu was alone with her husband when he died on May 8, 1819. She emerged to announce that in his final moments Kamehameha had appointed her *kuhina nui*, the person whom he chose to administer his kingdom and care for his heir, twenty-year-old Liholiho. This was a most extraordinary assumption of power, but Kaahumanu's stature and ability were such that no one dared to challenge her. In death, Kamehameha seemed to have said, "Let the gods decide," for he had made contention and possible breaking up of his kingdom possible by bequeathing his precious stone-and-feather war god, his own talisman of power, to a chief whose conservatism put him in direct opposition to the bold plans of Kaahumanu.

Before they could hurry him out of the atmosphere of death that hung over Kailua-Kona, Kaahumanu immediately disclosed her secret plans to Liholiho and then publicly proclaimed him to now be the ruling chief of the kingdom, Kamehameha II. The new king spent the next several months of the ritual mourning period at the *heiau* of Puukohola, thirty miles north of Kailua-Kona. There he brooded over what he was not sure he could bring himself to do, whiling away the time in drink and gaming, only too aware of the intrigue beginning against him. In November, the message that he dreaded came. All was in readiness. His mother, Keopuolani, and his *kuhina nui*, Kaahumanu, wanted him to return to Kailua at once.

Reluctantly, he set out with several companions and a supply of rum. For two days he sailed aimlessly back and forth the thirty miles to Kailua. He knew his indecision could cost his throne. Delay could minimize the impact of what so far had been a well-kept secret. He was torn by his loyalty to the traditions of his past. He realized that what his mother and his *kuhina nui* expected of him was the only way for him to remain king, and yet how could he, who had been trained as a priest in the service of the gods, now challenge their power? How could he, for whose benefit and protection the *kapu* existed, perform the acts that would signal its end?

He was offshore from Kailua on the second day when the wind died. Kaahumanu sent a canoe and paddlers to tow him in. It was as if the decision were making itself, for when he stepped ashore he acquiesced as his mother, his *kuhina nui,* and numerous of his father's widows offered him food which they had prepared in the *imu,* the earth oven, with their own hands. They offered him dogmeat and other foods *kapu* to men. In full view of an awed crowd of chiefs and commoners he sat down and ate these forbidden foods in the company of the women. He went with them into a taboo house. All things previously prohibited he—the ruling chief of the kingdom—did! It was a symbolic defiance ending the power of the old gods in Hawaii, and at Kaahumanu's urging he sent messengers to every part of the kingdom, even to Kauai, proclaiming the end of all *kapu.*

As Kaahumanu had anticipated, there was adverse reaction from conservative chiefs. She had forces ready. In December, the chief who had inherited Kamehameha's war god led a rebellion against Liholiho and was defeated and killed in a great battle in Kona. That same month, in the Hamakua district of the Big Island, a similar, smaller uprising was quelled. With this, overt opposition ceased. For the most part, the ending of *kapu* was met with jubilation. Temple walls were torn down. Sacred images were burned or thrown into the sea. With the overthrow of their old gods by Hawaiians themselves, an existential freedom was opened to chiefs and commoners that was, in itself, the most stunning in a half century of changes in Hawaii.

The visible differences in the kingdom were no longer a veneer. The freeing from *kapu* brought a deep inner change to Hawaiians who would never again feel the swift death-dealing blow of a club against the skull for failing to prostrate at the approach of even the shadow of a chief. Never again would a woman who ate with a man, or a girl who tasted banana, coconut, or pork, risk death. There were in almost every district places where a *heiau* remained untouched, the sacred images hidden away, and to those few of the young who cared to listen, *kahunas* taught the legends and chants and ritual of the gods who no longer ruled over life and death in Hawaiian society. Personal gods, the *aumakua* who were the clan deities of Hawaiian families, were not abandoned. Those whose *aumakua* was the shark continued to regard the shark as their patron and brother. Those whose *aumakua* was lizard or owl maintained their family pattern of reliance and interdependence with those creatures. Pele, the goddess of the volcanoes, was still worshipped at her Big Island firepit, Halemaumau, with old-style offerings of ohelo berries and new-style ones of gin.

The end of *kapu* and the fading away of the old gods and their power did not affect the basic system of Hawaiian values. The chiefs themselves had turned from *aloha aina* in their exploitation of the sandalwood. *Kokua* continued to be freely given, even to foreigners. Aloha not only remained an ideal as well as a personal practice and greeting but blossomed into a new "aloha spirit," not yet expressed as such, but felt and appreciated by most newcomers who as individuals were welcomed into Hawaiian homes and families and accepted readily as mates. The Hawaiian dislike of *haole* and Chinese was expressed, but it was an abstract group disdain seldom translated into personal relationships. This new dimension of aloha spirit, offered to strangers and exchanged between Hawaiians and resident foreigners, sped cultural transition, permeating island life in a way that had not had to be during the isolation of *ka poe kahiko*.

Mana, the spiritual energy that invested all things, did not flow off into oblivion when the power of the old gods ended. Hawaiians everywhere believed that *mana* still invested the lands and all that existed in and on them, that *mana* coursed in precious abundance in the bloodlines of the *alii*—particularly in the bloodline of Liholiho, his young brother Kauikeaouli, and his sister Nahienaena, the children of Kamehameha the Great and his "sacred" chiefess, Keopuolani.

The kingdom had entered a brief period when conditions did seem ideal for both Hawaiians and foreigners, when these islands truly were the paradise romanticized by foreign visitors. It was brief because when Liholiho's proclamation ended the *kapu* in November 1819, a new and more psychologically devastating set of prohibitions were already en route, one month out of Boston, bound for Hawaii in the persons of the first American mission company to the Sandwich Islands.

The death of Henry Obookaiah (the former Konan, Opukahaia) from pneumonia in Connecticut during the winter of 1818 had stimulated the American Board of Foreign Missions to accept recruits for a Sandwich Islands mission. The three Hawaiian mission assistants in this first company were all former classmates of Obookaiah, graduates of the Foreign Missions School of Cornwall, Connecticut, as was a fourth Hawaiian, George Kaumualii ("George Sandwich"), son of the ruling chief of Kauai. The young Kauai chief, who had finished his American education and also served with distinction as the first Hawaiian in the United States Navy, was returning home on the *Thaddeus* on this mission voyage as a passenger, having promised to pay his thousand-dollar fare in sandalwood once the brig reached his home island. He and the three Hawaiian mission assistants— Thomas Hopu, John Honolii, and William Kanui—used the six months of the voyage to give lessons in the Hawaiian language to the fourteen American missionaries. These were mostly young couples, brimming with an enthusiasm and earnestness much like that of those Americans who 150 years later set off on the twentieth century mission of the Peace Corps.

During the voyage, because of his ability and strong personality, the Reverend Hiram Bingham became the mission leader. He was thirty-one years of age, a native of Bennington, Vermont, graduate of Middlebury College and Andover Theological Seminary, married to Sybil Moseley of Hartford, Connecticut, two weeks before the *Thaddeus*'s departure. Bingham was a handsome man with prominent features, heavy dark eyebrows, determined eyes, and a sensuous mouth. His was not the face of a puritan, but puritanism was his ideal, and his intention was, at the sacrifice of his life if necessary, to make the Kingdom of Hawaii over into a Kingdom of God. He and his colleagues had pledged themselves to a mission of mercy in which their hearts would be opened wide and their marks set high to achieve the very civilization for which Golovnin had predicted such success in these islands.

The mission goals were "to aim at nothing short of covering those islands with fruitful fields and pleasant dwellings and schools and churches; of raising up the whole people to an elevated state of Christian civilization" and, specifically, to "obtain an adequate knowledge of the language of the people; to make them acquainted with letters; to give them the Bible with skill to read it; to turn them from their barbarous courses and habits; to introduce and get into extended operation among them the arts and institutions and usages of civilized life and society." All this was to be means to the end of "bringing thousands and millions of the present and succeeding generations to the mansions of eternal blessedness." [1]

The *Thaddeus* sighted the snowy summits of Mauna Kea and Mauna Loa on March 30. In a brief stop at the port of Kawaihae they heard the news that Kamehameha the Great had died the previous May, that Kamehameha II had already accomplished the primary goal of the mission: the overthrow of "idolatry." On April 4, the captain of the *Thaddeus* dropped anchor in the bay at Kailua-Kona, but the missionaries were told they might not go ashore until the king gave his permission. This was four days in coming, for Liholiho was reluctant to let such a large party of Americans enter his kingdom at one time. He stipulated that they were all to remain in Kailua-Kona, although he himself was in the process of moving his capital to Honolulu, and he made the further restriction that they could stay only for the trial period of one year.

The Daniel Chamberlains and their five children, Dr. and

1. Ralph S. Kuykendall, *The Hawaiian Kingdom: 1778–1854* (Honolulu: The University of Hawaii, 1938), p. 101.

Mrs. Thomas Holman, Mr. and Mrs. Elisha Loomis, Mr. and Mrs. Samuel Ruggles, Mr. and Mrs. Samuel Whitney, Thomas Hopu, William Kanui, and John Honolii came ashore to wait the success of Mr. Bingham's attempt to persuade the king to allow half of the company to continue on to Oahu and two of the couples to accompany George Kaumualii on to Kauai. Liholiho's wry comment, when he finally consented to this was, "White men all prefer Oahu. I think the Americans would like to have that island!" [2]

In his journal a few days later, Bingham described *Honoruru* as "an irregular village of some thousands of inhabitants whose grass thatched habitations were mostly small and mean while some were more spacious." [3] He led the mission men on an excursion up Punchbowl, an extinct volcanic crater whose summit afforded a wide view. To the left was an amphitheater of low barren hills stretching to Diamond Head. Waikiki was a fringe of palm trees along a white sand beach with a fringe of rolling surf offshore. Immediately below was the town with its fishponds and salt-making pools along the shore, the new fort, and the harbor busy with sandalwood traders. The previous winter, a foreign resident informed Bingham, two whaling ships had called, forerunner of what was to become the mainstay of the kingdom's economy when the sandalwood was gone.

To the north, Bingham saw in the interior that is now crowded subdivisions, freeway, high-rise buildings, shopping centers, and military reservations

an array of numerous beds of *kalo* (*Arum esculentum*) in its various stages of growth, with its large green leaves, beautifully embossed in the silvery water in which it flourishes. Through the valley, several streams descending from the mountains in the interior wend their way some six or seven miles, watering and overflowing by means of numerous artificial canals, the bottom of *kalo* patches and then, by one mouth, fall into the peaceful harbor.[4]

2. Hiram S. Bingham, *A Residence of Twenty-one Years in the Sandwich Islands,* 3rd ed. rev. and corr. (New York, Washington, London: Praeger Publishers, 1969), p. 89.

3. Bingham, p. 92.

4. Bingham, p. 93.

To the west, where an oil refinery now silhouettes the sky on Barber's Point, was a plain that embraced the volcanic hills of Moanalua and—converted into condominiums and a golf course now—"a singular little lake of seawater, abounding in salt crystallized through evaporation by the heat of the sun; the ravine of Moanalua, the lagoon of Ewa, and numerous little plantations and hamlets, scattered trees and cocoanut groves." [5] Of the latter, only Ewa Plantation is now left in Honolulu's urban and suburban sprawl. Then, in 1820, Hiram Bingham found the scene interesting "partly from its novelty, singularity, and natural beauty, its volcanic character, its commercial importance, its peculiar location in the midst of the Pacific Ocean . . . but chiefly as the dwelling places of some thousands of heathen, to whom we were commissioned to offer salvation." [6]

The mission's first year was an experience of almost total failure. Initial cordiality from Honolulu's foreign residents shifted to aggressive dislike as Bingham tried to urge constraints of puritan morality on the easy-going port and thrust words like "incest," "fornication," "whoredom," and "prostitution" into baffled Hawaiian ears and minds. Stephen Reynolds, an American who liked the Hawaiian lifestyle, complained in his diary that "missionaries are always the ruin of the whole world." [7] An adequate knowledge of the very subtle, poetic Hawaiian language, with its words more explicit than missionary ears cared to hear, was not quickly obtained. Hundreds, sometimes thousands, attended Sunday services but only out of curiosity for this foreign novelty.

A mission house was built on a plot of land a long, dusty walk from town and an even longer walk to the sweet water of Punahou Spring. Privation was the missionaries' choice as, in October temperatures that hovered in the mid-eighties, they donned the long underwear, flannels, and woolen clothing that was the autumnal necessity of New England. They sweat,

5. Bingham, p. 93.
6. Bingham, p. 94.
7. *Stephen Reynolds Journal:* November 27, 1823, to June 27, 1845. Excerpts from original journal copied by his daughter (Honolulu: Hawaii State Archives, Single Copy Typescript).

chafed, and itched through Honolulu's hot, humid winter with a discomfort they convinced themselves must be good for their souls. Plants whose seeds had been brought from New England were cultivated Massachusetts style by farmer Daniel Chamberlain, but withered and died as he refused advice from local experts like Don Marin. The crowning blow for Bingham was at the end of the year when the Chamberlains and Dr. and Mrs. Holman demanded a release from their commitments and immediate passage home. Bingham's single consolation was that the king seemed to have forgotten all about his stipulation of a one-year trial period.

During the second year, Thomas Hopu's conversion of the king's mother, Keopuolani, was a real breakthrough, for only if they saw their chiefs following the new religion would the commoners do so. From the king there continued indifference to the missionaries' message. Kaahumanu took no interest. She was preoccupied with political problems and to keep Kauai under control she had taken its aging ruler, Kaumualii, and one of his younger sons as her husbands. It was the good fortune of the mission that when the *kuhina nui* was struck with a serious illness in 1823, Sybil Bingham nursed her to recovery. Kaahumanu's whole personality became transformed by her belief that only Mrs. Bingham's prayers had helped her become well. Immediately, Kaahumanu became a Christian and applied all her strength and vigor to seeing to it her people listened to the word of God. Hiram Bingham became her religious mentor and the one person on whom she depended for advice in every detail for direction of Hawaii's government. Through her, in just three years, the missionary status shifted from discouraging failure to undreamed-of success.

The kingdom was once again a rigid theocracy. The people were warned not to wear flower leis, not to dance the hula, not to fly the kites that were their traditional pastime, and to abandon the foreign habits of tobacco and drink. Kamehameha II and his Queen Kamamalu, with a small retinue that included Oahu's Governor Boki, left on an impulsive trip to visit the king of England and in faroff London, in July of 1824, the royal couple fell ill with measles and both died. Kamehameha II's nine-year-old brother was proclaimed Kamehameha III with Kaahumanu in a position of still greater power, *kuhina nui* and regent. The boy king was given over to the Reverend Mr. Bingham for a Christian education. Only occasionally could he escape to the respite of being an *alii*, indulged and pampered, free to be with his beloved sister, Nahienaena.

Mission influence flooded Hawaiian life. Laws prohibited the kindling of fires on the Sabbath and the old sports of boxing and wrestling. Kaahumanu proclaimed that "when schools are established, all shall learn the *palapala*," and she herself set the example by learning to read in five days. For Hawaiians, to be able to read the black marks printed in mission Bibles was to be able to partake of the *mana* of Jehovah. Chiefs and commoners flocked to the mission stations being set up at areas throughout the kingdom recommended by the Reverend William Ellis in his survey commissioned by Bingham's group in 1823.

Ellis, a London Missionary Society veteran from the Tahitian island of Huahine, had also taken a census which confirmed impressions of the alarmingly rapid decline of the Hawaiian population: from sterility due to the spread of foreigner-introduced venereal disease, from what Ellis insisted was an ancient custom of infanticide, but most of all from the death toll of Kamehameha's wars of conquest, and from the terrible epidemics of other foreign diseases to which Hawaiians had absolutely no natural immunity. Only 140,000 survived: 85,000 on the Big Island; 20,000 on Maui; 3,000 on Molokai; 2,000 on Lanai; 20,000 on Oahu (6,000 concentrated in Honolulu); and 10,000 on Kauai.

Death and Hiram Bingham were laying an equally heavy hand on paradise, for those Hawaiians alive in 1825 were burdened with a weight of sin, with guilt, and with remorse for the ineradicably dark past of their being Hawaiian. In 1826, when the U.S.S. *Dolphin* arrived in Honolulu, the first U.S. naval vessel to visit that port, American sailors could not believe the difference between what they had heard about Hawaii and its reality under missionary rule. Their commander, Captain "Mad Jack" Perceval, abetted them in a riot during which they terrorized the town by breaking a number of fences and crashing into the house where women charged with prostitution were confined. The official business of Perceval and the *Dolphin*'s visit was to lay another heavy burden on Hawaiians: that of repaying the old sandalwood notes owed American traders. The sum was staggering for those times: $150,000 which the United States government insisted the government of the Kingdom of Hawaii must assume as a national debt.

Perhaps it was an ameliorating influence, a new view of human relationships brought by the missionaries, who had been reinforced with a second company in 1823, but Kaahumanu's direction of every able-bodied commoner in the kingdom to cut a half picul of sandalwood as his tax to help repay the huge debt was made palatable to commoners by a new and unusual provision of the Tax Law of 1826, the kingdom's first. Those who cut sandalwood for a tax payment were to be allowed to cut half a picul to keep and sell for their own profit, an unprecedented access to the product of their own labor, which for the more than one thousand years of island history had belonged without exception or question to the chiefs. Alternative payment was provided in the law: either four Spanish dollars or a commodity of equal value. The new foreign, and missionary, attitudes toward women surfaced in the difference in the tax levied on every woman: only one Spanish dollar, a mat six by twelve, or tapa of equivalent value.

The sole inequity for women in ancient times had been in diet and access to certain temples. Now, with Christianity, church membership was open to them on the same strict basis of moral award as to men. Few of either sex qualified, and the mission board back in Boston began to ask Bingham questions that during his first few heady years of power he shrugged off or explained away. In a kingdom where he was making Protestant Christianity a state religion, a kingdom of 140,000 Hawaiian souls, only a few hundred were being given the coveted status of church membership.

Kaahumanu's strong rule of the kingdom was typical of the political power chiefesses had traditionally possessed and often exercised, but like the 1826 tax law the new education—the *palapala* to which she mandated her people by decree—introduced to Hawaiian minds the western view of women as incapable of political action, financial decisions, or responsibility for themselves and their property. Under missionary tutelage, Hawaiian girls covered their graceful seminaked bodies with a high-necked, long-sleeved, ankle length, loose fitting garment, the progenitor of today's *muumuu,* designed by missionary wives bent on producing modesty in their pupils. Life was a grim business for most of these American missionaries who were appalled by the frankness and candor of Hawaiians on subjects taboo to New England culture and by the spontaneity with which Hawaiians lived each present moment, usually with innate exuberance whether the challenge was that of a surfing wave, a game, a job to be done, sex, or the chance to learn to read, write, and cipher.

The missionary education of the Hawaiian nation was coeducational, a network of schools in every district of each island—seven such schools on tiny Niihau. By 1822 the first spelling sheet of written Hawaiian had been run off on the mission press, but it was several years before a standard orthography was settled by a mission committee who met month after month at Lahaina, Maui, to devise a phonetic standard for writing this language that had been totally oral and mnemonic in its rich literature and subtle vocabulary.

As their basis, the committee followed the method proposed by the Honorable John Pickering of Salem, Massachusetts, in his "Essay on a Uniform Orthography for the Indian Languages of North America," published in the *Memoirs* of the American Academy of Arts and Sciences. However, missionary phoneticization of Hawaiian presented problems no method could resolve. New England ears were insensitive to the aural territory that lay between *t* and *k, l* and *r* in many Hawaiian words. The only possible solution was a committee vote on which sound most missionaries thought they heard in Hawaiians' pronunciation. That democratic settlement changed the *aroha* heard by Cook and Golovnin to "aloha"; the staple starch *kalo* (from which Hawaiians pounded their *poi*) to "taro." *Honoruru* became Honolulu. *Tamaahmaah* became Kamehameha. Fifty years later, visitors to Hawaii were to remark on the strange way older Hawaiians pronounced their own language, saying "Mauna Roa" for Mauna Loa and "Ranai" for Lanai. The mission committee ruefully described their own work as having done surgery on Hawaiian, but it was even so a laudable and monumental task. The way was prepared for a million pages of Hawaiian, primers and Hawaiian Bibles, to be run off on the mission press, and for Hawaiians to become one of the most literate peoples on earth. This they did, by 1846.

Bingham suffered only two frustrations: the independence of thought and behavior, the unassailable Hawaiian-ness of Kamehameha III (who refused to allow the Ten Commandments to be made the law of his kingdom); and the competition that arrived on the French ship *Comete* in July 1827, a Catholic mission of members of the Congregation of the Order of the Sacred Hearts of Jesus and Mary. Father Abraham Armand, Father Alexis Bachelot, Father Patrick Short, and Brothers Theodore Boissier, Melchior Bondu, and Leonore Portal ignored Kaahumanu's directive that they depart on the same ship on which they had arrived. They settled quietly into rented quarters in Honolulu and concentrated on learning Hawaiian. A few months later, through Auguste de Morineau, a young lawyer who hoped to be named French consul, they obtained lands on what is now Fort Street and built a small house and chapel on the site of the present Our Lady of Peace Cathedral. By July of 1829, two years after their arrival, they had sixty-five Hawaiian converts, and in the churchyard a young algaroba tree, which Hawaiians called *kiawe,* was shooting to a substantial size. Father Bachelot had brought the seeds from the Royal Conservatory in Paris, seeds originally from the California missions where this tree is known as mesquite. As the *kiawe* flourishes, so shall Catholicism in these islands, was the priest's prediction, but while the young tree spread strong roots and stretched wide branches, the cause of Catholicism itself was temporarily stunted by persecution so vigorous and severe that between 1829 and 1832 English and American naval commanders visiting Honolulu called upon Kaahumanu to plead that she desist. For her, Catholicism was insubordination. She insisted her people must have only one religion—that of Bingham's Protestantism. Her death, in June 1832, gave Catholics in the kingdom a brief respite from imprisonment and cruel punishments.

Kamehameha III was now eighteen, of an age to take direction of his own affairs. He chose as Kaahumanu's successor his half-sister Kinau, and their close relationship was such that, at first, she administered the kingdom as had Kaahumanu, with the same dependence on the guidance of the Reverend Mr. Bingham. Early in 1833, Kamehameha became angered over Kinau's refusal to allow him to purchase a brig he desired. Abruptly, he announced the termination of her office as *kuhina nui*. He sent a crier through the streets proclaiming the lifting of all prohibitions except those against theft and murder. He banished Bingham from court. Rumors circulated Honolulu that all American missionaries were to be banned from the kingdom. To the delight of American residents like Stephen Reynolds, self-taught lawyer, harbor pilot, and dancing master, there was a spontaneous and immediate return by Hawaiians to the customs of their past. On February 28, 1833, a few days after the break with Kinau and Bingham, Reynolds wrote in his diary: "At daylight the natives assembled in the yard next mine and had a great dance. The streets, lanes, fences, were filled with people to witness one of their former pastimes." Reynolds rejoiced with them in the return of the old relaxed freedom and went on to detail that "the native at whose house the dance took place (by name of Keomi) was first to be Baptized, first to be married in a Christian ceremony, 1st to turn off his wife, 1st in the dance, 1st in all turnings." [8]

Another American, Henry Peirce, wrote that "the King and his party have thrown off that ecclesiastical restraint which they have been under for so long a time. All their ancient games and customs are revived again." [9] For two years a lack of all restraint continued. Then, in 1835, Kamehameha III reinstated Kinau, of whom he was truly fond, and to make amends promised that her youngest son, Alex Liholiho, then an infant, would

8. Reynolds, pp. 20–21.
9. Kuykendall, p. 134n.

become next in succession to the throne. The return of Kinau was accompanied by the temporary return of Bingham's influence.

Persecution of Catholics was not only resumed but intensified. One elderly woman, condemned to hard labor in the fort because of her beliefs, insisted she would rather die. At Kinau's order, the old woman was rolled in human excrement in the prison yard.

From Boston in 1837 came censure of Hiram Bingham for his having forgotten that his was a mission of mercy and that his message was that of God's love. Only thirteen hundred Hawaiians had been admitted to church membership in the seventeen years of mission labors in the kingdom. Bingham was ordered to lower his standards and to open church membership rolls, a welcome change to many of the several companies of missionaries now in Hawaii, whose own personal emphasis was democracy rather than Calvinist authoritarianism.

As he approached the end of his power over the government, Bingham strove to accomplish his ends by legal strictures, which he hoped would continue after he left. He and Kinau set up exile colonies on Kahoolawe and Lanai, the former for men convicted of adultery, theft, or murder (all three crimes equal in Bingham's eyes) and the latter for adulteresses, female thieves, and murderesses. In 1837 he saw to it that Kamehameha III approved a set of laws banishing all Catholic teachers from the kingdom and making the teaching of Catholicism illegal. In 1838 he sought to encourage temperance by a set of liquor laws forbidding the sale of spirits by the glass and levying such a heavy duty on imports as to make drinking a prohibitive luxury. In France, these latter two edicts were interpreted as direct insults to French religion and French products, and it was determined the Hawaiian Kingdom should be confronted on both issues as well as on its favoritism to English as a second language. By 1839, the year of Kinau's death, trouble from those two edicts was on its way to Honolulu in the form of a French man-of-war.

Poor Bingham. Everything he had desired and everything he thought he had accomplished was now eluding him. On Kahoo-

lawe the male prisoners watched wind and current, swam to
Maui, stole canoes and food, rescued the women from Lanai,
and took them to Kahoolawe where they survived in a Robin
Hood existence, raiding Maui for supplies, until the environment of government changed. Bereft of political clout after the
death of Kinau, stripped of his leadership of the mission by the
Boston board, Bingham turned his energy to building the great
stone church of Kawaiahao. If he could not succeed in making
these islands a kingdom of God, he would build a church that
would dominate the landscape of Honolulu as he hoped his particular variety of Protestant Christianity would dominate the
hearts and minds of the future generations of Hawaii.

Kawaiahao was to be the largest structure in the kingdom and
loom as such for many years, but Hiram Bingham had to leave
without seeing it completed. Ostensibly because of Sybil
Bingham's failing health, he left Hawaii in 1841. His twenty-
one years of dedication and effort ended with a failure he did
not understand and a success he did not appreciate. Paradox, indeed. He sailed for Boston, leaving a literate Christian nation
that he had helped to bring into being, but a nation of people on
whose spirit he had left such deep wounds that it would be more
than a century before Hawaiians once again began to take pride
in who and what they were.

5

The Advent of Democracy

*F*OR years the Binghams and their mission colleagues had suffered varying degrees of cultural shock at rumors the king was sleeping with his sister. Hawaiian commoners and chiefs saw only good in such a union, for what could be more desirable than the joining of the precious *mana* of these last two surviving children of Kamehameha the Great and his sacred Queen Keopuolani? From earliest childhood, a relationship between the two had been encouraged and their marriage urged.

In 1825, Robert Dampier, artist with Lord Byron's *Blonde,* the British ship that returned the bodies of Kamehameha II and his consort to Hawaii, did a sketch of Nahienaena, a charming portrait of a ten-year-old who looks fourteen. There is an expression of composure in the great solemn eyes under the perfectly shaped dark wings of her eyebrows, a confidence with no trace of arrogance in the set of her full-lipped mouth and firm rounded chin. A coronet of feathers rests lightly on the cloud of her wavy black hair. She wears a feather cape of intricate design and in one hand holds the symbol of Hawaiian royalty, a feather-tipped standard, *kahili.* In the background is a thatch-roofed village under palms that soar skyward, a scene that evokes the old Hawaii in which Nahienaena and her brother were born. In a bay at the edge of the village, a three-masted ship rides at anchor, symbolic of the new Hawaii in which Nahienaena was to lose herself.

During their childhood and adolescence, the king and his sister moved back and forth from Honolulu to Lahaina, sometimes apart, sometimes together, sometimes each in a mission household chafing at its foreign restrictiveness and yet—in the case of Nahienaena and the William Richardses of Lahaina, Maui—warmed by genuine affection. There were frequent periods when, together, Nahienaena and her brother enjoyed an essentially Hawaiian environment, cloistered by their rank, indulged in the ancient way by chiefs and retainers. There are accounts that at one of these periods the white tapa of Hawaiian custom had been placed over the pair, and that they had been wed in the fashion of their own tradition.

Rumors of this having happened reached missionary ears, and the particular pressure placed on Nahienaena finally induced her to bolt from the household and teachings of William Richards, in whose care Keopuolani had placed her.

William Richards had arrived in Hawaii with the second company of missionaries in 1823. In morality he was as hardline as Hiram Bingham, and his encounters with whaling captains at the rowdy port of Lahaina were even stormier than those of Bingham in Honolulu. In 1831, Richards built the high school at Lahainaluna, high on the red dirt slopes above Lahaina. There he began to teach young Hawaiians the principles of democracy on which, unlike Bingham, he felt the emphasis of governance in this kingdom should be placed. It was this more open mind of Richards's that led the rebellious Nahienaena to never lose her affection for him, and puritan though he was in his own moral outlook, Richards's aloha for the princess never altered though she took to drink and a series of lovers, including an American sailor, Abe Russell, who received a lifetime pension from the government of Hawaii because of Nahienaena's fondness for him. Even though now each had other loves, at times Kamehameha III and Nahienaena continued their own relationship. A consort of suitable rank was found for the princess, but like so many of her generation and like her older brother Liholiho before her, she could not find herself in the confusion of new standards and old traditions that were tormenting crosscurrents in her life. Dissipated, unhappy, in despair, there was, as she reached the age of twenty, little trace left of the wide-eyed composure and naturalness that Dampier had painted in the lovely face of Nahienaena at ten. In December 1836, as if her body could no longer bear either the weight of flesh or guilt placed upon it, she died soon after bearing a still-born child.

For Kamehameha III this was the end of his youth, this death of his beloved sister. At the same time, it was the stimulus to his direct interest in the shape and function of his government. He moved the capital from Honolulu to Lahaina to be near the mausoleum he had built to house the coffins of Nahienaena and of their mother, who had died more than a decade earlier. In Lahaina, he put himself under the astute democratic influence of his sister's teacher, William Richards, asking Richards to instruct the chiefs daily in "political economy," discourses on the rights of free men in a democratic society to which on occasion the young king came to listen.

The previous year, 1835, the king had shown signs of a new maturity in his handling of the trouble between chiefs and commoners at Koloa, Kauai. Three Americans doing business as Ladd and Company had been granted the first agricultural lease ever given foreigners—one thousand acres and rights to an adjacent waterfall, at an annual rental of three hundred dollars. The lease was itself a sign of revolutionary change from Hawaiian tradition, giving to lessees the right to hire commoners for their labor force without going through the chiefs. There was specified a company payment of twenty-five cents a month to the government for each commoner hired to offset the loss of working days that that commoner owed as his tax. Laborers were to be provided with subsistence—fish and *poi* at the cost of approximately one cent per day per laborer—and a fair wage, which Ladd and Company proposed be a *hapawalu*—twelve and one-half cents a day.

In Honolulu and Lahaina in 1835, there were thousands of commoners moved in from country districts working at a going wage of twenty-five cents, but in places as remote as Koloa, times had not yet so changed. A myth persists that the contract labor brought in to work Hawaiian plantations in the latter half of the nineteenth century was brought because Hawaiians were either unwilling to work or too lazy. Nothing could be farther from the truth. It was the declining population that forced the kingdom to go abroad for labor as each decade saw a drop in the Hawaiian birthrate and a sharp decrease in their numbers. Hawaiians then as now worked at a broad range of jobs and professions, and the Hawaiian who is an unskilled laborer still works at a phenomenally fast and steady pace, willing to undertake the heaviest physical demands. What the Hawaiian was unwilling to do in 1835 and still is reluctant to do in the late twentieth century is to time-serve. The "busy work" syndrome is anathema to Hawaiians and was in missionary days. In modern Hawaii, those Hawaiians who do unskilled labor or work in the construction trades perform at a fast, steady pace even the most demanding physical labor. In jobs such as Honolulu's garbage collection services, Hawaiians prefer to negotiate for a workday of "tasks to be accomplished" rather than a time-serving number of hours.

In 1835, the commoners hired by the Koloa Plantation yoked themselves fifteen together to pull plows across the field. The workday began at dawn and ended at dusk, but they were jubilant at the chance given to them by the king to earn something for themselves from the labor of their hands and backs. When the chiefs posted armed guards to prevent their commoners from going to work for Ladd and Company, the king had sent his agent to intervene and to insist on this right for Koloa commoners. By 1837, he had himself abolished the old custom of "working days" and paid his workmen. In 1839 this was one of the freedoms guaranteed to all Hawaiians in the Magna Charta of the Hawaiian Kingdom, the proclamation of the shift from feudalism to democracy made by Kamehameha III in a Hawaiian Bill of Rights. Translated, in part, from its poetic Hawaiian, this bill resounded with the influence of the American Declaration of Independence:

> God hath made of one blood all nations of men, to dwell on the face of the earth in unity and blessedness. God has also bestowed certain rights alike on all men, and all chiefs, and all people of all lands. These are some of the rights which he has given alike to every man,

and every chief—life, limb, liberty, the labor of his hands, and productions of his mind.[1]

No foreigner drafted this. It was authored by Boaz Mahune, a Lahainaluna graduate, revised by the chiefs and signed by the king only one month before that indignant French man-of-war, spurred by the anti-Catholic and liquor laws of 1837 and 1838, sailed into Honolulu harbor. French consul Dudoit hurried aboard, gave his suggestion to Admiral LaPlace, and to the astonishment of Honolulu, the cannons of the man-of-war were pointed at the town with the ultimatum that unless French demands to end the 1837 anti-Catholic edicts and remove the 1838 liquor prohibitions were met within five hours, *L'Artemise* would bombard the town. In five hours not even word of the ultimatum could be sailed to Kamehameha III in his capital at Lahaina. The governor and chiefs of Oahu, faced with the decision, saw no way but to comply. Honolulu's Chinese and *haole* merchants offered quick *kokua* in loaning the $20,000 cash guarantee demanded by LaPlace that the Hawaiian agreement would be kept.

A day and a half later, when the king arrived in Honolulu, LaPlace and his French marines had been ashore to celebrate mass in the Catholic mission, grog shops were doing a brisk business in liquor by the glass, and a new freedom—that of religion—had been forced by France into island life. It was useless for Kamehameha to contemplate arming his small kingdom against the might of such a power and the possible recurrence of such an assault. He preferred the diplomatic alternative of trying for a tripartite treaty of respect for his independence from Great Britain, the United States, and France, as suggested by an American visitor, William Farnham, a few months after the French crisis.

In 1840 Farnham was commissioned to pursue such a treaty, while in domestic affairs the process of democracy was resumed. The Constitution adopted that year was protested by commoners, who insisted they were not yet ready for freedom

---

1. Ralph S. Kuykendall, *The Hawaiian Kingdom: 1778–1854* (Honolulu: The University of Hawaii, 1938), p. 160.

and responsibility. The king's use of foreigners in his government was another major complaint by Hawaiians. William Richards and Dr. Gerrit P. Judd, both former missionaries, were in high posts in the government. When Dr. and Mrs. Judd renounced their American citizenship to swear allegiance to Kamehameha III, both commoners and chiefs grumbled that foreigners ought not to be allowed Hawaiian citizenship.

The Hawaiian commoner of the 1840s was the particular victim of missionary attitudes that communicated a not so subtle cultural inferiority—a message received by the *alii* as well. The mission schools in which Hawaiians became quickly literate, and the churches where they sought God's love and grace, taught them that the Hawaiian past, Hawaiian culture with all its music, literature, dance, knowledge, and celebration of life, was dark and evil, an ineradicable blot staining the Hawaiian soul, a burden to be weighed on Judgment Day.

As a nation, Hawaiians understood the missionary's unspoken message: although in the eyes of God all men might be equal, in the eyes of the American Protestant missionaries, those with a heathen past and dark skin could never be so. The burden of their own heritage, laid on Hawaiians for twenty years in such a negative fashion, became so agonizing that along with the high mortality rate from epidemics of physical disease, there were in the 1840s hundreds of deaths from the effects of this psychological trauma. Depression and morbid awareness of the hopelessness of their condition as Hawaiians was a phenomenon described in a popular saying of the time as *na kanaka okuu wale aku no i kau uhane,* "the people freely dismissed their souls and died."

For those who could resist mission pressures and to travelers visiting Hawaii at the time, the outward appearance of island life was not that grim. The sun shone each day in its benign and ameliorating way. The surf rose in exhilarating temptation to polished koa boards. Hawaiians and foreigners together raced horses over the hard sand of Oahu and Maui and Hilo beaches, drank in the grog shops of port towns, lay together exchanging music, poetry, and love under the star-studded sky, or prowled the reefs by torchlight in the balmy nights to lure fish to net and spears. For the *alii* and well-to-do foreigners, for the increasing numbers of part-Hawaiians of comfortable economic status, there was in Honolulu and in such towns as Hilo a pleasant social life of picnics, balls, dancing school, and flirtations that redeemed the pall so long cast by mission dominance. The opening of church standards after the departure of Bingham gave rise to an authentic Hawaiian style of Christianity, with Hawaiians becoming ministers. Hawaiian ministers like the Reverend James Kekela of Hilo volunteered to take the gospel to those still heathen islands of his ancestors' homeland, the Marquesas.

In 1841, Hawaiians who had been most vociferous against the new style of government avidly discussed the ballot letters by which they were to elect "men of wisdom and prudence" to the seven-member House of Representatives of the new legislature. One man was to be elected from Kauai and Niihau, two from Oahu, two from the islands of Maui, Molokai, Lanai, and Kahoolawe, and two from the island of Hawaii. Women were to be seated only in the far larger and more powerful House of Nobles, *alii* given lifetime appointments by the king. That first legislature ought to have been in session in 1843, but again foreign assault intervened at the very time William Richards and Timothy Haalilio were abroad to continue Farnham's groundwork on a tripartite treaty to prevent such crises.

In December 1842, Richards and Haalilio had consulted with the then American secretary of state, Daniel Webster. As a result, for the first time, the Kingdom of Hawaii had been mentioned in the president's State of the Union message to the American Congress. In February 1843, the two envoys were on their way across the Atlantic to discuss the treaty with Great Britain when a British naval commander, Lord George Paulet, took it upon himself to use force to settle the long-standing land litigation claims in Honolulu of his old friend, the former British consul, Richard Charlton.

Paulet sailed into Honolulu harbor on February 10 in the same bold fashion as had the French man-of-war in 1839. This time the king was in Honolulu, however, and the ultimatum given him to acquiesce to British demands was eight hours.

Laura Fish Judd, wife of the good doctor, was a faithful, able diarist who recorded the frantic parade of foreigners and their wagonloads of household goods to Honolulu's water front that morning. In the harbor, British subjects took asylum on a British frigate towed offshore for that purpose. Americans took sanctuary on the U.S.S. *Boston* which happened to be in port. No nation could have been so defenseless as Kamehameha's kingdom. No longer were *alii* trained in or interested in the arts of war. The whitewashed walls of the fort Golovnin had admired held only a battery of obsolete cannon, and its interior was used as headquarters for the governor of Oahu, a parade ground for the few Hawaiian guards in the king's service, as well as for a prison for striking or miscreant foreign seamen and Hawaiian lawbreakers.

The foreign community was generous in its advice to the king.

> Unfortunately, [wrote Laura Judd] each had a separate plan to
> propose. Some said, "Don't yield a single iota; let them fire!"
> Others asked, "In that case, who will pay for American property
> thus destroyed?" One proposed cession of the islands to the U.S.
> and France, pro tem. Another inquired, "Will the U.S. government
> accept and protect, and the French ever relinquish their hold, if once
> in possession?" The interest of some of us was identified with that
> of the nation. With it we must live or die! [2]

By the end of the eight hours, Kamehameha had made his courageous decision. "I will not die piecemeal. They may cut off my head at once. I will yield the breath of my kingdom and trust to my commissioners in London, and the magnanimity of the British government to redress the wrong and restore my rights." As Paulet brought his men ashore to take possession of the town, as the Hawaiian flag was hauled down and the Union Jack raised in its place, the king made an agonized proclamation to his people: "Hear Ye! I make known to you that I am in perplexity by reason of the difficulties into which I have been brought without cause; therefore, I have given away the life of

2. Laura Fish Judd, *Honolulu: Sketches of Life in the Hawaiian Islands 1828–1861* (Honolulu: Reprinted by *The Honolulu Star Bulletin*, 1928), p. 94.

our land, hear ye! But my rule over you, my people, and your privilege will continue, for I have hope that the life of the land will be restored when my conduct is justified." [3]

It was May before news of Paulet's action reached his government. London's decision, meriting Kamehameha III's trust in the magnanimity of the British government and the diplomatic skill of Richards and Haalilio, was to dispatch Admiral Thomas from Valparaiso to Honolulu to settle the affair, but this order, and Thomas's execution of it, took until July. For those five months Hawaii had no way of knowing whether the Hawaiian flag would ever be restored. Lord Paulet tended to business by beginning the registration of land claims, a necessary change from feudal land tenure to modern land title that Hawaii had delayed. Paulet relaxed with a handsome chiefess from Waianae, the social life of Honolulu continued in all its gaiety, mission churches and mission schools operated as usual, the new Catholic cathedral rose to completion under the shade of Father Bachelot's *kiawe* tree, and in the secrecy of the royal mausoleum, Dr. Judd wrote documents by candlelight, using Kaahumanu's coffin as his desk.

It was not until July 31 that Kamehameha's kingdom was formally given back to him, the ceremony taking place on a plain east of Honolulu which is now Thomas Square. For years, July 31 was celebrated as a day of Thanksgiving in Hawaii, and in the first Thanksgiving service that afternoon at Kawaiahao Church, Kamehameha spoke the words that became the motto of his kingdom, and remain the motto of this state: *Ua mau ke ea o ka aina i ka pono*, "the life of the land is preserved in righteousness."

At last, on May 20, 1845, on a red carpet laid especially for opening day, the first legislature convened in Honolulu, which the king had again made the capital. Travelers arriving there then were not greeted by any vision of tropical beauty. At one side of the fort a slaughterhouse hung out over the waters of the harbor, and on the other side was a row of shanties, reeking of dead fish and decaying vegetables. The town was a mishmash of

3. Judd, p. 94.

flimsy adobe structures, frame buildings, some stone houses, still many grass shacks, all crowded onto narrow streets. Trees were scarce, with the only greenery being that around the European-style house which the king had built on the site now occupied by Iolani Palace.

There were three physicians in Honolulu and eleven mercantile establishments, several of them owned by Chinese and stocking such goods as grass matting and velvet jackets. The import list for 1843 showed the cosmopolitan nature of Honolulu's tastes: 51 French accordions, 2 bear skins, 16 dozen brass door bolts, 1 church bell, 12 cases of soy sauce, 400 gallons of rum, and 236 cases of gin. Carpenters, masons, wheelwrights, a saddle and harness maker, a barber, and a cigar maker all had business establishments in the capital. There were two hotels accommodating an unusual number of tourist visitors for so remote a part of the world. Rates were one dollar a day or six dollars a week for room and board.

In Honolulu all summer and into the fall the new legislature earnestly discussed the best way to modernize the government and in October passed an Organic Act, the kingdom's first, establishing executive departments of finance, foreign affairs, education (which was also assigned health care, care of indigents, prison supervision, and the keeping of vital statistics), and a ministry of interior through which the last leap out of feudalism was to be accomplished by resolving the question that had spurred Paulet's takeover: land title. An attorney general was also mandated by the act.

The outcry of Hawaiian commoners was intense against the king's selection of foreigners for four of the five posts in his new cabinet. A Scots visitor, Robert Crichton Wyllie, whose shrewd assessment of the kingdom had been published in a six-month series in Honolulu's newspaper, *The Friend,* was persuaded by Kamehameha III to remain in the kingdom and become minister of foreign affairs. Since Wyllie felt no British subject could ever renounce the citizenship that was his birthright, he proposed a new class of Hawaiian that was to make room for the carpetbaggers who took control of the government in the final years of the monarchy. At Wyllie's suggestion, letters of denization were awarded by the privy council to foreigners who announced their intent to reside in the kingdom. As denizens, they would be entitled to all the rights and privileges of native-born Hawaiians, including the right to serve in high posts in the king's government.

In the new cabinet with Denizen Wyllie were Dr. Judd as minister of finance, William Richards as minister of education, and Keoni Ana (John Young II) as minister of interior. John Ricord, the only bona fide law graduate in Hawaii, was made attorney general although he had a difficult personality and the record of a drifter, having practiced law in Florida, Texas, California, and Oregon. Ricord was the first legal adviser to the Board of Commissioners to Quiet Land Title, a predominantly Hawaiian commission who began what they believed to be a two-year task early in 1846.

The Hawaiian word *mahele* means "separation," a sorting out or division. Its use to describe the difficult sorting out of land titles in Hawaii is exact, for what had to be done was to separate the vested feudal interest of the king in each acre of land in the kingdom before any clear titles could be awarded to those whose land claims the commissioners found valid. Land in Hawaii had always been a trust, administered under the communal subsistence and conservation ethic, *aloha aina,* with control the prerogative of the ruling chiefs to award to those *alii* who supported them. Commoners had never been anything other than tenants, with their persons and labor regarded as simply one more resource at the disposal of the chiefs. The changed economy and governance of the kingdom now demanded that land be made available as a commodity, as it had been in the 1835 Koloa Plantation lease, that it become "real estate," a concept Hawaiians found difficult to comprehend. Need for a *mahele* stemmed not only from the pressures of foreign land claimants like Paulet's friend, the former British consul, but was apparent from any assessment of changed land use patterns throughout the kingdom.

In the most southerly Big Island district of Kau (now the southernmost area in the United States), where one third of the population of five thousand Hawaiians were Catholics, the old subsistence crops of taro, bananas, and sweet potatoes were still being raised, but much land area that later became canelands was planted to export crops: oranges, mangoes, custard apples, and figs for the booming California market that depended on Hawaii at that period for citrus and for shipments of salt beef, for fine laundering of its linens in Honolulu, and for the higher education of its children at privately operated Punahou School.

There had been little use in ancient times of the interior or semibarren uplands on Hawaii island. John Parker, an American, had started a small ranch in Kohala during the reign of Kamehameha the Great, tamed wild cattle descended from Vancouver's original gift for his spread, and added hundreds of thousands of acres to his ranch by marrying a landed chiefess. In the 1840s Parker Ranch pioneered a new land use in the kingdom and offered a new profession to Hawaiians—that of cowboy, *paniolo,* a word adapted from the *vaqueros* who came from Mexico to teach them how to ride and rope and herd cattle, and whose identification of themselves was "español." On Maui's upland slopes, there were also new ranches. Land title was an important aspect in the wide-scale grazing of cattle, sheep, and goats, but the new large-scale industry for which clear title was a necessity to attract venture capital was sugar cane. Wheat, cotton, tobacco, silk, and sugar cane were all experimental crops, but the promise of Hawaii's future was in cane, and in the 1840s there were already a number of small sugar plantations on Maui. Most of these were owned by Chinese, and Chinese sugarmasters directed the early sugar mills.

The goals of the missionaries who arrived in 1820 had been to transform the kingdom into a nation of small independent freeholders, with lands divided into New England–style farms of a few acres each. The Great *Mahele* discouraged that dream, although the land commissioners were men convinced that it was necessary commoners be given their own lands. The obstacle to any equitable land division in Hawaii was that it had never been equitably divided to begin with. The land holdings of the chiefs were vast tracts. The *kuleana* tenanted by Hawaiian commoners were never more than several acres in size, and the sum total of all of these for which clear title was petitioned was only 30,000 acres. In the Great *Mahele*, four-fifths of the land area of the kingdom was the rightful claim of the chiefs and of the crown—the latter dividing his share into one and one-half million acres of public lands for support of the government and one million acres of crown lands for support of the royal family. Two-fifths of all the lands, 1,600,000 acres, was awarded to the *alii*. Included in these vast estates of chiefs, king, and government lands were hundreds of thousands of acres of mountain tops and gorges, lava flows, desert, stony beaches, wastelands, the entire island of Niihau, and the semi-arid small island of Kahoolawe.

The reality of the Great *Mahele* was thus not the redistribution of lands, but a clearing of their titles. Key in this was a determination of the value of the king's interest in all lands as an amount equivalent to one-third of that land's unimproved value. Payment of that fee commuted the king's interest and gained chiefs, commoners, and the few foreign land claimants a clear title registered in a royal patent and so listed on the pages of the *mahele* book. Months of negotiation were required, with the king and chiefs sitting in consultation on each division of lands, signing facing pages of the *mahele* book to testify certain lands had been given by the chiefs to the king in payment of the commutation fee, and certain lands had been awarded clear title by the king through such commutation payment.

For commoners, the commutation fee was set at only one-fourth the unimproved value, but even so, few commoners chose to clear their titles. In 1906, the territorial government was still dealing with unresolved certificates of award for titles still clouded by the feudal interest of a defunct monarchy.

The *Mahele* took not two years, but nine, extending beyond the reign and lifetime of Kamehameha III, who died in 1854. A prominent influence on the *Mahele* was the policy advice of Judge William Little Lee, a Harvard law graduate from Troy, New York, who stopped over in Honolulu en route to Oregon in 1846. He was persuaded by Dr. Judd to stay, take out letters of denization, and accept an appointment as a judge. When John Ricord moved on in 1847, Lee succeeded him as counsel to the Board of Commissioners to Quiet Land Title. Lee also served as

Kamehameha III's envoy when in August 1849 Hawaii was
again subjected to a crisis by the arrival of a hostile French admiral. This second French assault in a decade was by Admiral
Legorant deTromelin who came into Honolulu harbor with two
ships, *La Poursuivante* and *Le Gassendi*. French consul Dillon
had long complained to the government of Hawaii about what
France considered the untenable supervision of the dual public
school system, Catholic and Protestant, by former missionary
Richard Armstrong, who succeeded to the post of minister of
education after William Richards's death. Records prove that
Armstrong had indeed favored Protestant schools in per-pupil
allocation and construction grants, but M. Dillon, the current
French consul, was so disliked in Honolulu that his complaints
concerning discrimination against Catholic schools, which were
also part of the public school system, were not heeded. Dillon
was always protesting—about the schools, about the duty on
brandy and wines being discriminatory against French products,
about the lack of compliance with the 1839 agreement which
stated French would be used as an official language on certain
Hawaiian customs documents.

No ultimatum accompanied Admiral deTromelin's August
22, 1849, demands that all these issues be promptly resolved.
Dr. Judd accompanied Judge Lee to discuss these items aboard
the admiral's flagship, but while they were there, the French
marched ashore, sacked the fort, spiked the cannon, threw the
Hawaiian supply of gunpowder into the harbor, and seized the
new government building that housed Hawaii's first post office
and the customs house. They also confiscated the king's yacht.
DeTromelin's cannons remained poised at Honolulu for seven
days until, as inexplicably as he had arrived and without resolution of any of his demands, the admiral departed with M. Dillon
and family aboard and the king's yacht in tow.

This third threat to his sovereignty left the king in despair. He
dispatched Dr. Judd to Europe and America for one last try at a
tripartite treaty. Should this final effort fail, Judd was provided
by the king with secret instructions to offer the Kingdom of
Hawaii to the highest bidder. Lucy Judd wrote in her journal
that she had seen these documents and was frightened by the

knowledge that such unlimited power and responsibility had been delegated to her husband.

Judd, accompanied by the princes Alex Liholiho and Lot Kamehameha, was gone for nearly a year, with such encouraging reception by the governments of the United States, Britain, and France that the unlimited power given him did not have to be used. Word of that secret instruction had leaked, however, and the third visit of a French warship, *LaSérieuse* in 1851, pushed the king into agreement with many Americans in his kingdom that there was no alternative but to offer his islands to the United States. In 1852 a bill to annex the Hawaiian Kingdom was first introduced into the U.S. Congress. The United States commissioner to Hawaii, David L. Gregg, was empowered to work with Robert Crichton Wyllie, whom Kamehameha III had chosen to draft a treaty by which annexation could be accomplished. Gregg advised Wyllie that the U.S. Senate was likely to find the king's terms unacceptable: immediate entry of Hawaii as a state, $75,000 a year for ten years to maintain the centrally administered public school system, and a $300,000 annual pension for support of the royal family and the chiefs.

Men like Princess Bernice Pauahi's husband, Charles Reed Bishop, missionaries, sugar planters, and businessmen who sought domestic steamer routes between Honolulu and San Francisco signed petitions urging this annexation to the United States. Those against such a treaty were strong chiefs like John Papa Ii, and Princess Bernice Pauahi's father, Chief Paki. Most effective in arguing against his uncle's action was Kinau's son Alex Liholiho, the king's nephew, heir to the throne and together with his brother Lot a companion on Dr. Judd's 1849–1850 mission abroad. It was on that trip, in the United States, that Prince Alex had suffered a bad experience with Americans. A conductor on a Pullman car had mistaken the prince for someone's colored manservant and summarily ordered him to leave.

Alex's reaction is preserved in his own words:

Confounded fool! The first time that I ever received such treatment, not in England, or France, or anywhere else. But in this country I

must be treated like a dog to come and go at an American's bidding.
Here I must say that I am disappointed at the Americans. They have
no manners, no politeness, not even common civilities to a stranger.
And not only in this single case, but almost everybody that one
meets in the United States are saucy. Even the waiters in their hotels
in answering a bell, instead of coming and knocking at the door,
they stalk into the room as if they were paying one a visit, and after
one has given an order for something they pretend not to hear—give
a grunt which cannot be exactly imitated by pen and paper, but
would go something like—hu! In England an African can pay his
fare for the Cars, and he can sit alongside of Queen Victoria. The
Americans talk, and they think a great deal of their liberty, and
strangers often find that too many liberties are taken of their
comfort, just because his hosts are a free people.[4]

Late in 1854, U.S. Commissioner Gregg took the liberty of
presuming that he could hurry Kamehameha III's signature to
the annexation agreement by alarming him with a rumor of
American freebooters arriving from California to seize the Hawaiian government. It was a strategy that backfired. A British, a
French, and two American warships lay in Honolulu harbor.
Robert Wyllie, to whom Gregg and a United States naval officer
told their story of the supposed plot, called in the French and
British consuls who offered the aid of their vessels should such
an attempt be made. Wyllie then called Gregg, told him of the
French and British offers, which left Gregg with no alternative
except to also pledge the aid of the United States. How else but
to interpret the assurance from these three nations? Could it be
anything other than the tripartite guarantee which Hawaii had
sought for the past fourteen years?

Kamehameha III was ecstatic. The need for his pursuit of annexation was no more. On December 8 he published a proclamation: "My independence is more firmly established than ever
before." [5] Only one week later, after an illness of two days, he

4. *The Journal of Prince Alexander Liholiho*, edited by Jacob Adler (Honolulu: The
University of Hawaii Press for the Hawaiian Historical Society, 1967), p. 108.
5. Proclamation published in *Polynesian*, December 9, 1854.

died. He had reigned through thirty critical years as ruling chief, as *Ka Moi* (the King), and since the Constitution of 1852, as Supreme Executive Magistrate of the kingdom his father had created.

6

The Last of the Kamehamehas

$\mathcal{A}$ NEW era was announced as his intention by Alexander Liholiho, Kamehameha IV, who succeeded his uncle in January 1855. In a way quite different from Alex's idealistic inference, a new era had already begun in 1850 with legislative passage of an Act for the Governance of Masters and Servants. Under this permission to import indentured labor into Hawaii, Captain Cass of the brig *Thetis* brought three hundred Chinese from Amoy, Fukien province, in 1852 and 1853. They were all males, most of them contracted as labor for the plantations, and a few bound to contracts for domestic service in the homes of sugar planters or wealthy Honoluluans.

This was the first influx of immigrant labor, spurred by the needs of cane planters. It was the beginning of a contract labor pattern that was to confront the democratic ideals launched in the kingdom by William Richards, to change the population patterns of Hawaii, and to return the work environment of the islands to a quasi feudalism. The 1850 act making all this possible was at first condemned and then condoned by missionaries like Elias Bond of Kohala. Bond, who had arrived at his mission station in 1841, was among the ardent abolitionists who complained that the passage of the 1850 act permitted conditions tantamount to slavery on Hawaii's plantations. Withdrawal of the Boston board's support of the Hawaiian missions forced Elias Bond, and many of his colleagues like the Baldwins of

Maui, to go into business to be able to keep their missions operable. In 1863, when Elias Bond founded Kohala Sugar Company, the plantation that was to be the economic sustenance of his district for over a century, he used contract labor.

Such contradictory missionary attitudes were no surprise and constituted no paradox to the opposition editor Abraham Fornander of the *Argus* and later of the *Argus and New Era*. Fornander, a Swede who had attended the universities of Upsala and Lund, a former whaler, husband of the chiefess Pinao, protégé of Dr. T. C. B. Rooke, and admirer of Kamehameha IV, was an outspoken critic of missionary influence on the government of the Hawaiian Kingdom. He referred to Dr. Judd as "the White King," charged that Richards, Judd, Armstrong, and their colleagues had put forth only a mask of platitudes, a paper semblance of democracy to hide the true fact of their oligarchy. Fornander urged a return to the rule of the chiefs, a curtailment of franchise until education in responsibility for self-government should be effected by drastic improvements in the kingdom's public school system. That once contagious zeal for learning had fallen off. Hawaiian education was no longer of the quality it had been when schools were a part of the Protestant mission stations, and the *palapala* a conduit to the *mana* of the Christian God.

An equal concern of the fiery Swedish editor was the health and survival of the Hawaiian people. In 1853, the penurious attitude of the king's cabinet had circumvented a mass vaccination program, with the result that in the terrible smallpox epidemic of 1853, on Oahu alone, the private estimate was not the official 2,500 deaths, but a cost of 6,000 Hawaiian lives. Whole villages in Oahu's rural areas and on the neighbor islands lay abandoned either from the ravages of such epidemics or from the steady migration of Hawaiians to the towns of Honolulu, Lahaina, or overseas to California and the Pacific Northwest.

There was, as Kamehameha IV began his nine-year reign, no more one Hawaiian stereotype than there was one predictable kind of island *haole* or one kind of Chinese. Freed from their traditional obligations of labor to chiefs and king, many Hawaiians chose lives of idleness and what mission puritans labeled as dissipation. Because these drifters among the population concentrated in Honolulu and Lahaina, they were visible in an impression of numbers far beyond their actual percentage in a Hawaiian population whose dwindling majority continued to be independent farmers, fishermen, harbor pilots, longshoremen, cowboys, ranchers, schoolteachers, writers and editors, scholars, government workers, policemen, ministers, and like the Reverend Mr. Kekela of Hilo, Christian missionaries. Hawaiians were the backbone of the plantation labor force during the reigns of both Kamehameha IV and his brother, Kamehameha V, who succeeded to the throne in November 1863 after Alex's tragic early death.

These two brothers, sons of Kinau, grandsons of Kamehameha the Great, were the last two rulers of the direct Kamehameha line. Both of them had a preference for things British, including the Anglican church. Both were vehement opponents of annexation to the United States, an option still cherished by many in the missionary and business group of American residents. Both were responsible for what was, perhaps, the most pleasant of all periods in the history of the Hawaiian Kingdom—a time when Hawaii was still predominantly Hawaiian in population, when all the arts and institutions of civilization had become Hawaiian custom, and when the great progress prophesied by Vassily Golovnin in 1818 seemed on the threshold of fruition.

The mixture of Hawaiian, Chinese, American, English, and French influences were a harmonious balance. Whalers, diversified agriculture, and the new sugar industry gave promise to the economy, with the finalization of the Great *Mahele* in 1855 freeing land to be sold, leased, used, and transferred as its owners so pleased without the traditional uncertainty of interference from the government. The foreign crises of the 1840s were over. The worst pressures of missionary puritanism were relaxed as their influence in the government lessened. Opera, musical concerts, and the theater—boycotted by adamant Calvinists—were much enjoyed by Hawaiians, part-Hawaiians, and the more urbane of the foreign community. Islanders such as Swedish Lutheran Abraham Fornander and pro-Anglican Kamehameha IV attended Christmas Day mass in the Catholic cathedral. The Mormons had founded a temporary Hawaiian Zion on the island of Lanai. Grog shops and brothels and dance halls on Honolulu's water front gave visiting sailors the wild brawls and roistering dissipation they expected in such a port.

A postal service provided efficient delivery of mail throughout the kingdom, a welcome change from the former need to depend on the mail pouch of visiting ships and the shuffling through a sack of letters dumped on the floor of a ship agent's office. The public school system, criticized though it was by such as Fornander, gave a basic education of varying quality to most children aged four to fourteen. The Board of Health, a pioneer in its attempt to attack public health problems on a nationwide basis, wrestled with control of the spread of such new diseases as leprosy, which first struck Hawaiians in Kamehameha IV's reign. It was then called the Chinese Pox and was believed to have been brought in by the contract laborers who arrived by the shipload following the three hundred Fukienese who came on the voyages of the *Thetis*.

The Chinese already longtime residents of the kingdom were Cantonese, and with the exception of the passengers on the *Thetis*, subsequent contract labor immigrants also came from the area of Canton and Hong Kong. The Amoy men of the *Thetis* were unable to converse with their fellow countrymen except in Hawaiian. Its use, grafted onto a simple English vocabulary, pronounced with the familiar speech rhythms of the speaker, became the basis for Hawaiian pidgin, the lingua franca that is still the familiar street language of islanders today. This was the constantly changing dialect English used by the many peoples of the "new era" that began in 1850 with legalization of contract labor. Thousands of foreign laborers imported from Asia and Europe used pidgin to communicate with each other, with the clerks in plantation stores, with government officials, with the often heavy-handed *luna* (plantation supervisors), and with the *wahine* whose aloha was almost never discriminatory.

Language alone did not separate the first contract labor immigrants from Hawaii's pioneer Chinese. The newcomers were what planters called "coolies," beginning their lives in the islands at the bottom of the economic and the social scale. Theirs was a far different Hawaiian experience from the Chinese merchants and planters who were an integral part of the gay social life of Kamehameha IV's early years on the throne. Balls, picnics, celebrations of all kinds had a cosmopolitan guest list. In 1856, when the king wed part-Hawaiian Emma Rooke, granddaughter of the *haole* chief John Young, Chinese merchants of Honolulu and Lahaina gave a lavishly elegant wedding reception for the royal couple. In 1858, when the prince of Hawaii was born to Alex and Emma, the entire population of the kingdom rejoiced at the birth of the first royal heir to a reigning monarch since the days of Kamehameha the Great.

The little prince was three years old when the American Civil War began, with a distinctly beneficial economic effect on the kingdom that it was expected he would one day rule. Sugar prices soared, with profits so high that the 30 percent American import tariff on Hawaiian sugar hardly made a difference to the new plantations that opened on Kauai, Oahu, Maui, and Hawaii. Charles Reed Bishop, who founded the first Hawaiian bank in 1858, floated loans for many of the new planters. Samuel Northrup Castle and Amos Starr Cooke, former missionaries, did the "factoring," purchase of supplies, keeping of accounts, and marketing for many of the new plantations in their firm that is today a strong multinational corporation— Castle and Cooke. For a time it was projected by enthusiasts like John Papa Ii that Hawaii might also capture the cotton market from the war-torn Confederacy, but Ii was able to persuade only a few Hawaiian landowners to plant cotton, the largest project being several hundred acres at Waimea, on the Big Island.

That intrepid Scots bachelor, Denizen Robert Crichton Wyllie, was Kamehameha IV's mentor, close friend, and minister of foreign affairs. It was Wyllie's very British conviction that the Confederacy was bound to be victorious, but the king disagreed with him. At Alex's insistence, the political stance of Hawaii toward the War Between the States was one of strict neutrality. Among Hawaiians themselves, the preference—due to missionary influence—was for the northern side. Several hundred Hawaiians volunteered for service in the Union Army. Southerners in Hawaii were generally regarded with suspicion, as was the case with Walter Murray Gibson, who arrived as a Mormon missionary in 1861 to carry forward the work on Lanai that had been interrupted by the recall of the Mormon elders during the Utah wars. Gibson, a native Virginian, one-time homesteader on the banks of the Savannah River, veteran of international intrigue in central America and in Java, was—like Abraham Fornander—ostracized by Hawaii's establishment *haole* community, particularly by those loyal to the American Protestant Mission, which was now independently organized as the Hawaiian Evangelical Association.

In late August 1862, the four-year-old prince of Hawaii fell suddenly ill and died, leaving his parents so devastated by grief that fifteen months later, suffering the double burden of his accidental shooting of an American friend, Kamehameha IV, only twenty-nine years of age, followed his small son to the grave. On the last day of November 1863, his older brother Lot was proclaimed Kamehameha V, and for the next eight years the ideals of return to chiefly governance, the return to a Hawaiian cultural identity, the exploration of an economic alternative to sugar, and the strong personal rule of a Hawaiian king (which Alex had intended) were the "new era" of this last ruler in the Kamehameha dynasty.

Change was advertised by Lot's refusal on accession to swear to uphold the Constitution of 1852, which had supplanted the old ballot letter with the improvement of universal franchise to all males but which had demoted the title of the king to the peculiarly American term Supreme Executive Magistrate. Kamehameha V himself drafted the Constitution of 1864, imposing the old order of power and privilege through rank and wealth onto a nation that had learned to regard itself through that "paper mask" of democracy, which had been more real than Fornander was willing to believe. Now editor of the government-supported paper, the *Polynesian,* Abraham Fornander endorsed Kamehameha V's removal of the franchise and privilege of serving in the legislature from the poor, the landless, the Hawaiian commoner.

No protest rose from the *makaainana* who remembered from the past that such arbitrariness was to be expected from a ruling chief. Their love and their loyalty were constant. How could they be critical of a king with the cultural confidence to bring the sight and sound of hula back to his palace, and to include *kahuna* in his retinue? The majority of American residents who might in William Richards's day have been critical of this return to Hawaiian autocracy kept silence, for in this first year of his reign, 1864, Kamehameha V gave them the economic assistance of a government-funded Bureau of Immigration to recruit contract labor for their expanding cane acreage.

In both physical appearance and temperament, Lot Kamehameha was much like his grandfather, Kamehameha I. He was described by his contemporaries as the last of the great chiefs, and he carried out that role with natural power and dignity. His hand was strong, decisive, traditional. Yet, it was this very Hawaiian king who directed the Board of Education for the kingdom to effect the transfer of instruction in all public schools from Hawaiian to the English language, a change called for a decade earlier by Fornander and begged in petitions by parents such as those of several of the public schools on the island of Niihau. To compete with the foreigners arriving in such numbers to settle in these islands, Lot knew his people must become well educated in English, skilled in subjects not then in the average Hawaiian public school curriculum. He saw to it that Abraham Fornander was appointed the first inspector-general of schools in the kingdom. He appreciated the efforts of that other *haole* champion of the Hawaiian people, Walter Murray Gibson, still on Lanai but no longer Mormon. Gibson, whom Hawaiians called *Kipikona,* now personally controlled the three thousand fertile acres of Lanai's interior Palawai Basin and dreamed that old missionary dream of populating his small, lovely island with colonists from the United States who would be freeholders cultivating New England-style farms.

A free and independent yeoman class was not what Hawaii's planters sought as Hawaii's future. They were explicit in their desire for peasants who would be content to till the soil and wield a hoe and who would remain a docile, stable resource willing to work long hours at low pay—another improbable dream! Chinese contract laborers as they ended their indenture periods streamed off the plantations. Planters were faced with the need to replace much of their labor force at the expiration of each contract period. At the urging of the planters' association, and out of his own concern for the rapid decline of the Hawaiian population, Kamehameha V's 1864 Bureau of Immigration was to fund and supervise recruitment of "cognate races" (the anthropological term of the day) who would serve as a stable labor force for the plantations and at the same time be a compatible race with whom Hawaiians could intermarry to restore the vitality and replenish the numbers of what was, undeniably by now, a people otherwise doomed to extinction.

To those fearful of importing so many Chinese, Robert Crichton Wyllie suggested that the Japanese, islanders with a strong peasant stock, a tradition of loyalty to their lords such as the *makaainana* had to their *alii,* and a reputation for hard work and amenability, would be such a "cognate race." In 1865, Wyllie began correspondence with an American living in Japan, businessman Thomas Van Reed of Kanagawa, one of those foreign residents who had seized the opportunity presented by Commodore Perry's American naval visit forcing an Open Door policy on Japan in 1854. Three hundred years of isolation of those islands were now ended. The Hawaiian experience of a few shipwrecked Japanese who had been washed up on the shores of the kingdom and remained to become Hawaiian citizens had been positive. Wyllie wrote Van Reed that he could assure the Japanese government that any of its subjects who immigrated to Hawaii on labor contracts would be well treated, enjoy all the rights of free men, and perhaps be far better off as permanent settlers in the benign political climate of the Hawaiian Kingdom than in their own islands.

Wyllie died soon after beginning this correspondence, which his successor, the popular former French consul, Charles de Varigny, continued. The result, on May 17, 1868, was that 141 men, 6 women, and 2 small boys sailed from Yokohama as contract laborers bound for Hawaii, departing just one day before the Tokugawa government was taken over by the Mikado. They were not farmers, but mostly city people whom Van Reed had recruited in great haste, knowing that the change of regime would delay any such effort for the next several years. Among the group were palanquin bearers, roustabouts, and, so it is rumored, a number of displaced samurai who hid their true identity. They had no idea where Hawaii might be or what awaited them, but referred to their destination as *Tenjiku*— heaven. At their departure, they cut their topknots as a sign of farewell to the gods of their country, and overwhelmed by what might lie ahead, they entered into a covenant of brotherhood, pledging not to quarrel but to help and protect each other in every way in their new lives as contract laborers. Because of the historic date of their departure, they were ever after called First Year Meiji Men.

In addition to the beginning of group immigration on labor contracts, there continued the steady small flow of free settlers that had persisted since 1786. A number of Germans came in the 1860s, many of them settling into plantation life on Kauai, and a number of German firms, such as H. Hackfeld and Company, establishing branches in Honolulu. In 1864, Mrs. Eliza Sinclair, a Scots widow from New Zealand, sailed in with her own ship, captained by her son-in-law Francis Gay. Aboard were the members of her large family, livestock and farm implements, and household goods from the family's former homestead at that southern base of the Polynesian triangle. Mrs. Sinclair had been in Honolulu the previous year, gone on to British Columbia where the climate proved discouraging, and returned to purchase the entire island of Niihau fee simple from Kamehameha V for ten thousand dollars in gold. A rumor persists over the years that part of the purchase price was also her grand piano.

In 1865, a young American, Benjamin Franklin Dillingham, stayed on in the islands after breaking his leg in a horse accident on treacherous Nuuanu Pali and having to be left behind by his whaling ship. After his recovery, Dillingham was advised by another young newcomer, P. C. Jones, that he might as well move on, since everything in the islands was all taken up. Jones, who was later to found the Bank of Hawaii, announced however that he himself was going to remain in Honolulu. Dillingham decided to stay on to watch what happened to P.C. and seized the opportunity to found his own business. He pioneered railroads on Oahu and his company survived a series of crises to become the modern multinational island corporation that has branches in Australia, New Guinea, and the U.S. mainland as well as prime investments like Honolulu's Ala Moana Shopping Center.

The main flow of immigration, contract labor and free settlers, was not to reach Hawaii for another twenty years, but during Kamehameha V's reign the Chinese vanguard of contract laborers were to total 1,700. The dietary preference of these new residents led to large-scale rice planting in the islands, to such an extent that by the end of the century rice would become Hawaii's number two crop.

The "new era" of Kamehameha V included economic adventure in a direction quite different from that of agriculture. A major attempt was made to develop tourism at government expense. Cabinet Minister de Varigny was convinced that Honolulu might well become the Nice of the Pacific, and he so persuaded the king. The number of tourist visitors to the islands continued to be as unusually high as Wyllie had remarked on his 1845 survey of economic potential. The only obstacle to attracting more of this usually well-to-do, money-spending business was the lack of quality accommodations. Hotel Street's offerings were less than elegant—more boarding-house-type facilities. In 1866 Mark Twain stimulated American visitor interest with his *Letters from the Sandwich Islands,* in which he described his tour of Hawaii. "Roughing it" was his description, particularly on the Big Island where he spent one memorable night in the grass-thatch Volcano House on the rim of Madam Pele's firepit at Kilauea. Such primitive accommodations on the outer islands were part of the excitement of such a journey, but the growing sophistication of cosmopolitan Honolulu, and its fortunate location as a stopping place on steamer runs across the Pacific, seemed to de Varigny and like-minded enthusiasts in Kamehameha V's government to call for a first-class resort hotel. Private capital was not likely to undertake such a venture,

so the legislature was persuaded to authorize a $50,000 bond
issue to fund site purchase and construction of the Hawaiian
Hotel.

Two cabinet members, Charles C. Harris, former attorney
general who succeeded de Varigny as minister of foreign affairs,
and Dr. John Mott-Smith, minister of finance, were asked to
direct the project. Only $42,500 worth of bonds were sold, but
enthusiasm for the new hotel ran high, especially on the part of
Harris and Mott-Smith. They purchased the choice site at the
corner of Richards and Hotel streets, a block from the palace.
On May 5, 1871, construction began. In less than a year the in-
disputably elegant, first-class concrete structure was completed,
but at a price that made for a scandal in government and cost
Harris and Mott-Smith their cabinet posts. Grudgingly, with ac-
cusations and a resolve to never again invest government
monies in such a venture, the legislature appropriated the difference between the amount raised from the bond sale and the
actual expenditures authorized by the two cabinet ministers:
$116,528.16 for building, grounds, and standing furniture. The
Hawaiian Hotel did attract visitors from all over the world, and
leased to Allen Herbert, was a well-run handsome addition to
the amenities of Honolulu, but the financial problems of its construction so discouraged Kamehameha V that his government
abandoned its pursuit of tourism. Sugar was to be the primary
economic interest of Hawaii for the next century.

In 1872, the strain of Kamehameha V's years in office and
the burden of a weight that made it impossible for him to walk
without assistance left the kingdom on the brink of that catastro-
phe for which only the despised Constitution of 1852 provided a
resolution. Lot had remained a bachelor. He had once confided
to de Varigny that he was in love with Emma, his brother's
widow, but that she would not have him. In his youth he had
been engaged to Bernice Pauahi, an engagement broken to permit her to marry the American with whom she fell in love,
Charles Reed Bishop. On his deathbed, that December, Lot
tried to persuade Bernice Pauahi Bishop to allow him to name
her his heir to the throne. She refused. Queen Emma, whose

hand he had once sought, now was eager to be his heir and this he refused.

Emma plagued the last hours of his life, sitting beside his bed and pleading in vain with him to name her his successor. On the morning of December 11, 1872, Lot Kamehameha, fifth and last of his line, passed away, leaving the kingdom of the Kamehamehas, the kingdom that he had made once again Hawaiian and autocratic, with the strangely democratic prospect of having to elect a new king—or queen.

7

The Beginning of the End

IT was nearly one hundred years since the people of Waimea, Kauai, had gasped at their first sight of foreign sails entering the bay, nearly one hundred years since Cook's positioning of these lovely islands on his charts led to the phenomenon of foreign residents whose numbers in the kingdom were now a more than substantial minority.

In 1873, as Hawaii prepared to elect a new king, an astute American journalist recorded what the kingdom looked and felt like to a foreign visitor and what impressed him most here. Charles Nordhoff, whose son was to become famous as coauthor of the Bounty trilogy, came on the pleasant nine-day voyage of the Pacific Mail Company's monthly steamer from San Francisco to Honolulu. Not until he entered the recently dredged, enlarged harbor did Nordhoff catch his first glimpse of the Hawaiian capital, a city now, embowered in palms and tall tamarind trees, with the lofty fronds of bananas peering above the low roofs of the houses. The old fort, the slaughterhouse, the dilapidated shanties of 1846 were gone. The harbor was busy with men-of-war and Hawaiian canoes. The wharf was crowded with ladies in carriages and fruit vendors dressed in what to Nordhoff appeared to be brightly colored nightgowns—the *muumuu*. He stayed, of course, at the elegant new Hawaiian Hotel, with its spacious shaded courtyards, its deep verandas and breezy corridors. The rooms were large, well appointed, and the baths so luxurious that he was moved to write: "You might imagine yourself in San Francisco were it not that you drive in under the shade of cocoa-nut, tamarind, guava and algaroba trees and find all the doors and windows open in mid-winter."

In an unhurried tour of the kingdom, Nordhoff sailed to Hilo, was impressed by the green coast line of the Hamakua district there, surprised by the number of "quaint little churches which mark the distances almost with the regularity of milestones." Riding overland from Hilo, he saw that for every church there was also a schoolhouse, where the quality and equality of public education intrigued him. "On the benches sit, and in the classes recite, Hawaiian, Chinese, Portuguese, half-white and half-Chinese children; and the little pig-tailed Celestial reads out of his primer as well as any." He was charmed by Hilo.

> If you are so fortunate as to enter the bay on a fine day, you will see a very tropical landscape—a long, pleasant, curved sweep of beach, on which the surf is breaking, and beyond, white houses nestling among cocoa-nut groves, and bread-fruit, pandanus, and other Southern trees, many of them bearing brilliant flowers; with shops and stores along the beach. Men and boys sporting in the surf, and men and women dashing on horseback over the beach, make up the life of the scene.[1]

He advised energetic travelers to see the active volcano of Kilauea, thirty miles from Hilo, and to ascend Mauna Loa and Mauna Kea, whose snow-clad summits were a spectacular view from Hilo on a clear winter day. Listening to the Hawaiians' speech and comparing it to Hawaiian words he saw in print, he commented on the strange fashion in which islanders pronounced their language: "Lanai is indifferently called *Ranai* and Mauna Loa is, in the mouths of most Hawaiians, *Mauna Roa.*"

Back in Honolulu he visited the new public hospital named for Queen Emma and admired Aliiolani Hale, a new government building designed by Sydney architects as a royal palace but used for offices instead. Traveling around rural Oahu he

---

1. Charles Nordhoff, *Northern California, Oregon, and the Sandwich Islands* (Berkeley, California: Ten Speed Press, Centennial Printing 1874–1974), pp. 19–20.

wrote, "If you are American, and familiar with New England, it will be revealed to you why all the countryside looks so familiar is that it is really a very accurate description of New England country scenery." He described the stone walls marking off fields and pastures, the whitewashed picket fences, the little white frame houses—often with green blinds—the narrow front yards, the verandas where at the close of day Hawaiians could be seen sitting down to read their newspapers. "There is," Nordhoff observed, "not a country in the world where the stranger may travel in such absolute safety as these islands. Even in Honolulu people leave their houses open all day and unlocked all night without thought of theft."

In the spirit of the people, in their "often quaint habits," in their universal free public education, in all that made these islands unique, Nordhoff recognized the marks of "the Puritans who came here but fifty years ago. No intelligent American can visit the islands and remain even a month, without feeling proud that the civilization which has here been created in so marvelously short a time was the work of his country men and women." This sentiment was shared by those Americans resident in the Kingdom of Hawaii, most of whom were qualified by wealth or landownership under the Constitution of 1864 to be either electors or elected representatives in the legislature whose unprecedented task was to elect Hawaii's new king.

There were two candidates: Colonel David Kalakaua, whose slogan "Hawaii for Hawaiians" affronted many *haole* residents and found little sympathy with wealthy *alii* whose lands were profitably leased to *haole* planters; and William Charles Lunalilo, a relative of the Kamehamehas, a bright and gentle man known as *Ke alii lokomaikai*—the kind chief. It was Lunalilo who won the election by a substantial majority. His concern for the Hawaiian people was no less intense or genuine than Kalakaua's, but he felt impelled to work within the slow and orderly constraints of constitutional amendment. In the one year and twenty-five days of his reign, this able but ailing ruler devised two constitutional amendments which would return the franchise and the privilege of holding elective office to the Hawaiian commoner, or to any poor landless citizen of the Hawaiian Kingdom.

Lunalilo died just one day after the February 4, 1874, election of a legislature whose triple burden of decisions would include the election of his successor, the ratification of his proposed constitutional amendments, and approval of a treaty to be negotiated with the United States government trading certain concessions in return for relief from the 30 percent import tariff on Hawaiian sugar. Recessions and a drop from the high wartime sugar prices forced this last issue. Debate on all three items was heated, and concerns were interrelated, for the choice of a monarch would determine basic policies in which the reopening of the franchise and the possible concession of Pearl Harbor as a U.S. naval coaling station in the reciprocity treaty would determine the future course of the kingdom. Paradox: Americans whose national ideals were touted to be those of democracy and equal privilege were now openly supportive of the franchise restrictions. Among the voices raised against such restriction was that of Walter Murray Gibson, the ambitious white-bearded "Shepherd of Lanai," whose colony of mainlanders had left, discouraged by drought, insect blights, and isolation. Gibson's property was now a successful sheep and goat ranch, and Gibson had left Lanai in the care of his son-in-law Fred Hayselden to become an eloquent political voice in the kingdom. For a time this was editorially, in Fornander's tradition, through the columns of the Hawaiian-language paper *Nuhou* and later through the *Advertiser*. In the 1874 election of Lunalilo's successor, Gibson backed the candidacy of Colonel David Kalakaua.

Queen Emma, widow of Kamehameha IV, was the favored candidate in Honolulu, whose citizens were inclined to forget the interests or welfare of the predominantly rural outer islands of the kingdom. Emma's confidence was in that narrow base of the capital. Her anti-American, antimission attitudes were well known. She had great personal popularity. Neither she nor Kalakaua favored Pearl Harbor as the bargaining price of reciprocity, but pre-election rumors had it that Americans preferred her.

If Kalakaua were to be elected, the belief was that a strong group of Americans stood ready to stage an insurrection and take over the government.

America's interest in Hawaii was such that in 1873 Major General John M. Schofield and Brevet Brigadier General B. S. Alexander made a secret surveillance of the kingdom under the pretext of a visit for health reasons and a renewal of civilian acquaintanceships. Historian Ralph Kuykendall felt that Charles Reed Bishop, a member of Lunalilo's cabinet, was privy to U.S. Secretary of War W. W. Belknap's confidential orders to the two generals "to ascertain the defensive responsibilities of the different ports and their commercial facilities, to examine into any other subject that may occur to you is desirable, in order to collect all information that would be of service to the country in the event of war with a powerful maritime nation." [2]

Generals Schofield and Alexander surveyed Pearl Harbor, a series of natural lochs near Honolulu, decided it would make an ideal naval base, and in a report kept top secret for the next twenty years recommended that it be acquired in whatever manner possible. These two were not the first American spies in Hawaii. At the end of the Civil War, Colonel Zephaniah Spaulding, a congressman's son traveling in the guise of a prospective cotton planter, assessed the kingdom for the United States government, sending his reports in the form of letters to his father who then turned them over to the U.S. secretary of state.

Charles Reed Bishop and the Honolulu Chamber of Commerce committee whose interest was the representation of the thirty-five sugar plantations of the kingdom made no secret of their feeling that if reciprocity negating the adverse tariff on Hawaiian sugar was not approved, the only alternative was for Hawaii to become a possession of the United States. Annexation, the last-ditch proposal of Kamehameha III, the bugaboo of Kamehameha IV, the worst possible alternative in the eyes of

2. Ralph S. Kuykendall, *The Hawaiian Kingdom, 1854–1874* (Honolulu: University of Hawaii Press, 1953), p. 248.

the Hawaiian people, guaranteed duty-free sugar shipments to American markets.

It was at this period that the United States representative in Hawaii, Henry A. Peirce, received lengthy instructions from U.S. Secretary of State Fish to "not discourage the feeling which may exist in favor of annexation to the United States. If there be any idea entertained in that direction among those in official position, you will endeavor to sound them and ascertain their views as to the manner and the terms on which such a project could be carried into execution." [3]

The 1874 legislature faced with such crucial decisions represented most of the nearly 3,000 *haole* residents of the kingdom, some of the 45,759 Hawaiians, a few of the 2,038 Chinese, none of the 200 Gilbert Islanders who had been imported on labor contracts, and none of the 90 Japanese who had stayed on after their 1868 labor contracts expired. It was a total surprise when this new elitist legislature elected Kalakaua king.

Emma was so confident of victory that on election day as the legislators cast their ballots, her supporters gathered outside the courthouse ready to celebrate her accession as queen. At the announcement that the results were 39 to 6 in Kalakaua's favor, the Emma-ites went berserk. They stormed into the building breaking windows and furniture and physically attacking legislators. Twelve legislators were wounded, one fatally so. Kalakaua's brother-in-law, Governor John Dominis of Oahu, sent an S O S to the two American and one British men-of-war that fortunately happened to be in Honolulu harbor. One hundred and fifty American marines from the U.S.S. *Tuscarora* and the U.S.S. *Portsmouth* joined British marines from the H.M.S. *Tenedos* in a march on the courthouse where, to the dismay of the Emma-ites, they enforced order on behalf of the newly elected king. The dowager queen's supporters could not believe that the men of the *Tenedos* were not there to stand up for their pro-British Emma or that the Americans would come forward to stand up for Kalakaua. They refused to accept defeat, appealing

3. Kuykendall, p. 253.

to the French to intervene and place Emma on the throne, but as had the British, the French diplomats in Honolulu advised the would-be queen that affairs in the kingdom must be allowed to take their democratic course.

The main strength of the charismatic Kalakaua came from rural Oahu and the neighbor islands, all of which were still administered under four governors in a local level of government that maintained the geographic boundaries of the four former chiefdoms of *ka poe kahiko*. In a splendid triumphal procession with his queen, Kapiolani, Kalakaua spent his first weeks in office touring the kingdom to consolidate his support, marshal new strength, and in particular reassure the planters who so distrusted him. Over and over, in every district, Kalakaua made the promises that he hoped to be able to carry out. To the planters, he affirmed that his primary goal was the advance of commerce and agriculture, and that he was about to go in person to the United States to push for a reciprocity treaty. To his own people, he promised renewal of Hawaiian culture and the restoration of their franchise.

As the date of his planned departure for the American trip approached, Kalakaua became increasingly apprehensive about what might happen at home during his absence. An American, Henry Whitney, founder of the *Pacific Commercial Advertiser,* a missionary son who had been the first postmaster under Kamehameha III, had convinced the king that such a trip was essential. It remained for the British consul, J. Hay Wodehouse, to convince the king that he should have no fears about the venture. "Sir!" Wodehouse advised, "Pardon me for speaking so frankly! Do not, when you are about to visit the United States in one of its national vessels, distrust the intentions of the Government with regard to your islands. I do not believe it capable of such an act as the seizure of your Kingdom in your absence." [4]

Wodehouse well knew the popularity of foreign royalty and the admiration of titles that was a paradox of a people so adamantly democratic as the Americans. Kalakaua was the first

4. Ralph S. Kuykendall, *The Hawaiian Kingdom, 1874–1893* (Honolulu: University of Hawaii Press, 1967), p. 22.

king ever to visit the United States, and his reception during his three months' visit was one of tremendous aloha. He was feted from the time of his arrival in San Francisco on the U.S.S. *Benicia* through the cross-country railroad journey. The president and the Congress gave him receptions in Washington, D.C. Kalakaua continued on to tour Boston, New Bedford (because of the whalers originating there), Niagara Falls, Chicago, St. Louis, Omaha, and from San Francisco returned home on the U.S.S. *Pensacola* full of a passion for travel.

The American minister to Hawaii, Henry Peirce, who had accompanied the king to Washington, remained there to argue before the Senate Foreign Relations Committee that a reciprocity treaty with Kalakaua's kingdom would have the effect of holding the islands "with hooks of steel in the interests of the United States, and to result finally in their annexation to the United States." [5] He warned the senators in blunt language. "Refuse the offered treaty, necessity will drive the islands to seek for more intimate political and commercial relations with the British colonies of (British) Columbia, New Zealand, Feejee, and Australia, and to eventuate in the Hawaiian Islands becoming a colony of the British crown." [6]

The ratification of the treaty by the Senate was won, but passage of the necessary enabling law by Congress was no easy victory. The final vote there was 115 to 101, with 74 members of the Congress abstaining. Strong opposition had come from the sugar-growing southern states. The lieutenant governor of Louisiana, a black, claimed competition resulting from reciprocity would be injurious to the black sugar workers of his home state. The enabling law, and the treaty ratifications, which Hawaii's planters viewed as an economic necessity, carried out Kalakaua's pledge to advance commerce and industry by assuring Hawaiian sugar a duty-free entry into United States markets.

The Pearl Harbor concession was not a part of the 1875 treaty agreement. An amendment added by Hawaii's envoy, H. A. P. Carter, put the American foot in Hawaii's door by stating that

5. Kuykendall, p. 27.
6. Kuykendall, p. 27.

the kingdom agreed not to let any other nation have the use of Pearl Harbor lochs during the seven years of the treaty period. Charles Reed Bishop confidently expected American capital to take advantage of the treaty and the high profits possible through reciprocity relief, but only one shrewd financier, Californian Claus Spreckels, invested in the kingdom and its sugar industry. Spreckels, a German emigrant, arrived on the vessel that brought news of the final victory of reciprocity to Honolulu and immediately bought up half of the year's sugar crop. He personally acquired by purchase and manipulation of *alii* land interests the Maui plantation that remains the largest and most prosperous in the islands: HC&S—the Hawaiian Commercial and Sugar Company.

Under the stimulus of the reciprocity agreement, the acreage planted to cane was to increase tenfold during the next fifteen years: from 12,000 acres in 1876 to 125,000 acres in 1891. Before reciprocity, 2,627 *kane*, 364 *wahine*, and fewer than 1,000 Chinese, Gilbert Islanders, Germans, Portuguese, First Year Meiji Men, and others made up the plantation workforce. With reciprocity came a new era of massive contract labor immigration that was to transform the population patterns and effect a century of social change in Hawaii. More than 8,000 Chinese were brought into the kingdom in the first four years of sugar expansion.

In 1882 young Frank Damon, son of Abraham Fornander's friend the Reverend Samuel Damon of the Seamen's Bethel and the temperance paper the *Friend*, made a tour of island plantations to take the gospel to these newly arrived Chinese contract laborers. With indignation Damon described the living quarters provided the newcomers by *haole* managers, all of whom were Christians and not a few of whom were themselves former missionaries or missionary sons. "It seemed unnatural, inhuman, this herding together in quarters of scores of laborers as if they were so many animals. We speak of Chinese immigration to these islands. It is, properly speaking, no immigration. It is simply the transplanting of so many working machines to our fields and valleys." [7]

7. Tin-Yuke Char, *The Sandalwood Mountains, Readings and Stories of the Early Chinese in Hawaii* (Honolulu: University Press of Hawaii, 1975), p. 205.

A space approximately three by six feet was allotted each man, and here he must keep all his possessions, enjoy his only privacy, and take his nightly rest. On some plantations, Damon saw that reading rooms were provided for *haole* workers, but for the Chinese the recreation offered was usually only a loft where they could smoke opium. On Kauai, Damon felt that the small cabins, with two or three laborers to each, were far better than the big room lined with beds like ship bunks and a common eating table in the middle of the room as was the case on Oahu. He commented on the contrast between the conditions on sugar plantations managed by members of his own race and religion and the conditions on the rice plantations conducted by Chinese: "The houses [on the Chinese plantations] are as a rule much larger and better ventilated. Some little attention seems to be paid to the morals of the men. Opium smoking is entirely prohibited and gambling is allowed as a special privilege for 3 days only at New Year's time." [8] Over the door of one quarters he noted a sign, "In-coming, out-going, Peace!"

As soon as their contracts were completed, most Chinese left the plantations. As more of their countrymen came to replace them and to work as field labor and mill hands in new plantations, the numbers of Chinese throughout the kingdom escalated to one-fifth and later to one-fourth of the total population. Many settled in homesteads on Maui's Mt. Haleakala at Kula. Others set up shop or took peddlers' routes in island towns. In Honolulu, Chinatown was bounded by River Street, near Don Marin's former vineyards, and by the business heart of town, a few blocks *mauka* of the harbor. The area, dominated by the twin towers of Kaumakapili Church, was shared by some Hawaiians and, after 1885, by a few Japanese. Stores, small eating places, boardinghouses, individual homes, and the headquarters of Tong societies (never as contentious as those of San Francisco) located here in a comfortable environment where a newcomer from the plantations or from China could buy a bowl of noodles or a steamed pork bun (*manapua*), where he could hear and speak the familiar dialects of home, where wearing a queue, a collarless jacket, and loose trousers did not set one apart,

8. Char, p. 208.

where the Chinese custom of as many wives as a man could afford could be discreetly followed and the ancestors given proper respect.

In 1883, when King Kalakaua awarded the prizes at the graduation ceremony of the school established by Episcopal Bishop and Mrs. Willis, the second prize in English grammar was won by a young Chinese immigrant, Sun Yat-sen. Bishop's College School, later renamed Iolani School, was for boys of Hawaiian birth, but by special arrangement a few Chinese boys were admitted. Fourteen-year-old Sun Yat-sen had arrived in Honolulu in 1879, having persuaded his parents to permit him to join his elder brother, who had a store in Honolulu. At first, Sun Yat-sen worked in this store, but his brother decided that the boy's brilliance demanded a special education.

It was during these impressionable years at Iolani, in the cosmopolitan democracy of the first thirteen years of Kalakaua's reign, that Sun Yat-sen became fired with the idea of political freedom for the Chinese in his homeland. He dreamed and talked and planned the overthrow of the Manchu emperors and the drafting for China of a new form of government: that of consent by the governed. The Christian doctrines that William Richards had taught Nahienaena—in the eyes of God all men are equal—became Sun Yat-sen's commitment. If democracy worked this well for the United States and for the tiny Hawaiian Kingdom, why not for the vast country and six-thousand-year-old civilization of the Chinese? Through this young idealist, the ties between Hawaii and China began to develop in new ways.

By the time Kalakaua awarded his prize in English grammar to the boy who was to make the liberation of the Chinese people a twentieth century reality, the king had himself established new ties between Hawaii and China during his 1881 trip around the world, the first such ever to be made by any ruling monarch in history. Like his American visit of 1874–1875, Kalakaua's round-the-world journey was a memorable success, despite the disadvantage of having William Armstrong, missionary son and Bureau of Immigration director, as his traveling companion. To the convivial, liberal Kalakaua, Armstrong's presence was often an embarrassment. No statement of the prevalent American missionary bias, which during Kalakaua's reign was translated into plantation colonialism, was ever more explicit than Armstrong's, written by him in an account of the 1881 tour: "All the nations of Christendom were agreed that the Chinese, Japanese, and East Indians were 'pagan' without noble traits and, according to the creeds of Christendom, were incapable of moral and intellectual progress, though they included more than two thirds of the inhabitants of the earth." [9]

For Armstrong, everything he experienced around the world with the king re-enforced his prejudice. For Kalakaua, the trip extended the range of his friendships and many interests. He was overwhelmed by the tremendous welcome given him in Japan, where he arranged for young Hawaiians to enroll at the Imperial University in Tokyo and discussed the possibility of betrothing his little niece, Princess Kaiulani, to Prince Komatsu of the emperor's family. In China, where the welcome was equally warm, Kalakaua arranged for young Hawaiians to study at the great Chinese universities, and traveled from Shanghai to attend a banquet given in his honor by Viceroy Li Hung Chang in Tientsin on the steamer *Pautah,* which was specially outfitted and put at his disposal by the Chinese government.

William Armstrong was astonished to discover an American managing the Chinese steamer, disclosing the selectivity of his own prejudices by his journal comment that the manager of the *Pautah* was

> a fine American Negro who had shown much ability when employed by the American Legation in Peking; he was not only well educated, but spoke several languages, including Chinese; his father was a Negro preacher in Washington, D.C. He had married a handsome English girl in Shanghai, who was an artist; but his marriage to a white person had much incensed the Americans living in Shanghai, though it was cordially approved by the English, German, and French residents. He caused some cabins of the "Pautah" to be refurnished and made provisions for a sumptuous table. [10]

9. William N. Armstrong, *Around the World with a King* (New York: Frederick A. Stokes Co., 1904), p. 277.

10. Armstrong, pp. 89–90.

Armstrong surmised that the cost of all this had been great but
that the Chinese no doubt expected favors in their future trade
with the Kingdom of Hawaii.

The cost of the trip was high, but money was no problem,
with Claus Spreckels generously loaning money to king and
kingdom and floating a mortgage loan for Walter Murray Gibson who was elected to the Hawaiian legislature in 1882. With a
new awareness of the customs and habitats of the royalty of the
world, Kalakaua went forward with two plans that were much
criticized by those who shared the prejudices and apprehensions
of William Armstrong. After nine years on the throne, the king
determined to hold a formal coronation that would belatedly celebrate the beginning of his new *Keawe-a-heulai* dynasty. This
event was to take place upon completion of the new Iolani Palace being built to replace the former modest story-and-a-half
coral-block structure built by Kamehameha III when he returned
his capital to Honolulu. Inspired by the royal palaces he had
seen in India, Kalakaua also built an airy pink bungalow on the
palace grounds, where he and his family could retreat for privacy.

Such expenditures much irritated the *haole* business and
planter group whom outsiders referred to as "the missionary
party." Kalakaua's continuance and expansion of the revival of
Hawaiian culture initiated by Kamehameha V, his interest in
Judaism and in Buddhism, his fondness for poker, good times,
and rum offended their puritanism. The restoration of the franchise to all male citizens of the kingdom aggravated them as the
Chinese population climbed toward one-fourth, and in Honolulu
alone 600 Chinese mechanics were registered to vote. In the
private offices of American residents in Honolulu as in plantation managers' offices on the outer islands there was heard increasing talk of the 1882 Chinese Exclusion Laws of the United
States as a possible model to solve what "the missionary party"
began to think of as the Chinese problem. They distrusted the
king. They hated Gibson, who became his premier. They
loathed Claus Spreckels, since they were at the mercy of his
money, and they were indignant when Kalakaua, creating royal
orders such as those he had observed in the courts of Europe,

made Spreckels a knight commander of the Order of Kalakaua in gratitude for the sugar magnate underwriting the first Hawaiian coinage.

In 1883, Kalakaua had appointed American Robert Walker Irwin, a great grandson of Benjamin Franklin, to be Hawaii's consul general in Tokyo. He then sent Governor John Kapena of Maui to Japan as envoy extraordinary to plead the emperor's permission of Japanese immigration to Hawaii. Kapena gave a dinner in Tokyo honoring the three imperial princes and all the heads of Japanese government. In an impassioned speech, the Maui governor declared,

> His Majesty Kalakaua believes that the Japanese and Hawaiian spring from one cognate race and this enhances his love for you. He hopes our people will more and more be brought closer in a common brotherhood. Hawaii holds out her loving hand and heart to Japan and desires that your people may come and cast in their lots with ours and repeople our Island Home with a race which may blend with ours and produce a new and vigorous nation.[11]

It was an opportune invitation for thousands of Japanese displaced from their lands and their livelihood in the economic and social upheaval, the civil wars of the Meiji era. The first group of 943 Japanese—farmers, dispossessed temple families, a few former samurai—arrived in Honolulu on the *City of Tokio* on February 8, 1885. The city turned out to welcome them in a gala reception at the Kakaako Immigration Station. Hawaiians brought aloha gifts of fresh vegetables, *poi,* and fish to the Japanese newcomers. Hawaiian policemen took them on sightseeing tours of the town. The *Hawaiian Gazette* noted that ''this may mark an important era in Hawaiian affairs. These people are probably coming to stay, to raise families of their nationality and to become part and parcel of the Hawaiian community.''

In appreciation for this welcome, the Japanese—eighty-four of whom were wives and children—put on a *sumo* tournament, the first in Hawaii. Six young Japanese women dressed in kimonos sat on zabuton on opposite sides of the wrestling ring and entertained spectators with samisen music and song. *Sake*

11. Kuykendall, *Hawaiian Kingdom: 1874–1893,* pp. 159–160.

flowed for all who wished it from great tubs eighteen inches in diameter and two feet high. King Kalakaua was among those present, applauding this vanguard of 28,695 Japanese who were to migrate to Hawaii in the last years of the Hawaiian Kingdom.

The labor contracts under which they and the thousands of Chinese, Portuguese, hundreds of Germans, Norwegians, and others were recruited as cheap field hands bound to work through at least three years or face imprisonment had received the righteous censure of the United States Congress since 1867, when the first resolution was passed condemning Hawaii's "coolie trade." In the 1880s there continued the American mis-impression of the kingdom's contract labor immigration—a mis-impression that still lingers in some islanders and many Americans today. In China, Japan, and Europe, Hawaii-bound immigrants voluntarily signed those labor contracts and set off on their ocean journeys with as much anticipation and fervor— and sometimes apprehension—as did the free European immigrants who hoped to find sweatshop jobs of any kind once they made the steerage passage across the Atlantic and passed through the inspection nightmare of Ellis Island.

Knowledge of what Hawaii might be like was seldom accurate in the home countries of labor contract immigrants. A young Portuguese who left the Azores on a Hawaii labor contract in 1883 later recalled that when he left Punta Dagolda his uncle told him, "John, you crazy go *Terra Nova*. The people there just like wild animals. They eat you up." [12] John, whose pidgin was faithfully recorded by his sociologist interviewer, remembered being frightened by this, but his fear dissipated once he got under way when "we get plenty to eat and everybody good to us. The Portuguese all good sailors so nobody get sea-sick. First thing you know, they get their guitars, their harmonicas, and everybody get good time." [13] To John's family, Hilo looked like the Azores.

12. Hideko Sasaki, "The Life History of a Portuguese Immigrant," *Social Process in Hawaii,* vol. 1, 1935, p. 26.
13. Sasaki, *Social Process,* vol. 1, p. 27.

We went to live in the Long House, Camp 4, Waiakea. Six families. Everything was new so my mother never grumble. Little by little the Japanese come. Every time a green bunch come, the Portuguese go help them fix the house. The Portuguese smart. They know the Japanese get good *sake* and if they help, they all get good drink. Our camp, the Portuguese and Japanese all good friends. No fights any time. They all like family and early in the morning on the way to work we hear them say, "Jo-san, o-ha-yo!" (Joe, Good Morning!) I like the Japanese very much. They invite me to their parties and everytime I sing for them. I sing Japanese, Chinese, Portuguese, and Spanish songs.[14]

The Portuguese were good mixers, sturdy and stable citizens. The 1,300 German contract laborers were similarly adaptive to island life, but the few hundred Norwegians complained about everything, disliked Hawaii, and quickly left. The experience of the planters was that it was cheaper, and more satisfactory, to go to Japan for their contract labor needs. Wherever they came from, the new immigrants on the plantations had at least replenished the population totals and sent the birth rate soaring. They had also demonstrated the impossibility of the slogan Kalakaua did not mention during the jubilee celebration of his fiftieth birthday, November 26, 1886. Hawaii could never again be simply for the Hawaiians alone. By 1886, they had become a minority in their own land.

14. Sasaki, *Social Process,* vol. 1, p. 28.

8

The "Reform Party"

IN his autocratic exuberance, buoyed by Gibson, Kalakaua sought to extend the influence of the Hawaiian Kingdom across the Pacific, encouraging the preservation of independence and self-government for the islands of Micronesia, Tonga, the Gilbert and Ellice group, and supporting Malietoa, ruling chief of Samoa, against German-sponsored rebel chiefs by sending the former guano ship, *Kaimiloa,* as a token of Hawaiian aid. It was a grandiose and somewhat ridiculous gesture. *Kaimiloa* was captained by an alcoholic *haole* and had a number of Hawaiian boys from the Reform School among the crew. These latter demonstrated exemplary behavior in Samoa, while the drunken captain, the officers, and others in the crew were a disgrace to the Hawaiian flag and a discredit to Kalakaua.

In 1884, the Honolulu Rifles, a private citizens' militia almost entirely *haole* in membership, provided an honor guard for the funeral of Princess Bernice Pauahi Bishop, whose large estate of lands was left in trust for the education of Hawaiian children and whose fine collection of Hawaiian antiquities was housed in her memory by her husband in the Bernice P. Bishop Museum. The Honolulu Rifles also honored the memory of Queen Emma, who died the following year. Early in 1887, their membership became the nucleus of a Hawaiian League, formed with the desperate resolve to curb what they considered the recklessness and irresponsibility of Kalakaua and to get Walter Murray Gibson out of the government. The opium scandal (in which Kalakaua had accepted $71,000 from one Chinese to secure the government license for opium imports and then awarded the license to another Chinese without returning the first man's money) was only a small part of the league's complaint against the king and his premier. The basis of the league's political moves was their fear of the increasing competition of Chinese business, the increasing numbers of Chinese voters, and the apprehension that if universal suffrage continued, *haole* economic and political power in the kingdom would diminish and all hope of annexation to the United States forever disappear.

In June 1887, Mrs. Thomas Lack, a Honolulu merchant, advertised that in addition to her usual stock of corsets, silk thread, and yardgoods she had a supply of rifles and ammunition. Before the month was over, her supply was sold out. On July 1, the Hawaiian League and the Honolulu Rifles had armed men patrolling Honolulu's streets. Walter Murray Gibson and his son-in-law Fred Hayselden were kidnapped, held for two days at gunpoint in a warehouse, threatened with being hanged or shot, and then taken to prison and jailed on charges of embezzlement. Kalakaua, as soon as he was informed that Gibson and Hayselden had been captured, called in the foreign diplomatic community of Honolulu to gauge support and solicit advice. He knew his powerlessness—the King's Guards were a largely ceremonial group, no match for the crack shots of the Rifles—but he told the British, French, Portuguese, Japanese, and American representatives that his men were ready to meet force with force.

Unanimously, they urged him to yield to the demands of the league in order to preserve the peace of his kingdom, even though, in so doing, he would be king in name only. His concern, with the ugliness of the situation, was to preserve his kingdom. One of the league's demands was that he dismiss his present cabinet, and this he immediately did. On July 6, he signed the constitution that relegated him to a figurehead and that imposed a fairly high property ownership qualification on those running for the new legislature, which for the first time was officially given that name. Both the king and his new all-*haole* "reform party" cabinet swore to uphold this 1887 "Bayonet" Constitution. Only those who swore allegiance to this constitution were to be permitted to vote in the September elections for the new legislature. Abraham Fornander, now old and terminally ill, did so on August 4 in order to be able to vote for legislative candidates who pledged their support to his good friend Kalakaua.

On the surface, life seemed to go on as usual after this bloodless revolution of 1887. Schools continued to teach, still mostly in Hawaiian. The Board of Health continued its forced exile of lepers to the cliff-walled peninsula of Kalaupapa, on Molokai, where Father Damien DeVeuster had gone in 1873 to minister to those victims and had become a victim of the disease himself. Electricity, the telephone, and a tram out to the new race track at Kapiolani Park were additions to Honolulu, and railroads were additions in the sugar-growing areas of the neighbor islands and Oahu. New contract-labor immigrants came in by the steamerload. The extension of the reciprocity treaty, ordered by the king's new cabinet, granted the United States an eight-year lease on the use of Pearl Harbor as a naval coaling station. Since even unnaturalized American and European aliens, illiterate or literate, were given the vote by the "Bayonet" Constitution, the *haole* minority of the population now controlled the political destiny of the kingdom.

Organizing in secret, a group of Hawaiians, Chinese, and whites like Belgian Albert Loomens met month after month to plot a counterrevolution that would restore power to the king and return democratic freedom to the kingdom. Ho-Fun, manager of one of the Chinese newspapers, was one of the leaders, and the sympathies of most Chinese were with Kalakaua. The "Bayonet" Constitution denied them the franchise, and the new *haole*-controlled legislature had come close to passing laws curtailing the right of Chinese in the kingdom to free enterprise and mobility of occupation. Robert Wilcox, one of the young Hawaiians whom the king had sent abroad for an education, led the military arm of the counterrevolutionary group—the Kamehameha Rifles. Wilcox, graduate of an Italian military academy, led the charge on the night of July 30, 1889, when the counter-revolution began with an attack on Iolani Palace grounds.

Wilcox and his men had assumed that the king's guards, Hawaiians most of them, would either promptly yield or be eager to join with them. Neither happened. Marines came marching ashore from the U.S.S. *Adams* to protect the American legation, bringing ammunition and reinforcement to fight off Wilcox's forces. The Honolulu Rifles turned out. Strangely enough, not even Kalakaua supported this attempt on his behalf. Rumors of ammunition smuggled into the city, of meetings held in Princess Liliuokalani's home, and of the possibility that the counter-revolution would replace her on his throne had much affected him. He was not at the palace that night when six of Wilcox's men were killed in the first skirmish on the palace grounds. By the following afternoon, it was all over. The ringleaders were captured and brought to trial. Albert Loomens was sentenced to be hanged. The judge then commuted the sentence to one year's imprisonment which was suspended when Loomens agreed to leave Hawaii forever. Ho-Fun was fined the inordinately large sum of $250. Wilcox, after the 9 to 3 vote of an all-Hawaiian jury, was found not guilty of conspiracy—a strange finding for the man who had led the counterrevolutionary force! There had been charges against Liliuokalani for abetting the insurrectionists by providing her home as a meeting place. These were dropped after her denial of knowing that the group had met there in her absence.

For Kalakaua, the 1889 attempt was the final straw. He retired to his boathouse in the spacious semi-isolation of Waikiki where only one hotel then graced the beach. Sans Souci, among whose guests was Robert Louis Stevenson, was owned by a Greek named George Lycurgus whose two sons later owned and operated the Hilo Hotel and the Volcano House. There was a cottage nearby where guests of Allen Herbert's Hawaiian Hotel came on day excursions. A long stretch of duckponds and open space separated the beach and the adjoining new race track at Kapiolani Park from the small city of 30,000 inhabitants that was Honolulu in 1889.

With apathy, Kalakaua lived through the last remaining year of his life. The year, 1890, was a difficult one for those who had usurped power from him. The McKinley Tariff Act nullified reciprocity. Planters and American businessmen spoke more and more ardently of annexation. Hawaiians spoke out with bitterness against the failure of the United States government to return Pearl Harbor now that the treaty leasing it to them was void. Americans he had met on his previous trip to the United States continued to extend friendly invitations to King David Kalakaua. A title was a title, and they enjoyed him as a personality. Late in 1890, the once-merry monarch took his last trip, back to California. He died there in San Francisco after a final whirl of being adulated, feted, and given the fond aloha of American friends. The end of his reign, and his life, came on January 20, 1891.

9

Aloha Oe: Farewell to Thee

ILIUOKALANI'S accession gave new heart to the Hawaiians. From Kohala, from Molokai, from every district of the kingdom came petitions for her to change from the hated Constitution of 1887. The nature of that constitution and its restriction of her sovereign powers made this a long, difficult maneuver, but Liliuokalani was a woman of great strength, patience, endurance, and talent. For two years she persisted until she had a cabinet amenable to constitutional change and yet men of whom the reform-party-controlled legislature approved.

The rumor circulated that her new constitution would deny the vote to any *haole* who was not married to a Hawaiian. The certainty of many Americans was that she would sooner see her kingdom placed in the hands of the British than continue a pattern of American influence and American political control. On the morning of January 14, 1893, the queen announced her intention to promulgate a new constitution that would restore actual rule of the kingdom to her as sovereign and return to all citizens the privilege of franchise and candidacy.

That afternoon leaders of the reform party organized themselves as a ''Committee of Safety''—five of whom were native-born Americans, four Hawaii-born sons of American missionaries, one Tasmanian, one Scotsman, and a German who had second thoughts and resigned before the committee made a declaration claiming that in their view the queen's action was

99

revolutionary. Their conviction that she was likely to persist in her course led to their approval of a motion by Lorrin A. Thurston to take immediate steps to form and declare a provisional government with the sole purpose of securing Hawaii's annexation to the United States. The committee justified its action by describing itself as the intelligent part of the community, which had decided to take matters into its own hands and establish law and order on its own terms.

The next day, January 15, the committee again met. Thurston reported that American minister John L. Stevens, apprised of the committee's declaration and proposed action, had offered support with troops from the U.S.S. *Boston,* which had just returned from Hilo. Judge Sanford Ballard Dole, an associate justice of the Supreme Court of the kingdom, a quiet missionary son much respected by Hawaiians, was nominated as head of the proposed provisional government. Dole's first impulse was refusal. He suggested that a moderate course be followed: that the queen be asked to abdicate in favor of Princess Kaiulani and the monarchy thus preserved. During the evening of January 15, American minister Stevens persuaded Dole otherwise, and the judge notified the committee he would acquiesce in their plans and accept the presidency offered to him. He was now confident, having discussed the subject with Stevens, that it would be only a matter of a few weeks or months before annexation to the United States took place.

On his own authority, Minister Stevens sent word to the *Boston* that he wanted their bluejackets ashore, and at his request at dusk on January 16, the American sailors and marines marched through Honolulu to Arion Hall, near the palace, where they tried to sleep through an onslaught of mosquitoes. Meanwhile, the queen had been informed of the Committee of Safety and their plans. Hoping to stave off their actions, she announced deferral of any constitutional change. W. D. Alexander, a contemporary historian of the times, later analyzed the strangeness of Liliuokalani's predicament and the lack of support given her by those whom she had trusted.

> To judge from their conduct, the Queen's Cabinet were overawed
> by the unanimity and determination of the foreign community and

probably had an exaggerated idea of the force at the command of the Committee of Safety. They shrank from the responsibility of causing fruitless bloodshed and sought a valid excuse for inaction, which they thought they found in the presence of the United States troops on shore, and in the well known sympathy of the American Minister with the opposition.[1]

On January 17, three days after it was conceived, the revolution was carried out. At three o'clock that afternoon, the proclamation of the provisional government was read and the government building occupied without difficulty. The only physical resistance was from Marshal Wilson at the police station, who refused to yield his headquarters until he received orders to do so from the queen. The single casualty of the revolution was a policeman named Leialoha, who tried to stop a wagon loaded with ammunition for the Honolulu Rifles armory. John Good, an ordnance officer of the Rifles, shot Leialoha in the shoulder.

At five o'clock, two hours after the proclamation of the provisional government and the takeover of government buildings by the Committee of Safety, Minister Stevens sent a note to Judge Dole, taking it upon himself to recognize the new government as the *de facto* government of the Hawaiian Islands. In his anticipation of immediate annexation to the United States, Stevens had the American flag raised over the post office.

By six o'clock the revolution was over. Marshal Wilson had surrendered the police station. The queen was under house arrest in her bedroom in the palace. Martial law was proclaimed before most of the population of Honolulu knew that the change of government had taken place or noticed that the post office was flying the stars and stripes instead of the flag of Hawaii. In Lorrin Thurston's view, a view shared by his colleagues on the Committee of Safety, the circumstances that had prompted their usurpation of power and governance were little different from the thirteen colonies effecting their independence from Great Britain in 1776. Thurston was earnestly convinced that the Hawaiians were an enfeebled and dying race, incapable of rule, and that had the committee not taken the bold step of revolu-

---

1. Ralph S. Kuykendall, *The Hawaiian Kingdom, 1874–1893* (Honolulu: University of Hawaii Press, 1967), p. 598.

tion, Liliuokalani was ready to give her kingdom to the British.

The Hawaiians and their queen and their loyal supporters throughout the kingdom—including a number of American residents who did not share the Committee of Safety's views—considered Stevens's part in the affair reprehensible. On the advice of lawyer Paul Neumann, the queen made a formal appeal to the United States government, protesting the acts of the provisional government against herself and against the constitutional government of Hawaii and placing the burden on the American government by formally yielding "to the superior force of the United States of America, whose minister plenipotentiary, His Excellency John L. Stevens, has caused United States troops to be landed at Honolulu and declared that he would support the said provisional government.'' [2] She called upon the United States, as Kamehameha III had in 1843 appealed to the magnanimity of the British government, to restore her as the constitutional sovereign of her island kingdom.

The first steamer departing for America carried members of the Committee of Safety, bound for Washington to ask President Harrison for the immediate annexation that Minister Stevens so confidently anticipated. The president was known to be receptive. On February 14, 1893, he concluded a Treaty of Annexation between his secretary of state, John W. Foster, and the visiting delegation from the provisional government of Hawaii. On February 15 the treaty was sent to the Senate, with his recommendation for its ratification. His message to the senators was that in his view the restoration of the Hawaiian queen was undesirable and impossible and possession of the islands an urgent necessity before some other great power should secure them.

The problem for the Committee of Safety, and the temporary saving grace for Liliuokalani's cause, was that Harrison was a lame duck president. The Senate was still debating Hawaiian annexation when Grover Cleveland took office and announced that he would withhold his recommendation of resolution of the

---

2. Liliuokalani, *Hawaii's Story by Hawaii's Queen*. (Tokyo, Japan: Charles E. Tuttle Co., Inc., 1964), app. B, p. 387.

Hawaiian problem until he had the report of his official investigator, former Georgia congressman James H. Blount, who had
been dispatched to Honolulu on a fact-finding mission. Blount's
first action in Honolulu was to order the American flag pulled
down and American troops returned to their naval vessels. He
notified President Cleveland that Minister Stevens should be replaced forthwith. From the neutral vantage point of a cottage on
the grounds of the Hawaiian Hotel, Blount began his careful in-
quiries.

Among the many groups to whom he listened with an impar-
tial ear were the Hawaiian political societies *Hui Aloha Aina*
and *Hui Kalaiaina,* whose combined memberships comprised
nearly half of the 40,612 Hawaiians counted in the kingdom's
last census. From lengthy private interviews with the deposed
queen—now in residence in her late husband's home, Washington Place—Blount learned of her belief that for fifteen years the
missionaries had been plotting so that their sons could control
Hawaii. Others might call them the "reform" party. To Liliuokalani, it was the "mission" party who had foisted the Bayonet
Constitution upon her brother and who now wrested sovereignty
from her.

Nine months of provisional government were endured and
nine long months of Minister Stevens's continued presence before his replacement, Albert S. Willis, arrived. Blount's report
led President Cleveland to lean toward restoration of the monarchy, and his instructions to Willis were to interview Liliuokalani
as to her intent should she be placed back upon her throne.
When she was adamant that she would use Hawaiian law to
punish or permanently exile those who had made the revolution
and formed the provisional government, Willis somehow
thought he heard her use the word *behead,* a verb neither common to her vocabulary nor to Hawaiian tradition. Emotion defeated reason. That one word skewed Willis's reactions, and he
advised Cleveland that only trouble would ensue if the queen
were restored. Willis's reports to him were so contrary to
Blount's findings that President Cleveland decided for the time
being to take no action whatever in regard to Hawaii.

President Dole's provisional government was thus left with a task it had neither wanted nor expected—maintaining and controlling their own government in Hawaii for the next five years. The name Republic of Hawaii was adopted by the oligarchy, who decided it no longer mattered whether the Hawaiian flag that had flown over the monarchy was replaced by a new banner designed for a republic its executives were certain would be temporary. The *Hawaiian Star* of February 14, 1894, carried an editorial on the question of changing the flag.

> There is another consideration that well may be weighed and that is the wish of the natives. They have lost a great deal, politically, and if they cherish the flag it might be best to keep it flying. These kindly and peace loving people, now and hereafter the wards of the nation, should not be needlessly affronted. We do not know that they wanted the cross and stripes. If they do, so much might properly be conceded to sentiment. If not, there would seem to be no reason why the flag should not be laid away with the throne, the tabu sticks, the feather cloaks, and other insignia of a vanished epoch.

That February 14, 1894, was a memorable day in Honolulu. At four o'clock in the afternoon all Honolulu's Chinese firms, with the exception of restaurants, closed their doors for the day. Nearly three thousand Chinese crowded into the Chinese Theater to protest the provisional government's proposal to limit their free enterprise under a licensing act directed solely against their race, prohibiting them from entering any trading or mechanical occupation in which they had not been previously engaged. This was an attempt previously made in 1887 and judged illegal by the Supreme Court of the kingdom in 1889. The exercise of the democracy whose influence had so swayed Sun Yat-sen was the challenge given by those at this meeting to the ruling oligarchy of Americans who supposedly cherished ideals of liberty, equality, and freedom for all.

There was no set program. Order prevailed. A number of Hawaiians, a handful of *haole* observers, and a squad of police were also in the audience. Fifty leaders of the Chinese community occupied the stage, and those with something to say spoke up, each one receiving the full attention of the crowd. Ing Chan began with a calm assessment of past and present conditions.

"Up to ten years ago the Chinese had been treated as men and as the equals of all. They are law abiding but their treatment is getting worse all the time. They do not meddle with the politics. They are now over twenty thousand strong, and in varied occupations do good for the country; and like one big family must unite their forces. The white people are dissatisfied and want to impose laws that other countries would not think of passing." [3]

Wong Wah-Toy followed him. "These foreigners do not remember their own scripture, which says, 'Do unto others as you would they should do unto you.' They claim to be an enlightened people, but I say they are not if they act in this way!" [4] Chung Kim, a lawyer's clerk from the law offices of Clarence Ashford, declared his belief that the proposed legislation was

> occasioned by the government to place Chinese under the ban and favor Portuguese. The government seems to have formed the opinion that no injustice heaped upon the Chinese will be opposed or resented. This is a mistake. Are we not all members of one great family? Is there any reason why any one of God's creatures should be trampled upon by his brothers? By what right do our white skinned brothers lord it over us to say that we shall do business and trade and live and breathe only by their consent? Is it only because our skins are brown and theirs are white? The Government is glad enough to collect the taxes from the Chinese, but when it comes to finding a class upon whom the spite of all cranks shall be expended, they at once light upon the patient and long-suffering Chinaman.[5]

There was one statement that the Geary Act in the United States was bad enough but that the proposed legislation of the new Hawaii government was worse. "The Hawaiian Constitution declares that the Government is established for equal right and benefit of all men and all classes, but if the Chinese license act shall pass, it will show the Government intends to deny us the equal benefits of the law." [6] Those assembled then passed a resolution: "We respectfully reassert our right under the princi-

3. Tin-Yuke Char, *The Sandalwood Mountains, Readings and Stories of the Early Chinese in Hawaii* (Honolulu: University Press of Hawaii, 1967), p. 289.
4. Char, p. 290.
5. Char, pp. 290–291.
6. Char, p. 291.

ples of enlightened justice and the provisions of the Hawaiian Constitution to dwell in Hawaii and be accorded the protection of the law upon terms of equality with those of other nationalities here sojourning.'' [7]

Reporting on this meeting in its February 15 edition, the *Hawaiian Star* observed that

> in no city of a state or territory of the American Union could the Chinese have made such a demonstration as last night. Here the *Pakes* have first been tolerated, then encouraged, until they assume an attitude plainly defiant and close bordering on the dominant and dictatorial. From the weak and lowly field hand of 1851 and the wage scale of $3 a month, they have, by an unparalleled and alarming revolution reached the station of an assertive element in the policy of the nation. The spectacle has not its counterpart elsewhere on the globe.

Chinese support went in strength to the queen as, throughout 1894, secret preparations were made to restore her through the forceful means of counterrevolution. John Wilson, son of the former police marshal, came home from his studies at newly opened Stanford University to help smuggle ammunition from Maui to Oahu. Robert Boyd, a classmate of Wilcox at the Italian military academy, took command of training and strategy. On January 6, 1895, the many friends of Queen Liliuokalani felt they were ready for their coup. During ten valiant days they struggled to regain control of their nation, but it had been one hundred years since Hawaiians practiced the skill of waging war. In 1895, the descendants of Kamehameha the Great's able warriors were neither well trained nor well organized enough to come close to victory.

The defeat was bitter. The terms of retribution by the republic's oligarchy were harsh. Boyd and his men were hunted down and taken prisoner. The queen was marched from Washington Place the block back to Iolani Palace where she was imprisoned in an austere room on the second floor, stripped of all comforts, and denied all visitors—even the Episcopal bishop being refused the privilege of consoling her. Night and day guards tramped

7. Char, p. 292.

back and forth across the lanai and corridor onto which her
room opened. Under the threat that should she not sign, the two
hundred loyalists in prison would be executed, Liliuokalani
filled out papers signifying her formal abdication and legalizing
the demise of the Hawaiian monarchy.

For nearly eight months Queen Liliuokalani suffered confine-
ment in that palace room. She was forced to endure the humilia-
tion of a court martial held in the throne room where she had
once presided as queen. Her crown lands, that portion allocated
to the monarch by the Great *Mahele,* were arbitrarily taken from
her. Her private papers had been ransacked by a company of
Portuguese soldiers instructed by the government to search
Washington Place for arms. There is no record as to whether, as
they rifled through Liliuokalani's personal papers, the soldiers
found the original manuscript of the song she had composed,
the hauntingly beautiful *Aloha Oe*—''Farewell to Thee.''

To Sun Yat-sen, returning to Hawaii in 1896 after his first
abortive attempt to dethrone the Manchu imperial regime, the
gap between ideals and practice of the political philosophy he
had learned from Hawaiians and Americans was revealed.
Queue cut, dressed in western clothes, he began using Hawaii
as his ''typhoon shelter,'' his friends providing him with a
counterfeit Hawaiian birth certificate to enable him to travel easily in the United States and Japan to raise support for his cause.
But, for his fellow Chinese in Hawaii, the paradox of the end of
the Hawaiian monarchy was that the democracy they sought to
help him achieve for their ancestral kingdom was to be denied
them as they became residents of an American territory.

10

Territoriality

*O*N December 22, 1897, Japan withdrew its formal protest against the proposed annexation of Hawaii by the United States. With Liliuokalani's abdication, her petition for redress became moot. There remained only two obstacles to what was now an inevitable transfer, and these were the indecision of a new American president, William G. McKinley, and the indecisiveness of the Congress concerning annexation.

In February 1898, Hawaiian-language newspapers split headline space between an account of the blowing up of the U.S. battleship *Maine* in Havana harbor and an account ridiculing the visit of republic president Sanford Ballard Dole to Washington, where, Hawaiian reporters charged, he had appeared at social functions dressed in an outfit looted from Iolani Palace— Kalakaua's helmet, Lunalilo's cape, diamond shirt studs from the Hawaiian crown jewels. Dole was in Washington to try to persuade an affirmative vote on annexation by the Congress. Opposition like that of Champ Clark, the senator from Missouri, was strong. "How can we justify either to ourselves or to our posterity the act we are about to commit?" demanded Senator Clark, speaking against the annexation of Hawaii. "How can we endure our shame when a Chinese senator from Hawaii, with his pigtail hanging down his back, his pagan joss in hand, shall rise from his curule chair and in pidgin English proceed to

108

chop logic with George Frisbie Hoar or Henry Cabot Lodge? A Chinaman can never be fit for American citizenship!'' [1]

The dozens of politically adept, articulate Chinese societies in Hawaii (among them Sun Yat-sen's Kuomintang) held their able tongues, kept their astonishing patience, and in the privacy of their meeting rooms—rather than decrying the prejudice of Americans like the senator from Missouri—continued plans to spur democratic rule in China. Many of the lawyers, scholars, teachers, doctors, and business leaders of the Chinese community, and the Chinese-Hawaiians who were noted for their brilliance, read news of the Spanish-American War in Hawaiian-language papers that shrewdly pointed out to their readers the shifts in idealism occurring in America as that strange, short war intensified.

Pearl Harbor was being used by the American navy as a coaling station. Hawaii was a stopover point for American troops en route to fight the war that was to delay the independence of the Philippines for over forty years. On Oahu, American soldiers set up Camp McKinley at the base of Diamond Head. Stationed there was a nineteen-year-old Kansan, Delbert Metzger, who saw much about Hawaii that appealed to him. With his comrades in arms he enjoyed Honolulu's hospitality: free haircuts for American soldiers and a *luau* entertaining three thousand of them at a time with roast chicken and potato salad (rather than the traditional *kalua* pig and *poi*) on the palace grounds. In July, the S.S. *Coptic* rounded Diamond Head with the news that annexation had finally passed in the Congress. The steamer carried an American flag stitched with a symbolic forty-sixth star, a special flag sent by the secretary of state to be used in the formal annexation ceremony, which president of the republic Dole scheduled for August 12, 1898.

A Chinese grandmother now in her nineties and still living in Honolulu has vivid memories of that day. She was fifteen years old, just two weeks in Hawaii, having come from her home village near Canton to marry an elderly man whom she had

1. Congressional Records, United States Senate, 1898, p. 5790.

never before seen. They lived in Pearl City, west of Honolulu,
and started at dawn to reach the palace grounds by 10 A.M.
when the gates were opened and ordinary people such as themselves could find places in the spectators' seats set out on either
side of the palace drive. To her husband, who had been many
years in Hawaii, this was a grave occasion. She remembers the
concern on his face, the wet eyes and cheeks of those seated
around her, the high keening lament of the women from Kawaiahao Church. The band music delighted her. So did the sight
of the foreign women in the galleries, in their elegant finery.
She had no real idea as to what was happening, or why, but she
was deeply touched as the Hawaiian anthem began, the Hawaiian flag fell, and the Hawaiian policemen hurried to leave in
order to avoid seeing the symbolic death of what they held so
dear. For months afterward, she remembers, Hawaiians wore a
special hat band as a sign of mourning—a band printed with the
legend: *Kuu hae aloha*—"My beloved flag."

To those who worked hard to achieve it, Annexation Day offered some unpleasant surprises. United States customs officials
took over the port of Honolulu. Duties were placed on all kinds
of imported merchandise with the result that prices of some
items doubled in Honolulu stores. It took more than a year for
the commission appointed by President McKinley to decide
upon the administrative design of a territorial government. In
some areas, the transition was smooth. The Board of Education
continued the centralized control it had exercised under monarchy and republic and the progressive education methods in
which John Dewey himself had indoctrinated Hawaii's teachers.
The Board of Health also continued its previous patterns and
personnel, initiating preventive measures of burning the possessions and homes of bubonic plague victims when in December
1899 an outbreak of that dread disease occurred in Honolulu.

The city was to remain the capital of the new territory, as it
had been of republic and kingdom. One of the most densely
populated areas of the city was Chinatown, where plague cases
were reported that first year following annexation. A strict quar-
antine was placed on the area. Military guards were stationed at
the boundaries of Chinatown. All schools were closed. No Ori-

ental was permitted to leave the city. Chinese suspicions were roused when the same restrictions were not applied to the few *haole* plague cases. When five deaths occurred in one block, Block 15 between Kaumakapili Church and Nuuanu Street, the fire department turned out as was its custom to burn the houses where the plague victims had lived.

At first, the controlled fire was kept within its planned limits. Unexpectedly, the wind shifted and rose. The blaze lunged into Chinatown. Residents who had been temporarily evacuated from nearby streets rushed to retrieve their possessions. They were held back by a cordon of citizens armed with sticks, pick handles, bats, and shovels. The Chinese consul and vice consul pleaded in vain for order. The Japanese consul had no better luck in trying to control the crowd of Japanese who lived in the neighborhood.

Ships left the harbor as the fire raged toward the wharves. Thirty-eight acres, the vast twin-towered structure of Kaumakapili Church, and almost the whole of Chinatown burned that day. Forty-five hundred people were left homeless with nothing but the clothes on their backs. No one could convince the Chinese that the Board of Health had not purposely burned their homes. It was, many of them believed (and still believe to this day), a retribution for their support of the Hawaiian monarchy, a lesson intended to dissuade them from petitioning for their rights as citizens as they had in 1894. The fire seemed to them ironic proof of the discrimination against the very ideals of American democracy that Sun Yat-sen was attempting to export from Hawaii in his creation of the first democracy in Asia, the Republic of China.

The shift in American ideals noted in the Hawaiian-language press during the Spanish-American War and the gap between democracy preached and democracy practiced experienced by Hawaii's Chinese was analyzed eight years after the annexation of the islands in a book, *National Ideals Historically Traced,* by Harvard historian Albert Bushnell Hart. For him, the twentieth century American dilemma was identified as the very gap and shift observable in Hawaii, the increasing difference between the ideals America preached at home and the practices by which it conducted its affairs both in domestic matters and, particularly, in its new possessions overseas.

"On top of the unsolved Indian problem, and the insoluble Negro question," wrote Hart, "the people of the United States by the annexations of 1898 and 1899 took to themselves a set of Spanish, Hawaiian and Malay race issues." [2] For Professor Hart, as for many thoughtful Americans of that day, this new imperialism posed the contradictions of manifest destiny and economic expedience to the high ideals of the Declaration of Independence. Was democracy to survive only in the eloquence of Fourth of July speeches? Were the peoples of the new dependencies entitled to the rights for which generations of Americans had been contending since 1776? Did the guarantees of a federal Constitution apply to the newly annexed Territory of Hawaii? Were islanders ready to receive the kinds of local and territorial government enjoyed by other communities not yet ready for statehood? Were they citizens of the United States, as were the citizens of the territories of Oklahoma, New Mexico, and Arizona, and with the same prerogatives?

The crowning paradox of Hart's book was that he dedicated it to that champion of manifest destiny, Theodore Roosevelt, and after long soliloquies on the ideals of democracy, Hart referred to the United States of America in 1906 as "this empire." The real question for Hawaii was whether as an overseas American possession it would be treated as an integral part of the American union, a territory with the same future potential and present privilege as those of Oklahoma, Arizona, and New Mexico. In 1787 the Congress of the Confederation of newly independent American states passed the Northwest Ordinance, establishing the steps by which a territory could progress toward statehood. The federal government established under the Constitution preserved that ordinance and the admission standards it set. By June 1900 when an Organic Act of the United States designated its new possession, the Hawaiian Islands, as the Territory of Hawaii, thirty-two territories had met those standards and been

2. Albert Bushnell Hart, *National Ideals Historically Traced* (New York, London: Harper and Bros., 1907), p. 63.

admitted as states. Oklahoma, New Mexico, and Arizona were in the process of qualifying for admission.

Like her three mainland sister territories, Hawaii was to be administered by a presidentially appointed governor, with her executive offices of territorial government budgeted and administered by the United States Department of the Interior. As did Oklahoma, New Mexico, and Arizona in 1900, Hawaii had only a small minority of Anglo-Saxon whites in her territorial population. Queen Liliuokalani's thousands of acres of former crown lands had been taken over as government lands in the coup of 1893 and were so transferred at annexation. New Mexico's large Spanish land grants, dissolved in public lands, were to be resurrected in public litigation in the latter half of the twentieth century. Similarly, the usurpation of Hawaii's crown lands was to face court challenges in the 1980s by Hawaiians experiencing a political, cultural, and demographic renaissance.

In common with the three mainland territories nearing statehood in 1900, Hawaii had a long tradition of independence, autonomy, and cultural heritage. Unlike her three mainland counterparts, Hawaii had had eighty years of experience in the practice of democracy and American-style government. Her record of friendship with the government of the United States went back to its inception and the unification of the kingdom by Kamehameha I. The Hawaiian people's trust in that government had persisted, despite their distrust and dislike for certain individual Americans such as those of the Hawaiian League, the Honolulu Rifles, the Provisional Government and the reform party oligarchy of the Republic of Hawaii (much the same roster of *haole* leadership).

The histories of the new Territory of Hawaii and those of the Southwest were vastly different. While the American West and Southwest were being penetrated by settlers and racked by Indian wars, the Hawaiian Kingdom had enjoyed peace, the progress of literacy, and the advent of commerce and industry. Hawaii's development remains a model for small nations in her building of government structure and services, the strengthening of her economy, the establishment of a network of post offices, roads, harbors, and railroads, the universality of public education, public health assistance, road maintenance, police and fire protection. In 1900, Hawaiians were literate and ardently political in the American style, whereas the Indians and Hispano-Americans of the Southwest were at ease only in their own languages and culture. Hawaiians had married *haole*, Chinese, members of each of the immigrant ethnic groups, with the exception of the Japanese whose custom favored marriage within their own racial group and who seldom took Hawaiian mates. Part-Hawaiian children (half-castes, the new formal census language of the territory described them) retained status and economic and social prestige in their territory. In the American Southwest territories, children born of mixed Spanish, Indian, and Anglo parentage were not socially accepted and were often pushed to the lowest level of economic and political participation.

In 1900, in the fields of social services, legislative experience, education, water and land development, along with progress in the amenities of western civilization, Oklahoma, New Mexico, and Arizona were primitive in contrast to the Territory of Hawaii. Yet, those three mainland territories were only seven and twelve years away from statehood. How far away was the Territory of Hawaii? What could islanders expect as the newest subjects of the federal government? How real and how imminent was that promise of the forty-sixth star in the flag flown at the annexation ceremony of August 12, 1898?

There were three steps a territory must pass to achieve statehood. First was the appointment of a territorial governor, a requirement fulfilled by the appointment of former president of the republic Sanford Ballard Dole to serve in that office in the Territory of Hawaii. The second step toward statehood directed that when a territory, or any division of it, attained a population of five thousand adult males, its citizens could elect a legislature with limited powers of local government lawmaking and a delegate to Congress who would have a voice but no vote. In June 1900, a majority of the Territory of Hawaii's population of 154,000 could not be counted in qualifying for this step since they were Asian born. The United States' Chinese Exclusion Acts of 1882–1884 denied citizenship privileges to all residents of Asian birth. The opportunity of naturalization, which the Kingdom of Hawaii had traditionally offered all her resident foreigners, was thus removed from the 25,767 Chinese and more than 61,000 Japanese immigrants residing in the Territory of Hawaii at its inception.

The substantial *haole* population and the Hawaiians who were legally declared Caucasians in an act of Congress at annexation more than met this second step. For Hawaiians, territoriality returned a political power that time and the growth of a new era population in their own kingdom had removed from them. Under the leadership of Robert Wilcox they organized a Home Rule party, with advice to the Hawaiian voters who were a clear majority in the new territorial electorate: *Nana i ka ili!*—"Look at the skin!"

The old oligarchy of the republic, the *haole* annexationists who had been members of the reform party and the Hawaiian League had become instant Republicans. There were only a few Democrats. Prince David Kawananakoa, adopted son of Kalakaua's consort, Queen Kapiolani, was the most prominent and one of the few Hawaiian Democrats. Well driller and later rancher and land developer Lincoln McCandless helped found the Democratic party in the territory. Another founding Democrat was Delbert K. Metzger, the Spanish-American War veteran who stayed on in Honolulu to drill artesian wells and help survey Pearl Harbor. In 1908 he moved to Hilo to supervise construction of the breakwater across Hilo Bay. David K. Trask, Sr., of Kauai and Oahu was another early party member along with prominent Hawaiian-Chinese families in Hilo and a few Portuguese on Maui.

The first territorial legislature elected in consonance with Hawaii's following the second step on the statehood path consisted of fourteen Home Rulers, nine Republicans, and four Democrats in the House. Nine of the thirteen in the territorial Senate were Home Rulers. Robert Wilcox, their party leader, was elected congressional delegate.

Territorial governor Dole fumed at the actions of this Hawaiian-controlled legislature, which insisted on conducting its business in Hawaiian rather than in English, tried to free Hawaiian prisoners, and forced Dole to use his gubernatorial veto on their lowering of the three-dollar-a-year tax on female dogs. In Dole's eyes, this last was nonsense legislation. In Hawaiian eyes this was a practical measure designed to aid the Hawaiian for whom dog was a favored *luau* food. One legislative action that the opposition could not condemn was their adoption of the Hawaiian flag as the official banner of the new territory.

Governor Dole and his colleagues could not stage a revolution to get rid of the Home Rulers. Their strategy had to be political. In 1902 they wooed the popular Prince Jonah Kuhio Kalanianaole to the Republican side, making him their candidate for congressional delegate—a seat he easily wrested from Robert Wilcox. Prince Kuhio was the brother of David Kawananakoa, and like him had been named by Queen Liliuokalani an heir to the throne after the death of Princess Kaiulani. Kuhio was a strange choice for the Republicans. He had fought for the queen in the counterrevolution of 1895. He had been one of those imprisoned loyalists whose lives she was convinced she saved by her signing of abdication papers. However, the alliance was clear eyed on both sides. The Republicans had a Hawaiian chief who drew support of his people away from the Home Rule party, which died away by 1914. Kuhio had a channel to get patronage, and several years later he tried to obtain lands for at least a few of his people with his Hawaiian Homes Commission Act.

It was the second territorial legislature, in 1905, that passed the Organic Act enabling the old gubernatorial divisions of the four former chiefdoms to assume the new legal status of counties. This fulfilled the second and final requirement of the second step toward statehood. Kauai and Niihau became the County of Kauai with its seat at Lihue. A tacit agreement assured the Sinclair and Robinson families that government interference on their privately owned island would be at a minimum. The owners' rights to control visitations and departures was a limitation so restrictive of travel to and from Niihau that it became known as the Forbidden Isle or the Mystery Island.

Oahu was organized as the City and County of Honolulu, adding the 1,100-mile-distant Line island of Palmyra to its jurisdiction after that island's acquisition by Honolulu's Fullard-Leo family in 1912. Honolulu was both territorial capital and county seat for the entire island and, after 1912, distant Palmyra.

The former chiefdom of Maui became Maui County, with Molokai, Lanai, and the lonely grazing lands of Kahoolawe administered from the county seat of Wailuku, Maui. The Big Island, Hawaii, became the County of Hawaii with the county seat shifted to Hilo, the windward town that had gained in importance from the sugar plantations surrounding it. Kailua-Kona, Kamehameha's former capital, had regressed into a sleepy seaside village. It was Hilo that had grown to be the island's central port and business community.

A fifth county jurisdiction was added to accommodate the leper colony at Kalaupapa, Molokai, which had the dubious privilege given to it of having its own local government—the County of Kalawao.

The third step toward statehood, a territorial population exceeding 60,000 eligible citizens, had already been met before 1900. By 1906, all constitutional requirements being asked of Oklahoma, New Mexico, and Arizona, and all that had been met by the thirty-two territories previously admitted to the union, had been met by the Territory of Hawaii. The struggle for statehood was even then recognized to be more of an emotional than a legal one. The heavily Oriental population of the islands made many of the prejudicially WASP Americans of the continental United States as uneasy as they made the *haole* leadership of the territory's Republican party. Professor Hart's book had contained many inferences that even a democratic empire would do well to keep its overseas possessions in the colonial status of territories, although as a conscientious historian and student of American ideals he believed such a stance would weight the United States with an almost unbearable burden of conscience in the twentieth century.

With confidence in those American ideals now introduced into the curriculum of Hawaii's public schools, the children of Hawaii's alien-born Orientals faced a future in which they understood they would have to prove their Americanism. Teachers of Hawaiian, Chinese, Portuguese, and idealistic young mainland *haole* backgrounds began to give, in English, a solid democratic education to the children who would one day become Hawaii's leaders and make statehood a reality.

The territory's school system continued to be centrally administered. Territorial government also maintained overall responsibility for public health, road construction, harbor maintenance, prisons, and tax collection. The county governments assumed responsibility for the repair and maintenance of roads, police and fire protection, and the building and repair of school and hospital facilities. At both levels of the government there was little change in personnel at the shift from independence to annexation. Postal employees became federal, subject to rules and regulations of the United States government. In 1911 the first government employee of Japanese ancestry in Hawaii's history was hired—Steere Noda, employed by the islands' first office of the Bureau of Internal Revenue. The paradox in racial attitudes of island *haoles* was displayed when strong protest was sent by Honolulu's leaders to Washington, D.C., at the appointment of a black to be the bureau's director in Hawaii and equally strong protest was raised by the same *haoles* at the bureau's transfer of the black director back to the mainland several years later. The aloha spirit often needed the stimulus of direct personal contact to begin to operate.

Under the monarchy, the majority of government jobs at the supervisory, clerical, teaching, inspector, tax collector, police officer, fireman, cantoneer, and custodian level had been held by Hawaiians. They retained these through the provisional government, under the republic, and were the core of government workers in the first half century of the Territory of Hawaii, along with cadres of Chinese and Portuguese. Though the emotional impact of the loss of their queen and their independence had been as severe a psychological assault on Hawaiians as had the missionary negation of their culture in the 1820s, they survived with two sources of sustenance. One was that of their inner reliance on the *mana* of themselves and of their islands, a spiritual sustenance with which they had infused Christianity whether of the Protestant, Catholic, or Mormon denominations. The second source of their salvation was their easy aloha in intermarriage. The federal government and Republican leadership in territorial circles spoke in patronizing terms throughout the first half of the century not so much of "the Hawaiians" as of "the Hawaiian problem." The real surprise of those first fifty years as an American territory was the resurgence of the Hawaiians in numbers, culture, and ethnic pride. That easy aloha of which the missionaries had so disapproved finally accomplished the replenishment of the Hawaiian population: 100,000 of the territory's 499,754 people counted in the 1950 census would identify themselves as Hawaiians.

The Hawaiian-Japanese antipathy that has colored the group relationships of each toward the other in the second decade of statehood was not felt nor expressed to any great degree in the early days of the territory. Then, Hawaiians had the monopoly on government jobs that islanders of Japanese ancestry now enjoy. Then, a majority of Hawaiians were well educated. That statistic reversed with a despondency that marked the Hawaiians of the 1920s and 1930s, in the days before they dared to look with open pride at their cultural roots. The great advantage to territoriality for the Japanese in 1900 was the abrogation of their labor contracts, which became illegal under federal law. As early as 1898 and 1899 courageous Japanese tore up the pieces of paper that bound them to a hated plantation and demanded their rights as free laborers. They might not become citizens of the new territory, but no longer could they be forced to work under harsh conditions, and brutal *lunas,* unless they chose to do so. No longer would they be hunted down by Hawaiian police, whose heaviest caseload in the 1890s had been capturing laborers who had jumped their contract and imprisoning them until they agreed to work their contracts out.

Debt and the economic necessity to survive was to continue to drive former contract laborers to hard work, for long hours, under difficult conditions for the next forty years, but those who had courage and the ability to make a go of it independently could and did leave the plantations to start small businesses, to become fishermen, to open family stores, to go into construction, which in Hawaii became a predominantly Japanese industry.

Planters now had to seek free labor, a much more expensive arrangement than the contracts, and with the flow of labor off the plantations, their need to seek new supplies of workers was as great as ever. Duty-free sugar had been purchased at the expense of the old cheap labor contract advantages. Annexation, which Americans like Governor Dole and Lorrin A. Thurston believed would solve all their problems, escalated the democratic social process that was to move Hawaii during the twentieth century from plantation colonialism through the agony of wartime and army rule to the political and labor revolutions that immediately preceded statehood.

Hawaii's new twentieth-century territorial labor immigrants came from the troubled places of the world. Between 1903 and 1905, five thousand Puerto Ricans arrived, grateful refugees from an island devastated by storms, epidemics, and the Spanish-American War. In that same period seventy-four hundred Koreans arrived, equally grateful to find refuge outside their country, which was about to fall under the rule of Japan. Three thousand Russian Molokans sought a place to practice their religion—a schism from the Doukhubors—but soon moved on, claiming that plantation labor conditions were not what had been promised them. Others who left plantation jobs at the first opportunity were many of the eight thousand Spanish workers and several hundred Tennessee blacks who came as field labor in the early years of the territory.

It was December 1906 when the first group of Filipino immigrants arrived. This was also the first year of immigration from Okinawa—the Ryukyuan Islands under Japanese rule. To outsiders, Okinawans were indistinguishable from Japanese, but between those two peoples, who differed in culture and language, the difference was as marked and the feelings as hostile as between the English and the Irish. For most of the new immigrants, the burdens of everyday life were no less harsh than had been those of the *makaainana* before the improvements of 1840. Plantation work in the first three decades of the twentieth century was still a backbreaking process involving the clearing of wastelands, the building of irrigation ditches, and the boring of water tunnels through mountain ranges. Planting, cultivating, and harvesting were hard hand labor, aided only by wagons and teams of oxen to haul the cut cane to the nearest mill. The milled sugar, in one-hundred-pound bags, either rode to the nearest shipping port by rail or was lightered to be hoisted by the slingload to freighters heaving in the offshore surge along the islands' windward coasts.

The plantation workday was dawn to dusk, six days a week. Everyone worked: women with babies on their backs, children as young as nine and ten years old. The necessity to feed, house, and clothe one's family was a powerful impetus to self-contract. Immigrants in plantation Hawaii under United States rule endured hardships much like those of the European immigrant in the sweatshops of early twentieth century America. The curses and sometimes the whips of *lunas* would haul a sick employee out of his bed to a plantation workday that began at sunrise. On some plantations, Chinese cooks brought lunch to the fields—big tubs of rice, a few pickles, vegetables seasoned with strips of meat or pieces of fish. Back in their own quarters at the end of the day, the laborers had to prepare their evening meal, and in the Japanese camps, light the fire to heat the water for their *o-furo,* evening bath. Conditions in the Territory of Hawaii in 1900 were little different than they had been in the Kingdom of Hawaii in 1890 for Benjamin Iida and his family, who were among the first immigrants arriving on the *City of Tokio.* Iida, who was three when that first shipload of contract labor brought him to Honolulu in 1885, recalled in later years that at Kilauea, Kauai, where his family was sent on a labor contract, one water pipe served an entire housing camp. His family of four had one room. They kept their water in a fifty-gallon barrel. His mother's stove was a kerosene drum opened at the top and on one side to be loaded with firewood. When it rained, the stove had to be moved inside their one room, where the smoke made the air almost unbearable. They watched birds and animals eat weeds to find out which ones were safe for them to eat, Iida recalled years later. When his family arrived, there were almost no vegetables, so they experimented: picking mill weeds to use for greens, cooking taro and pumpkin stems with Chinese soy.

Territorial politics were not yet of interest to these alien-born Orientals whom United States laws barred from citizenship. As did Hawaii's Chinese, the Koreans in the new territory involved themselves in the political causes of their homelands. Chinese support continued to go to Sun Yat-sen from Hawaii. Koreans new to the territory argued among themselves as to whether evolution or revolution was the best way to free their country from Japanese domination. The success of Sun Yat-sen in ousting the Manchu regime, and on October 10, 1910, establishing the Republic of China, encouraged Koreans in their struggle from the overseas base of Hawaii. In 1911, a Korean military academy operated for a time on windward Oahu. However, the eventual Korean decision was to abide by the counsel of their most conservative leader, Syngman Rhee, who used Hawaii as his home and organization base. Not until the conclusion of World War II would he achieve the slow painful evolution of an independent Republic of Korea, of which he became the president.

As with the Chinese and Koreans of the Territory of Hawaii, the Japanese and Okinawan populations were barred from participation in island politics. For these first generation immigrants, the *issei,* exclusion forced and emphasized the need to continue ties of loyalty with their home country. Japan's civil wars and social revolution of the 1860s and 1870s were over. The Meiji emperor was beyond political speculation, revered by his people at home and overseas as the sacred heir of the sun goddess, Amaterasu, ancestress of the Japanese people. As their children were born in Hawaii, the *issei* of the territory prudently registered their births with the Japanese consul in Honolulu or with representatives of the Japanese consulate appointed to serve in plantation communities and county seats throughout the islands. In 1908, a gentleman's agreement had been made between the United States and Japan. Its exact text was not made public but its implications led Japanese parents in the territory to doubt their American-born *nisei*—second generation—would receive the citizenship to which their American birth by rights entitled them.

Under the terms of the 1908 gentleman's agreement, Japanese

immigration to Hawaii was restricted to the sixteen-year period, 1908–1924, during which families of those already living in the Territory of Hawaii and brides coming from Japan to marry island husbands were to be permitted entry. All others were to be denied. On the basis of this selective relaxation of the 1882 Exclusion Laws, the United Chinese Societies of Hawaii in 1916 petitioned the United States Congress for this same opportunity to bring in families and brides for Chinese,

> not for the Chinese to the whole of the United States but for the benefit of the Territory of Hawaii only. Trusting that American justice will be accorded to us. The Constitution and flag of the United States are ours to live under, respect, and obey; to you we look to protection; to the United States we give our loyalty. That all men be equal under the law is the petition of all the Chinese in Hawaii.[3]

The petition of the Chinese was turned down. Only for the Japanese was this period in territorial history known as *Yobiyose Jidai*—"the period of summoning families." Brides were sought through an exchange of photographs, with both homely or older "picture brides" in Japan and unattractive or older prospective bridegrooms in Hawaii substituting the photographs of younger, better-looking friends to be used in the negotiations conducted through village matchmakers in the groom's home district. When a match was arranged, the prospective groom sent passage money, met the girl (who was presumably to be his lifetime companion) on her arrival at the Kakaako Immigration Depot, and married her there. Usually, such arranged marriages worked well. It was the Japanese custom. Both parties were eager to have a harmonious life. Values and backgrounds of bride and groom were compatible: hard work, thrift, filial piety, compassion, the inner strength of Buddhism, and a fierce desire that their children have the best possible chance at a new life. But there were also a great many exceptions to the rule that carefully matched couples would find happiness. At Kakaako, there were courageous girls who refused ugly husbands to marry the first stranger there waiting to pick up a disgruntled girl.

3. Tin-Yuke Char, *The Sandalwood Mountains, Readings and Stories of the Early Chinese in Hawaii* (Honolulu: University Press of Hawaii, 1967), p. 307.

Often the first years of "picture bride" marriages were private anguish, ending in wives running away, assuming new names, and marrying men of their own choice.

Many of these picture brides, and a large majority of the *issei* settled in the territory, quickly perceived that for them, Hawaii and in particular the harsh life of the plantations was far from paradise. Migration from Hawaii to California and the Pacific Northwest was prohibited to Japanese, but despite the need to go illegally, thousands of them moved from Hawaii to the mainland during these years. Between 1908 and 1924, 62,277 relatives and picture brides came to Hawaii from Japan. For most, life on the plantations was like imprisonment or slavery compared with the freedom and informality of the village life in Hiroshima or Yamaguchi. In Japan, the whole family had labored from dawn to dusk, as they did here, but in Japan the work had usually been done on their own land, their own initiative, and with a free spirit. Here, for the first time they worked in an alien caste system, baffled by a language difficult for them to learn, rejected as unassimilable by the laws of this United States territory.

How to meet this strange new situation? The path still followed by many *issei* and a number of *nisei* was to keep strictly to themselves, ignore the *haole* whenever possible, and follow the traditional ethic of *Yamato Damashii*—the Japanese spirit and tradition of the Meiji era, the customs of the homeland that had prevailed when they left it. Politeness was part of this ethic, for they were guests in the host country of the Americans, and one never behaved badly to one's host, no matter what the circumstances of one's own treatment by that host. Differences in culture, the clinging to their own language, isolated the *issei* into small beachheads of Japanese culture, with a social, religious, and often an economic life of their own. Ties with the rest of the community were pleasant but limited in much the same ways as the American missionaries who had once lived in their own insulated New England–style worlds in Hawaii-nei, and who like the *issei* continued to live in an insularity of their own kind, socially, in the increasingly cosmopolitan environment of territorial Hawaii.

11

The Rise of Labor

$\mathcal{T}$HE paradox of the years of territoriality was that the warmth of friendship and aloha, along with the interchange of *kokua,* prevailed between island neighbors, schoolmates, and between men and women who worked in the same gang on the plantation or in the same shop or mill; yet, separatism and racial divisiveness was encouraged by the plantation management custom of segregating employees in housing camps allocated by race and paying a wage scale with a racial bias.

Japanese contract laborers staged the prologue of the labor-management drama that was to be played through the two decades preceding and one following World War II. Management's response to the union activities, encouraged by their indifferent treatment of workers' grievances and by the same callous inhumanity Frank Damon had observed displayed toward Chinese labor in 1883, led eventually to a schism not between the various races of laborers but between management and labor itself.

One year after the arrival of the first large contract labor group from Japan, *haole* planters (whose economic visibility led them to be assumed to be the stereotype of all *haoles*) ignored the advice of Robert Walker Irwin that the newcomers be treated with "the silken thread of kindness." Too often a manager or his *luna* tried to solve communication problems by using a whip or harsh language and threats. The same bonds of racial brotherhood and compassion that had united the First Year Meiji Men continued to be strong among the Japanese immigrants of the *City of Tokio* and the thousands who followed them. Harsh treatment of one Japanese made several hundred coworkers immediately assume his cause as their own.

In 1886, fifty Japanese workers were jailed at Lihue, Kauai, for refusing to work under the harsh conditions at Lihue Plantation. Since the signing of a convention that year between the Kingdom of Hawaii and the government of the Meiji emperor provided official protection for Japanese contract workers in Hawaii, Consul General Taro Ando hurried from Honolulu to investigate the complaint. His intention was to scold the workers, but after listening to them, he found their complaints valid. They had been forced out of sick beds to work. They had not been allowed to prepare their own meals and were forced to eat *poi* rather than their accustomed staple, rice. The most trivial infraction resulted in excessive fines deducted from their already small wages. For example, if—just one time—a worker was ten minutes late in reporting to the field, he had to forfeit one-fourth of his month's earnings.

In 1890, on the Big Island, 400 Japanese marched from Hakalau to Hilo, more than fifteen miles, to protest being overworked. At Kukuihaele, on that same island, 150 workers marched seven miles to Honokaa to attend the trial of a *luna* who had shot and wounded a Japanese. On Oahu, 200 workers from Ewa Plantation marched twenty miles into Honolulu to present their grievances to the Japanese consul. Another 150 marched forty-five miles from Kahuku Plantation, through the mud of the narrow treacherous trail over Nuuanu Pali, to protest mistreatment. Each of these latter was fined five dollars and made to march the forty-five miles back to Kahuku, but a few months later, 120 of the same workers protested the continuing mistreatment by striking again. A second time they made the long march over the Pali to Honolulu. This time they were not fined, and they were returned to Kahuku by steamer.

Management did not alter its attitudes nor practices as between 1896 and 1900 the number of Japanese living in Hawaii and working on island plantations more than doubled. As Frank

Damon had noted in 1883, on the territory's plantations men and women were regarded as simply so many machines to be fed and housed as cheaply as possible and paid a minimal wage. The Organic Act that nullified labor contracts also imposed federal labor laws upon the islands, but in 1900 the major impact of these was a report to be published by the Bureau of Labor every five years on labor conditions in the new territory.

In 1902, a Japanese educated in America described the problem for plantation labor as being attributable to management's habit of ignoring employees grievances rather than taking the trouble to understand them. The grievances would accumulate, and finally, after months or even years of neglect, a strike would be called, much to the "surprise" of management. Such strikes could perhaps have been avoided had the laborers been able to make themselves understood.

The bulletins first prepared on labor conditions in Hawaii by the United States Bureau of Labor recounted numerous such strikes. One was in Lahaina, Maui, in April of 1900 when 1,160 out of 1,634 Japanese field workers took over the town until their demands were met for higher pay, improved working conditions, compensation for industrial injury, and a better water supply for their camps.

Two months later, in June 1900, Japanese workers at Olaa Plantation near Hilo struck because expired labor contracts were still being enforced. Between 1900 and 1903 there were twenty-five strikes involving 8,000 Japanese laborers over issues such as those in Lahaina and Olaa and more personal matters such as *lunas* forcing Japanese women laborers to have sexual relations with them or managers giving the choicest jobs to the prettiest Japanese girls. Between 1903 and 1906, at least 13,000 Japanese took part in fourteen strikes. In one of these, a strike on Maui in 1905, police fired on 1,700 Japanese workers who walked off the job. One worker was killed. Two others suffered injuries.

Planters were indignant that a supposedly docile people would be adamant in their demands to be treated in a fair and humane fashion. The *Honolulu Advertiser,* editorial voice of plantation interests in the territory, reflected the postannexation shift in idealism of Americans who having picked up the "white man's burden" assumed by Christendom were annoyed that the black-skinned, brown-skinned, and yellow-skinned brothers dared to be so ungrateful. Like President Theodore Roosevelt and Senators Albert Beveridge and Henry Cabot Lodge, territorial management *haoles* felt that all Orientals must be dealt with forcefully—and always as inferiors. Not a few of the wealthy *alii* landowners agreed. Americans in this early period of the century tended to believe that Asian countries could not govern themselves well, nor should Asiatics expect to gain a living standard or working conditions similar to those enjoyed by white residents of the United States. Paradoxically, these attitudes were often shared by Hawaiians who themselves had been the victims of Christian missionary intolerance and prejudice. A lingering dislike for the peoples to whom their own King Kalakaua had offered the loving hands and heart of the Hawaiians poisoned the aloha of some *alii* and some *makaainana* toward Japanese. Yet, marriages between Japanese and Hawaiians, though comparatively few, were generally happy, and on an individual basis personal friendships were frequent between Hawaiians and Japanese. In the labor movement, it would be another two decades before Hawaiian and Japanese workers united in organizations like the International Longshoremen's and Warehousemen's Union, the Hawaii Government Employees Association, the United Public Workers, and the AFL-CIO affiliated Teamsters Union.

Unions in the earliest territorial years were not the "all for one, one for all" organizations that came later. The Japanese who "respectfully suggested" a fair wage, and one not based on the worker's race, were not the first group to unionize, despite the numerous instances of demands, walk outs, and strikes by Japanese workers. In 1901 the Honolulu Federation of Trades was formed, and in 1902 the White Mechanics and Workingmen of Honolulu were the territory's first trade unions. Their sole aim was to preserve jobs for *haole* workers and to protest continuance of Oriental immigration to the islands. In 1903 a community-wide council was organized in Hilo for the same purposes. All three groups sought also to negate planter efforts to have the Chinese Exclusion Act waived for the territory. They agreed with the *Advertiser* in its stand to keep Japanese labor in check. "Yield to his demands, and he thinks he is the master and makes new demands. Use the strong hand and he recognizes the power to which, from immemorial times, he has abjectly bowed. There is one word which holds the lower classes of every nation in check and that is Authority." [1]

What the new trade unions, the Hilo council, the planters, and the *Advertiser* failed to realize was that exactly like the European immigrants to the continental United States, the Japanese laborers had expected a new freedom and opportunity in Hawaii. The Japanese had never known the yoke of colonialism. They had voluntarily left their own country to try for a better life for themselves and their children. They were a people with a tradition of peasant revolt whenever a feudal lord was oppressively heavy-handed. The most courageous, independent, free thinking among them had emigrated to Hawaii. Editorial columns of the Japanese-language papers asked the hard question that such Americans as Professor Hart were posing. Could this be the renowned American democracy?

When, in 1909, the first Japanese industrial union organized, the Japanese-language press became the voice of labor, speaking out for the new union, the Japanese Higher Wages Association, which struck all Oahu plantations to protest racially biased wage differentials.

If a laborer comes from Japan and he performs the same quantity of work of same quality within the same period of time as those who hail from opposite sides of the world, what good reason is there to discriminate one as against the other. It is not the color of the skin or hair, or the language that he speaks, or manner that grows cane in the field. It is labor that grows cane, and the more efficient the labor, the better the crop the cane field will bring. We demand higher wages of planters in the full confidence of the efficiency of our labor and, also, in the equally full confidence in the planters' sense of justice and equality in all things that pertain to human affairs, especially in the delicate relations between capital and labor. [2]

1. Lawrence H. Fuchs, *Hawaii Pono: A Social History* (New York: Harcourt, Brace & World, Inc., 1961), p. 208.
2. Gavan Daws, *Shoal of Time: A History of the Hawaiian Islands* (New York: The Macmillan Company, 1968), p. 304.

The 1909 strikers held out for a month, hoping for justice and equality along with a decent cottage and an acre of good land for each worker. To keep operating during that month, planters paid strikebreaking Hawaiians and Portuguese $1.50 a day. When the strike ended, management replaced many Japanese mechanics and *lunas* with Hawaiians and *haoles*. Some group benefit was won in the improvement of plantation sewerage and water systems in the housing camps and in expanded but still inadequate medical care for laborers and their families. But six years later, the Bureau of Labor reported that on all plantations in the territory, the basic monthly wage rate was $24 for all Europeans and Hawaiians, and $20 for all Orientals. Injustice and inequality prevailed.

The five major corporations exercising an economic monopoly over the territory in the first half of the century were not interested in redress for the Japanese who formed 60 percent of the plantation workforce. Although independent plantations still survived, each year more of them came under either the direct ownership or the indirect financial control of Castle and Cooke, C. Brewer, Theo Davies and Co., Alexander and Baldwin, or after World War I American Factors, a confiscation of the German alien assets of H. Hackfeld and Co. Ninety percent of the territory's income was from sugar. It mattered little that the number two crop, rice, was the province of Chinese entrepreneurs. Pineapple, which was soon to displace rice in that second position, was in the trustworthy hands of Sanford Ballard Dole's young cousin, Jim Dole, whose sixty acres of a promising new variety of pineapple was planted to the very gates of the United States Army's new Schofield Barracks.

The *haole* tradesmen leaving Hawaii because of the competition of lower-priced Japanese mechanics were being replaced by a new variety of transient *haole:* servicemen and their families. Neither in 1907 when four thousand regular army and navy personnel were assigned to federal defense installations at Pearl Harbor, Fort Shafter, and Schofield Barracks (all on Oahu) nor in the 1970s when a total of 58,300 army, navy, air force, Coast Guard, and marine personnel were stationed in Hawaii were these an easily assimilable group. Except for high-ranking officers, the servicemen both in territorial days and in the 1970s had little social contact with local residents. In 1907, a language barrier existed between the sailor who came from Kansas or the army private from Kentucky and the Hawaiian, Chinese, Japanese, Portuguese, Puerto Rican, or Korean who used pidgin as a comfortable common dialect. Service children like John Anthony Burns, son of an army sergeant, found themselves a minority in the public schools, an experience new to most American mainlanders who tended not to realize that the racial structure of Hawaii more closely approximated the demographic structure of majority races on the planet. Upper-class, well-to-do island *haole* families did not send their children to public schools. Punahou, Iolani, and St. Andrew's Priory were beyond the financial reach of most service families. The Kamehameha Schools were exclusively for children of Hawaiian ancestry and not yet then one of the private schools stressing quality academic achievement and college preparatory courses. Not until the 1970s would this institution, founded by the immense wealth in lands of Bernice Pauahi Bishop, change from a vocational and trades emphasis to top quality, broad-based educational preparation of young Hawaiians. Few *alii* families chose Kamehameha. They preferred to send their children to Punahou, Iolani, or the Catholic high school, St. Louis College.

The problem of *haole* service families was further compounded by there being so few families among the four thousand troops. Most were single men. Their experience of life in Hawaii was the rough drink-and-sex entertainment that the old roistering whalers and visiting ship crews had known. The difference in territorial days was that prostitution was now regulated by city authorities. The red-light district was Iwilei, a Dillingham fill just Ewa (west) of Honolulu harbor. There was a small neighborhood of brothels in the Kalihi district. Cheap bars, arcades, and dance halls lined Hotel Street and attracted a big servicemen's clientele.

John Burns's family was stranded in Honolulu when his army sergeant father deserted them. Mrs. Burns was befriended by Hawaiians. The slim tough *haole* boy who would grow up to achieve statehood for Hawaii acculturated in the street life of the

Kalihi district, acquiring fluency in pidgin and an insight into what being poor, local, and frustrated was all about. In the public schools of Honolulu, and at the Catholic high school he attended, Burns absorbed an enthusiasm for and commitment to the democratic ideals taught by a new young Peace Corps–type breed of liberal *haole* and by Chinese, Hawaiian, and Portuguese teachers who believed in the reality of those ideals as a potential in Hawaii's future.

All over the territory, by 1916, the thousands of *nisei,* growing up in home and camp neighborhoods cloistered by the insulating spirit of *Yamato Damashii,* were (like "Army brat" Burns) being infected in territorial classrooms with the Great American Dream. Unlike John Burns, his *nisei* contemporaries had a dual education. Once the public school day ended, most of them went for another few hours to Japanese Language Schools where they learned the language and how to write it, the ethical culture of Japanese tradition, and Japanese history— but where, also, American democratic ideals were re-enforced. Pictures of George Washington, Abraham Lincoln, and current presidents of the United States decorated Japanese Language classroom walls. Already the *nisei* was different in character from the parents to whom he gave his filial devotion. On the street, in school, at the beach, and in the part-time jobs he might have, the *nisei*—like *haole* Burns—was acquiring tastes for Chinese food, Portuguese music, and Hawaiian equanimity. While appreciating his own difference, he was at the same time accepting the differences of his friends and adopting some of their customs and attitudes. Bishop Yemyo Imamura of Honpa Hongwanji Mission in Honolulu was a vigorous supporter of this social process. In 1916 he was making public statements that the aim of his mission, the largest Buddhist group in the territory, was clear. It was to foster the Americanization process, to make the territory truly the cradle of democracy for the thousands of Japanese children who were the overwhelming majority in the student population of Hawaii's public schools.

In 1916 the famous writer Jack London made his second visit to the territory with his wife. Charmian London was herself an astute observer who put her impressions of both the 1907 and

1916 visits into a book titled *The New Hawaii,* which was published in 1923. For Charmian London it was evident that Hawaii was indeed still a paradise in the early twentieth century, but only so for the well-to-do. In Hilo, in 1907, as she and London prepared for the cruise of their yacht—the first such to sail to the Marquesas—and again in 1916 as they were feted by Honolulu society, she was struck by the paradox of those for whom paradise was a reality in this benign climate, with city houses, mountain houses, and beach homes all staffed by servants, with frequent trips to San Francisco and Europe, with a social life as gay as that of the season in London or New York. These cultured, cosmopolitan wealthy families—many *haole,* some Hawaiian—controlled the economy and political life and set the conditions for laborers in the territory of Hawaii. "Some," wrote Mrs. London, "contribute one-fourth to one-half of their income to good works in a distinctly feudal manner in a Hawaii where the coolie and peasant labor possess no vote." [3]

She warned those Americans who might not be aware of the labor situation in Hawaii that there was an advisory bulletin issued by the Hawaiian Promotion Committee to Americans not to come to the territory unless they had guaranteed employment waiting for them. "Clerical positions are well filled; common labor is largely performed by Japanese or native Hawaiians; the ranks of skilled labor are also well supplied." [4]

Tourist visitors in 1916 found delightful accommodations on Waikiki Beach where the Moana Hotel had a pier jutting out into the water. The old Hawaiian Hotel had passed its prime. Passengers on Captain Matson's cruise ship *Lurline* preferred to spend their Hawaiian holiday—often the entire winter season—in the tranquil resort atmosphere of palm trees, white sand, surf, and Hawaiian music at Waikiki.

Charmian London sampled the resort life there, along with the partying of Honolulu society in their luxurious homes out Nuunau, in cool Manoa Valley, in the choice view locations on the slopes above the city. She heard the views of admirals and

3. Charmian K. London, *The New Hawaii* (London: Mills and Born Ltd., 1923), p. 52.
4. London, p. 51.

generals stationed in the territory. Their feeling was that territorial status for Hawaii was only temporary, but their horizon was not statehood. The U.S. Navy administered American Samoa under a commission-form of government, and this was what high-ranking military personnel felt should be the eventual status of government in the Hawaiian Islands.

Mrs. London's insight was quite at variance with theirs. In 1916 the Japanese were the largest minority in the territory. She predicted that "it is merely a matter of time when the Hawaii-born Japanese vote will not only be larger than any other Hawaiian vote but will be practically equal to all other votes combined. If Hawaii should get statehood, a Japanese governor of the state of Hawaii would be not merely possible, but very probable." [5]

5. London, p. 54.

12

The Roaring Twenties

*H*AWAII was so ardently patriotic in its support of
the First World War that the attorney general of the United
States had to issue a reproof to islanders whose anti-German
hysteria went out of bounds. Life was most unpleasant for German nationals aboard ships interned in Honolulu harbor after
America entered the war, and they became "the enemy." The
confiscated assets of H. Hackfeld and Co. were assumed by
island investors who promptly renamed that venerable firm
American Factors and changed the name of its subsidiary, Honolulu's leading department store, from B. F. Ehlers and Co. to
Liberty House.

Everyone in the territory bought liberty bonds. Army volunteers came forward from every racial and ethnic group from
Honolulu and from most of the towns and plantations throughout the islands. Captain Kenichi Sakai, a *nisei* from Kohala, became the first American of Japanese ancestry to serve as a commissioned officer in the United States Army. In Washington,
after the November 11, 1918, armistice, Prince Jonah Kuhio
was so elated by territorial participation in the war that on February 11, 1919, he introduced the first bill for Hawaiian statehood into the United States Congress. The war, said Kuhio, had
proved Hawaii's loyalty. His people had become Americans
worthy of full membership in the Union. A politely hesitant
Congress decided to refer his bill to committee for study.

In the internal affairs of the territory, World War I was a pressure cooker that inflated prices on forty-five essential commodities (including food and clothing) by 115 percent. Plantation laborers were particularly caught in the squeeze of low and still racially discriminatory wages and prices that at plantation company-owned stores had always been inordinately high. The relatively short duration of American participation in the war, and Hawaii's enthusiastic role in that participation, did not change the pattern of labor protests, which in 1916 had spread to the McCabe, Hamilton and Renny docks in Honolulu. There, paradoxically, 150 Japanese strikebreakers kept freight moving when Hawaiian, Filipino, and 38 Japanese longshoremen struck.

In 1917, a grassroots union movement, the Plantation Laborers Wage Increase Investigative Association, organized five locals on the plantations along the Big Island's Hamakua Coast. On the pineapple plantations that had expanded from Jim Dole's original sixty-acre Wahiawa production of two thousand cases of canned pineapple in 1901, production by 1919 had reached nearly six million cases of canned pineapple a year. Pineapple plantations flourished on Kauai and Maui as well as the red dirt plains near Oahu's Schofield Barracks. Labor on those plantations was increasingly restive. Union groups were forming. Conditions were ripe for a major showdown with management.

In October 1919, seventy-five delegates from the Japanese Young Men's Association conferring in Hilo called for an eight-hour day, overtime pay, increased wages, and an end to the bonus system that was tied into piece work and current sugar prices. In December, the Japanese Federation of Labor, representing workers on every cane-growing island, sat down to discuss labor demands with Pablo Manlapit's Filipino Labor Union, whose membership included a number of Puerto Rican workers. Their cause was endorsed by Ray Stannard Baker, crusading American journalist, who visited the territory's plantations that year and labeled conditions for plantation laborers as "serfdom." On December 4, the two unions jointly brought the Hawaii Sugar Planters Association a series of demands: a wage increase from $0.72 to $1.25 a day, an eight-hour workday with overtime for Sundays and holidays, paid maternity leaves for women workers.

Against the advice of the Japanese Federation, Manlapit's Filipino Labor Union decided to strike for these demands on January 19, 1920. Reluctantly, the Japanese Federation supported them by striking on Oahu on February 1. Members on the neighbor islands continued to work, supporting the Oahu strike with strike fund contributions that were to mount to more than $600,000. The first big labor battle of the century was on. Divide and conquer became management strategy, and their first attempt was to force a rift between the Japanese and Filipino unions by charging the move of the Japanese Federation as being primarily an attempt to make Hawaii an Oriental province. *Nippu Jiji,* edited by Yasutaro Soga, retorted that the strike was not racial, not political, but a simple matter of asking economic justice.

The predominantly Buddhist religious affiliation of the Japanese in Hawaii, together with the culturally oriented Japanese Language Schools, had contributed to make a largely Christian community uneasy. The Chinese had readily become Christian. Methodist missions were successful among the Koreans. Japanese Christians such as Takie Okamura were in the minority. Most Japanese retained their Buddhist faith, and in this territory where missionary activity had been especially strong, and where many subscribed to William Armstrong's 1881 observation on the suspect nature of all who were not Christian, a religious bias was quick to rise during such a crisis as the 1920 strike. As if it were somehow an integral part of the strike posture of the Japanese Federation, the Planters' Association called for destruction of the Japanese-language press and immediate elimination of all Japanese Language Schools in Hawaii. Headline insinuations of this statement were designed to feed on Filipino suspicions that the allegation of "Oriental province" could be right.

At the end of the first week in February, Manlapit called back his union, urged his men to return to work, and accused the Japanese of wanting to take over in Hawaii. In vain, strike leader Takashi Tsutsumi of the Japanese Federation tried to set the record straight. "I am not an advocate of narrow Japanese im-

perial principle. I am a staunch believer in democracy. We have
started this labor movement in order to display American
spirit.'' [1] For a week, Tsutsumi's union continued the strike
alone. Manlapit rejoined the strike on February 14, but only 500
of his union were with him. Everything seemed against the
strikers. It was the peak of the post–World War I influenza epidemic on Oahu. Between February and April of 1920, 6,000
cases were reported to the Board of Health. Management
evicted 42,000 strikers and their families, many ill with the
disease. A large number of the 1,088 fatalities in that epidemic
were among the strike refugees. When some of them took
shelter in an old abandoned rat-and-roach-infested brewery, territorial government inspectors forced them to leave. Buddhist
temples housed as many as they could, but hundreds had to
sleep out on bare ground under the open showery trade-wind
skies. Strikers' children were refused admission to the public
schools in refugee areas.

The psychological devastation of this experience for the Japanese was similar to that of the Chinese in the plague epidemic of
1899. Both groups felt the ostracism from a vauntedly democratic society. By now, the Chinese had made their own inner
structure of banks, businesses, and a Chinese Chamber of
Commerce. Their sons were educated to law, medicine, and
dentistry with large practices inside—and often outside—the
Chinese community. To many Japanese, especially the *issei*
approaching middle age, the message of the 1920 strike experience was: retreat into the isolation and self-sufficiency of a Japanese world in Hawaii. Takie Okumura, the Christian missionary, was preaching a quite different message. Many listened
to his urging that Japanese should all become Christian, strive to
be like the *haoles,* be obedient workers on the plantations, and
become what he called "New Americans." Numbers did.

Plantations had prepared for the 1920 strike by insuring that
year's crop for $20 million. They had no difficulty hiring Ha-
waiian and Portuguese strikebreakers at $4 a day and Koreans

1. Lawrence H. Fuchs, *Hawaii Pono: A Social History* (New York: Harcourt, Brace & World, Inc., 1961), p. 219.

and Chinese at $3 a day to harvest the mature cane. Financial preparedness was insufficient, however. What the planters were after was military force to end the strike and to end all further strikes in the territory. As the weeks wore on, the National Guard was in readiness. The *haole* establishment of the territory took comfort in their belief that the regular army personnel stationed on Oahu could be called out to help them in an emergency.

Acting Governor Curtis Iaukea disagreed with the planters that any threat to law and order was posed by the continuance of the strike. With the bitter poignancy of a Hawaiian, he reminded them: "It is a matter of history that armed forces of the United States were used to overawe the Hawaiians at the time of the overthrow of the monarchy, and there seems a desire to repeat this measure of intimidation." [2] To territorial governor McCarthy, who was in Washington with Hawaii's unofficial territorial delegate, Walter Dillingham, he wrote: "I am convinced that the racial issue has been deliberately emphasized to cloud the economic issue." [3]

An unexpected supporter of the strike and strikers, who called his Big Five executive parishioners on the racial issue, was the Reverend Albert W. Palmer, minister of Honolulu's Central Union Church. He reminded his congregation, and the community, that "the Oriental who gives to the Red Cross and purchases Liberty Bonds would be capable of organizing a labor union which is, after all, a typically Anglo-Saxon organization." [4] Palmer's proposal of a plan to end the strike was turned down by management. So was his plea to recognize unions and begin collective bargaining, as was already being done in many mainland industries.

The one mainland union willing to support the strikers in Hawaii was the highly controversial "Wobblies," the International Workers of the World. New charges rose from management at this. The IWW was an extremely liberal union, ideologically. Words that were to echo uncomfortably in Hawaii's

2. Fuchs, p. 220.
3. Fuchs, p. 220.
4. Fuchs, p. 221.

future began to tag the strikers after the "Wobblies" offer of support. In April, in a conference of union leaders, the Japanese Federation passed a resolution to expel any member "tainted with radicalism, communism or anarchism." There was a joint reaffirmation of Tsutsumi's stand that the federation would never join the IWW and did not wish to be identified with them in any way. Then, in a last effort to negate the racial tactic of the planters, the federation changed its name to Hawaiian Federation of Labor, urging all workers of every race to join.

It was an uneasy conference. Rumors circulated that the planters had offered Manlapit a $25,000 bribe. There were internal allegations of misuse of the Japanese Federation's strike fund. Membership accused some of the leaders of embezzlement. The atmosphere of mounting internal problems in the two unions decided the strike. In June, both Manlapit and the leaders of the new Hawaiian Federation of Labor called on strikers to return to work in the spirit of aloha. Five months of eviction, influenza epidemic, loss of wages, and disrupted education for their children had discouraged many. Before the strike, there were 24,791 Japanese sugar workers. By 1924, only 12,781 remained in plantation jobs. Many emigrated illegally to California and the Pacific Northwest. Many found jobs in Honolulu or in the neighbor island towns.

For those who returned, concessions were made by management. The minimum wage was increased by 50 percent. Contract rates and rates of semiskilled employees were increased. The racial wage differential as such seemed to have been removed, but a method of carefully structured job descriptions gave *haoles* a higher pay for any job in any industry or business in the territory. Plantation housing and water systems were also improved as a result of the strike. Management wished no such recurrence. They hired camp police and set up spy systems to spot troublemakers and dissidents. Through a new system of industrial relations personnel on each plantation, they tried to give workers a paternalistic image of management by sponsoring employee sports and recreation programs.

This postwar period of the early twenties was also a difficult time for management outside the sugar industry in the territory.

Workers struck at Oahu Railway Company, at Mutual Telephone on Maui, at such Oahu firms as Catton Neill Co. Foundry, Honolulu Iron Works, HC&D, Inter-Island Steamship, California Feed, Hana Wharf, Libby Cannery, Allen and Robinson Stevedores, and Hawaiian Tuna Packers. The Big Five executives had their favorite sport disrupted when the caddies struck Honolulu golf courses.

Sugar workers returning to work with the aloha spirit asked of them found no such *kokua* offered by management. A year after the end of the 1920 sugar strike, punitive action was still being taken against its leaders. On the Big Island, twenty-one union leaders were arrested and charged with dynamiting the house of a conservative *issei* at Olaa. Fifteen were found guilty and sentenced to serve three years and one month. Fred Makino of *Hawaii Hochi* and Yasutaro Soga of *Nippu Jiji* were imprisoned for their editorial support of the strike.

In 1922 a *haole* named George Wright from the American Federation of Labor tried to organize a territory-wide interracial labor union, the United Workers of Hawaii—"the One Big Union." Racial solidarity and class consciousness were the two issues stressed by Wright in meetings at Aala Park, at the edge of Chinatown in downtown Honolulu. Few dared to come out to hear him, but Wright's bull horn carried to eager ears in the densely populated neighborhood. Wright's efforts were curtailed by Governor Wallace R. Farrington's refusal of a charter to his union on the grounds that it was "un-American."

In 1924, Wright was still in the islands, helping Pablo Manlapit in a seven months' strike that swept the Filipinos of the territory into the mainstream of territorial life, demonstrated their courage and tenacity, and lowered the curtain on the first act of the labor drama in Hawaii. It was Manlapit and his Filipino members who had kept the union thrust going after the 1920 strike ended. Among the Japanese, total despair kept union activity at a minimum, but Manlapit, working on Kauai, organized new arrivals from the Philippines into a Filipino Higher Wages Association.

As had the early Chinese, the Filipinos came to Hawaii without wives or families. Many had left wives and young children back in their home barrios, intending to work in Hawaii a few years, save their money, and either return home or send for their families. For the Filipinos, that dream seldom came true before the 1960s. The Great Depression of the 1930s was to hit them at a time when they hoped to be able to realize their dream, and although that depression was to hit the territory with less force than it did the United States mainland, the Filipinos—as last entrants into the workforce—were among the first ones to be let go. The Depression was no sooner ended than World War II engulfed Hawaii and the Philippines.

In the 1920s, as they would be in the 1960s, Filipinos were a lonely group of men. Cockfighting, gambling, dance halls, and the traveling brothels that plantation management encouraged to make scheduled visits to the plantations were their recreation in much the way that the Chinese bachelors of the 1880s had been left with little to do but gamble and smoke opium in their leisure time. As some Filipina women arrived, and the Hawaiian with her usual congeniality began to accept Filipino husbands, lonely bachelors indulged the children of their friends with gifts and affection. They were gentle, good looking, affectionate men whom other immigrants tended to avoid and distrust. Rumor was that Filipinos in Kona, which had become a coffee raising district, took Spanish fly and would attack any girl walking alone on the road. Koji Ariyoshi, later editor of the liberal *Honolulu Record,* recalled that girls in his home district of Kona crossed the road in panic when they saw a Filipino approach. His own experience was of several Filipino bachelors working on his family's coffee farm and living with his family as much respected members of the household. For the lonely Filipino, who sometimes hanged himself in despair over the emptiness of his life, union activity provided a social outlet as well as a just cause.

On April 1, 1924, the Filipino Labor Union struck. Again, management used the tactic of racial division. Strike action was centered in Kauai. Manlapit and many in his union were from the Visayan region of the Philippines. The planters brought in Ilocano strikebreakers, men from the area of northern Luzon whose language and culture were substantially different. Again, as in 1920, the strike dragged on. In September, at Hanapepe, Kauai, strikers captured two strikebreakers in their camp. When the police arrived, the two captives were released. Police were leaving the camp with the two strikebreakers when violence flared. A fight broke out. Dozens of men were wounded. Sixteen strikers and four of the policemen were killed.

This was the emergency Governor Farrington had feared. He ordered out the National Guard—with machine guns—to restore order on Kauai. The impulse to violence and punitive action was a contagion throughout the territory. Delbert Metzger, now a magistrate in Hilo after a mainland law education, heard that the sheriff and a detachment of men planned to ambush a group of Filipino union members marching in from Olaa. Metzger got in his car, drove to the place where the sheriff's forces lay in waiting, and declared he would try every last one of them in court for attempted manslaughter if they so much as pointed a gun at the union marchers. His threats ended the ambush. Those familiar with that situation insist his action averted a massacre.

The 1924 strike intensified management's determination to oppose any and all union efforts. They imprisoned and eventually exiled Pablo Manlapit at the end of the strike. Many of his followers were imprisoned. Camp police and surveillance were increased on those plantations where his union had members. On Lanai, which Jim Dole had purchased in 1921 to create "the world's largest pineapple plantation," Dole refused to hire Filipino laborers or to allow a Filipino to land at the harbor that he had hired Pearl Harbor's "Drydock" Smith to blast out of the rock cliffs at Kaumalapau. Most plantation managers shared Dole's conviction that Filipino labor meant trouble—especially if a laborer had acquired any education. In 1928, a number of newly arrived Filipinos were sent back when it was discovered they were literate. High school graduates like Pedro de la Cruz, later vice-speaker of the House of Representatives, and Hilario Camino Moncado, university graduate and founder of the Filipino Federation of America, a cultural and quasi-religious movement, were no longer the kind of immigrants acceptable to management in the territory. Those who did come with degrees or professions were quick to camouflage their ability by signing an X for their name. Paradoxically, in the 1920s, America was still the escape route for the Filipino whose own land was under the colonial rule of the United States. In the 1920s, so many were eager to emigrate to Hawaii, and so many convinced planters they were too ignorant to want to join a union, that Filipinos comprised 65 percent of the plantation workforce by 1930.

The Roaring Twenties ended in Hawaii with only a dim echo of the repercussions of the 1929 Wall Street crash. Of far greater impact in the territory that year was the sensational case of the murder of the nine-year-old son of a Hawaiian Trust Company executive by a young *nisei* hotel worker, Myles Fukunaga. Castle and Cooke's 1928 construction of the Royal Hawaiian Hotel, and a modest growth in luxury tourist facilities in Waikiki, expanded job opportunities there. Hawaii was not yet ready for a tourist boom. The fare on the *Lurline,* the ten-day round trip to the West Coast, the lack of budget-priced accommodations and tours, limited Hawaiian holidays to the well-to-do or the lucky, whom Hawaiian employees and a few *nisei* like Myles Fukunaga served. Conditions for hotel workers were little better than those for plantation laborers. Supervisory personnel and executives were always *haole.* The schism between that *haole* establishment and his own family was exacerbated for Fukunaga when Hawaiian Trust Company threatened his family with eviction for delinquency in their rent.

In the 1970s, Myles Fukunaga would have probably been adjudged insane. In 1928, tormented, confused, his mind the prey of wild delusions, he kidnapped the boy and killed him in retribution for the callous treatment of Fukunaga's family by the boy's father's company. The case broke just as the anti-Japanese sentiment remaining from the 1920 strike seemed to have disappeared. As Fukunaga asked for and received the death penalty in 1929, the law-abiding local Japanese asked: how could a *nisei* commit such a crime?

13

Social Process

$\mathcal{A}$LLEGED rape, and a murder committed in retribution, thrust Hawaii into headlines across the United States with a case more sensational and more racially divisive than that of poor Myles Fukunaga. In 1931 Thalia Massie, a young navy wife, left a party to walk alone at midnight along Honolulu's Ala Moana Boulevard. Several hours later she was found staggering along that busy thoroughfare near Waikiki, her clothes torn and bloodied, her jaw broken, her body covered with bruises. She claimed she had been attacked and gang raped by a number of dark-skinned local men. Immediately, police arrested four Hawaiians and one *nisei* who had been seen earlier in the evening driving in that area. The lurid press report did not mention the coincidence of a Honolulu police officer that same night, in that same general vicinity, having picked up a naval lieutenant commander who was wandering drunk and dazed along the highway. His uniform was ripped. There were scratches on the navy officer's face that, to the policeman, looked as if they might have been made by a woman's fingernails. The policeman took the officer to naval headquarters at Pearl Harbor, but when he returned next morning to question the lieutenant commander, he was refused the man's name and told that he had already been transferred to the mainland for duty and that the incident must be regarded as closed.

The local men were targeted as suspects, and scapegoats. The

145

nisei was freed after he was able to prove he had been somewhere else at the time of the crime. An ugliness permeated the usually pleasant atmosphere of Honolulu. Police who might have wished to push the investigation of the lieutenant commander kept quiet, for local knowledge was aware that the navy might seize on even the smallest controversy with the territory to plead their case for commission government of Hawaii. Thalia Massie's husband, Lieutenant Thomas Massie; her mother, who was from the South; and many *haoles* in the territory both in and out of the service were hysterical in their claims that white women were no longer safe on the streets of Honolulu. Commission government, as in Samoa, was much mentioned and recommended. Uneasiness between the non-*haole* and the *haole* population of the capital prevailed, with the Fukunaga case and its implications revived, and the old rumor of Filipinos and their eagerness for women circulating in plantation communities.

After a jury trial, the four Hawaiians who had been accused by Mrs. Massie were acquitted for lack of evidence. It was then that Lieutenant Massie and his mother-in-law decided to take justice into their own hands. With help from two navy enlisted men who shared their sentiments, they kidnapped and murdered one of the defendants, Joseph Kahahawai. Their trial was held in an atmosphere of high tension in Honolulu and on the mainland where the case was followed day by day in leading newspapers and on that new medium for public information, the radio. Whites in general exonerated Lieutenant Massie and his mother-in-law for having applied punishment according to their own code of honor, giving his just deserts to a brown-skinned "native" suspected of raping a white woman. The governor of the territory, Lawrence Judd, was no exception. He commuted their sentence of "guilty" to one hour, which he allowed them to serve while waiting in his office on the second floor of Iolani Palace, just across the hall from the room where Hawaii's last queen endured long months of imprisonment for having tried to keep her independent nation free.

The racial tensions resulting from the Fukunaga and in particular from the Massie case were still strong when Franklin Delano Roosevelt visited Honolulu in 1934. He was the first American president to visit Hawaii, and he was welcomed with cheers, leis, and genuine aloha. The Great Depression that he was combating with his New Deal programs was only then eddying through the territory. Ten thousand were unemployed. For the first time in its nearly a century of economic importance, the sugar industry was not looking for labor. Jim Dole was no longer hiring for Lanai. He was, in fact, no longer a part of the Dole Pineapple Company. The Big Five placed punitive action on any business or businessman who challenged their economic monopoly. It was their control of passenger and freight steamer lines to Hawaii that set freight rates favorable to them and unfavorable to big shippers like Dole. When he tried to negotiate shipping his canned pineapple on their rival, Isthmian Lines, they made him a horrendous example of their power by acquiring control of his company and running him out of the territory, a broken man.

It was in this environment of racial tension, depression, and the hope of the man and woman on the streets and plantation roads of Hawaii that Franklin Delano Roosevelt's New Deal would somehow reach them that the second act in Hawaii's labor drama began. In 1935, longshoreman Harry Kamoku began organizing a union in Hilo. He was encouraged, that year, by the National Labor Relations Act becoming law. A new deal and a fair deal were being offered labor, but the question in the minds of Kamoku and other early labor organizers was whether this new, fair deal would reach the territory.

Samuel Wilder King, a part-Hawaiian, was delegate to Congress in 1935. He persuaded a congressional committee to spend twelve days in the islands investigating the possibility of admitting Hawaii to the Union—a possibility that congressional committees had supposedly been studying since 1919. The inaugural year of Pan American Airways clipper service between the West Coast and Honolulu was 1935. The flying boats, slow and cumbersome by modern standards of jet travel, cut passage time to Honolulu from five days aboard ship from San Francisco or Los Angeles to less than sixteen hours flying time. The congressional visitors were impressed by this. Hawaii seemed now to be much closer to the American continent, but their cautious conclusion was to be the frustrating, familiar "out" of congressional committees: the question of territorial readiness for statehood needed further study.

Labor conditions, racial tension, the inequities of opportunity under the Republican dominance of the Big Five—none of these touched the very different Hawaiian world of the tourist who flew the new clippers or enjoyed the leisure of Matson steamers, or of the "armchair" tourist who sat at radios across America in the 1930s listening on Sunday evenings to "Hawaii Calls," Webley Edwards's nostalgic program of steel guitars, ukulele music, sweet Hawaiian melodies and aloha sentiment. *Paradise of the Pacific* sent its monthly subscribers on the mainland and around the world slick paper impressions of the idyllic Hawaii whose social life Charmian London had described. No hint of the coexisting realities of the territory's lack of a minimum wage law, inadequate child-labor law, or lack of legislation protecting women in industry marred its pages.

In 1937 a congressional committee who came for seventeen days of statehood hearings showed no curiosity as to why federal labor standards were not being applied in the territory. The seven senators and twelve congressmen were entertained with hulas, luaus, sight-seeing trips, and hours of testimony. Their honest conclusion was that Hawaii had fulfilled every requirement for statehood, but because Japan was invading China and Adolph Hitler was threatening the peace of Europe, still further study might be wise. The gap between federal labor standards and territorial labor practices, though not of interest to this committee, did engage the attention of the National Labor Relations Board that same year. Before 1937 ended, an NLRB examiner visited the islands to investigate a series of complaints, among which was one that Castle and Cooke had violated federal law by firing longshoremen who sought collective bargaining. The examiner's conclusion that Castle and Cooke had violated federal regulations was a breakthrough for the cause of organized labor in the territory.

In his report, the NLRB examiner further noted with disapproval that in Hawaii workers were not permitted to criticize employers, and alleged surveillance was maintained by employers through the cooperation of the local police, U.S. Army intelligence agents, and the industrial association—which in 1937 was managed by former governor Lawrence Judd, an attorney for Castle and Cooke. This assurance of federal concern over territorial labor conditions was good news to Harry Kamoku and his dockworkers. A major West Coast dock strike in 1936–1937 had affected shipping to Hawaii. In a delayed replay of the maritime union activity of the West Coast where Harry Bridges was organizing the ILWU, 1937 saw the opening of hiring halls by seamen's unions in Honolulu. Union activity among Hawaii dockworkers was a critical expansion of the labor unrest begun by the Japanese Federation and the Filipino unions on the plantations.

About this time Jack Hall, a nineteen-year-old *haole* seaman, arrived in Honolulu. Unionism was his consuming passion. Like Jack Burns, who by the late 1930s had become a Honolulu policeman, Jack Hall was a different kind of *haole,* ready to identify with the rights of labor in the territory and to fight for those rights. Hall's ambition was to gain for the *makaainana* of territorial plantation and dock labor the fair deal guaranteed by the National Labor Relations Act and the human rights and opportunities that King Kamehameha III and his *haole* adviser, William Richards, had granted the Hawaiian *makaainana* a century earlier.

By 1937, the old days of the polite Japanese labor unions were long past. The polite mask of plantation management as a kindly paternal figure was about to be ripped loose by the union activity of this short second act in Hawaii's labor drama. In May of 1938 Jack Hall, Edward Berman, and Jack Kawano were in Hilo organizing a dock strike against the Inter-Island Steamship and Navigation Company. Those longshoremen, fully aware of the retaliatory intentions of management, turned out in a large group—wives standing valiantly at their side—to form a picket line on the Hilo docks in protest against the use of scab labor on the interisland steamship *Waialeale*. Immediately, management called in the police, who confronted the picket line with submachine guns, tear gas, and bayonets. The strikers, armed only with clubs, refused to yield or withdraw. The "Battle of the Hilo Docks" ensued, with police wounding twenty-five picketers seriously enough to be hospitalized and inflicting minor injuries on as many more with birdshot and buckshot fired at close range. "The Hilo Massacre" was how Jack Hall described the bloody affray.

From Hilo, Hall moved to Kauai to develop a new strategy for union support. In the elections of 1938 the first union try at political clout for their cause was successful with the election of William "Billy" Fernandez to the territorial legislature. Jack Hall did not stop at condemning the antilabor practices of the Big Five or electing candidates like Fernandez to question those practices in a legislature that was still under the thumb of the Big Five–dominated Republicans. With equal vigor, Hall condemned the Big Five stranglehold on Hawaii's wholesale and retail businesses. Their control of competition among retail stores meant higher prices and less choice of merchandise for the working people who were the majority of the territory's population. Sears, Kress, Woolworth, and J.C. Penney were all denied access to the Hawaiian retail market until labor's voice was strong enough, the political pendulum showed signs of a swing, and the Big Five was forced to relax its barricades against mainland business firms setting up branches in Hawaii. Well-to-do *haoles* and Hawaiians could, and often did, shop in San Francisco, New York, and Paris. Wealthy Chinese sent to Shanghai, Peking, and Hong Kong for merchandise. Japanese who had grown affluent in business or the professions went on buying sprees to Los Angeles and New York or to Tokyo and Osaka. Most of the 68,600 citizens registered to vote in Hawaii's 1940 statehood plebiscite could shop only at company-owned stores of plantation communities or in small family-style general stores in Honolulu, Hilo, Wailuku, and Lihue. The 354,400 residents of the territory who were not eligible to vote had the same limited shopping choice.

Choice was also limited in opportunities for higher education in the territory. The University of Hawaii, on a campus in Manoa Valley, was an excellent institution, especially in education and tropical agriculture. An entrance requirement of ability to speak unaccented English drove many local students to mainland universities. Chinese, who faced discrimination in most mainland college communities, enrolled in one of the excellent universities in Peking or Shanghai. A considerable number of Japanese families sent their children away to be educated when they were very young. *Kibei* were second-generation island Japanese sent to school in Japan. Unlike their Chinese counterparts they returned to feel uncomfortable in island society, for their parents and contemporaries had become much altered in attitude and custom by living in Hawaii, and the Japanese language and culture acquired by *kibei* was quite different from the Meiji-era vocabulary and custom of their *issei* parents or the American-style outlook of their *nisei* peers.

Sung Dai Seu, first administrator of federal social security in the territory was a Chinese-Hawaiian graduate of the University of Peking. It was the program he administered rather than his racial or educational background that made him unwelcome in the offices of plantation management across the territory. On a number of plantations, managers ordered him off their domain, refusing to offer to their employees the benefits of "this federal scheme," which they regarded as dangerous socialism. One of Seu's amused memories is that several years later one of the very managers who threw him off a plantation surreptitiously called to inquire how he himself might qualify for social security benefits.

At the University of Hawaii's sociology department, Professors Andrew Lind and Bernhard Hormann encouraged their students to record the social process of this decade in ethnic studies projects, oral history interviews with first-generation parents and friends, and articles for the monthly publication of the Romanzo Adams Social Research Laboratory, a journal appropriately named *Social Process in Hawaii*. In one plantation housing camp, a young *nisei* told one of the interviewers from this pioneer program that there was no place in the plantation hierarchy for a person like himself but that through education and hard work he was determined to find the way to a better life. That determination was shared by many of the 139,000 Japanese in the 1940 territorial census total of 423,000. Seventy-five percent of those 139,000 Japanese were American citizens, born in Hawaii, qualified to vote as soon as they reached age twenty-one. Enough of them were already of age to constitute 25 percent of the voters registering in the 1940 statehood plebiscite election. Together with Hawaiians, part-Hawaiians, Hawaii-born Chinese, other Orientals, a few Filipinos, Portuguese, Puerto Ricans, and *haoles,* they voted two to one in favor of Hawaii's being accepted into the Union as a state.

By 1940 labor in Hawaii had won federal NLRB support for its right to organize units, the same right given to mainland states, the same protection under federal labor laws—much of this, however, still only on paper. Several collective-bargaining agreements had been negotiated in the territory. Art Rutledge, a Polish bartender who had anglicized his name on immigration, organized fellow bartenders and brewery workers into what eventually would become the ILWU's political rival, the Teamsters Union of the AFL-CIO.

James Shoemaker came to Hawaii in 1940 as an on-site investigator for the United States Bureau of Labor. He won the respect that he still retains as an economist for the Bank of Hawaii when he courageously weighed these gains against the working conditions, housing conditions, and medical care provided on territorial plantations. To him, the labor climate in Hawaii was still almost feudal, and he said so in print.

In his fine novel *All I Asking For Is My Body,* writer Milton Murayama, who grew up in those prewar plantation days of territorial Hawaii, tells a story that is universal in its application to most second-generation men and women who experienced the pressure of the 1920s and 1930s. Their only hope for escape from the economic hardships and dead-end employment of plantation life, and from the demands of their first-generation parents, was through American-style education. Inner strength, tremendous courage, and spiritual commitment were theirs in abundance. But few in 1940 had the means to go on to any university. The events of December 7, 1941, which ended the second act in Hawaii's labor drama, were to bring the eventual solution to the dreams of the *nisei* generation, to those of their peers like Maui's Elmer Cravalho, Oahu's Hawaiian-Chinese

William Richardson, Hawaii island's Filipino Benjamin Menor, and to make possible the new society sought by *malihini* Jack Hall and *kamaaina* John A. Burns.

Shoemaker's indictment would be the last such comment from a federal investigator. Times were about to be changed. Eighteen months before the Pearl Harbor attack, the territory's civilian population was preparing for just such an emergency. Paradox, indeed, that after all the readiness for what might happen, December 7, 1941, was such a fearful surprise. It was no paradox that what lay ahead—the crucial test of *nisei* loyalty and territorial strength, of the rights of American citizens placed under the duress of martial law, of internment of Americans whose ancestral homeland had become the enemy—would result in Hawaii's special gift to all fellow Americans, the restoration of democracy and civilian rights even in time of war, a gift made explicit through the December 7, 1945, decision of the United States Supreme Court.

Social process in Hawaii was about to be expedited by four years of national and territorial crisis. Across the territory's many-faceted realities of plantations and towns where despite labor troubles and hardships, the 1930s would be remembered as "the good old days"; across the Hawaii of a public school population segregated into English-standard and pidgin-speaking schools; across the tourist paradise of Waikiki, ukulele music, swaying palm trees, and the big pink Royal Hawaiian Hotel; into the lives of Hawaiians, Chinese, *nisei, kamaaina haole* (old-timers), Portuguese, Koreans, Puerto Ricans, and Filipinos, all of whom felt as American as any citizen of any mainland state; there cut the terrible swift sword of World War II.

14

The Bitter Test of War

EDWIN O. Reischauer places the beginning of World War II as July 7, 1937, in China, when fighting began between Chinese and Japanese troops near Peking. Numerous island students were there at the time, among them Sung Dai Seu, who became the territory's federal social security administrator when he returned to Hawaii that year. As the Japanese fought on into China and occupied the northern part of that republic and Manchuria, demonstrations against Imperial Japan's aggression erupted among University of Hawaii students, many of them *nisei* like Koji Ariyoshi of Kona.

The possibility of that war's enlarging in scope to include these islands became real when, after Hitler's troops marched through Europe in 1939, Japan pursued its Greater East Asia Co-Prosperity Sphere with further conquests. In co-operation with United States Army forces stationed on Oahu, the city of Honolulu organized a complete practice blackout. The following year, 1940, the City and County of Honolulu's Board of Supervisors discussed and adopted a Comprehensive Emergency Disaster Plan, and by April 1941, a city ordinance created a Major Disaster Council to co-ordinate and administer essential civilian activities in the event of war. M-Day plans were made by the Honolulu Medical Society. Provisional police were sworn in on plantations and in rural communities. The Honolulu Police Department and the army and navy commands in the territory co-operated and were in full communication with civilians involved in all readiness programs. The Preparedness Committee and the Hawaii chapter of the American Red Cross issued a joint warning that spring. In the event of a war emergency, the civilian population must be prepared to take care of itself.

On October 3, 1941, Governor Joseph Poindexter called a special session of the territorial legislature, asking members of both houses to pass a Hawaii Defense Act giving him powers to deal with any emergency that might arise. Thus, by mid-October 1941, the several city, county, and territorial governments were ready for war.

News from Japan that General Hideki Tojo, head of that country's military forces, had become prime minister was interpreted as meaning that war could begin at any time and that the American naval base at Pearl Harbor might be a prime target. University of Hawaii president David L. Crawford and fellow members of the Hawaii chapter of the Institute of Pacific Relations felt that negotiation and appeasement could still preserve peace. Crawford proposed, through the institute, to ask that the United States recognize Manchukuo, co-operate with Japan in the economic development of China, cease building fortifications on Guam and in the Philippines, and remove the United States Pacific Fleet from Hawaiian waters. In return for those concessions, Japan was expected to withdraw troops from China proper and pledge not to invade the Philippines. In addition, both Japan and the United States were urged to negotiate a mutually satisfactory commercial treaty and to agree jointly not to invade the Netherlands East Indies or any Asian territory of the British Commonwealth.

On the weekend of November 30, 1941, no progress had been made with that proposal, but Frank Midkiff, another member of the Institute of Pacific Relations was drafting a new proposal. Headlines in Honolulu's papers that Sunday morning screamed:

JAPANESE MAY STRIKE OVER WEEKEND:
KURUSU BLUNTLY WARNED NATION READY FOR BATTLE

Fred Spurlock, a black civilian-defense worker at Pearl Harbor, read these headlines with moderate interest and turned over to sleep off a bad hangover. The night before, he had been kicked out of a bar when he became drunk and had a small fracas with two Military Policemen. They had turned him over to the civilian police who booked him for being drunk and disorderly and assaulting a police officer. He had been released on bond and was to appear before a judge in mid-December. That Sunday morning of November 30, 1941, he viewed his charges as no big thing. The judge would impose the usual $25 fine, lecture him on the evils of drinking and fighting, and let him go. So, all that Sunday, Fred Spurlock peacefully slept his hangover away.

The following week, the first week of December, Yoshiaki Fujitani, eldest son of a Buddhist minister, went through his usual round of classes and ROTC drills on the University of Hawaii campus. Every evening he came home to his father's Hongwanji Temple in the neighboring district of Moiliili. When he left campus on Friday afternoon, December 5, members of the Institute of Pacific Relations were meeting downtown in Frank Midkiff's office to discuss Midkiff's new peace proposal, which General Walter C. Short had promised to forward to the president of the United States. Midkiff himself had to leave for a board of directors' meeting at Honolulu Iron Works, so he asked Riley H. Allen, editor of the *Honolulu Star-Bulletin,* to serve as chairman in his place. Everyone agreed that Midkiff's ideas might work: to induce Japan to withdraw from Indo-China in return for an American guarantee of oil supplies sufficient to meet current Japanese needs, to trade Japan's withdrawal to the north bank of China's Yangtze River for the United States promise to supply Japan with enough steel and cotton to keep Japanese industrial plants at current operating levels, and to offer a special loan of $500 million as compensation for relinquished territories and resources. In addition, in return for recognition of Manchukuo by America and the Allied Powers, Midkiff thought Japan might be persuaded to break with the Axis powers of Germany and Italy.

Washington, D.C.'s, time zone is six hours ahead of Hawaii. By the time the meeting in Honolulu ended, it was nearly midnight in the nation's capital. Riley Allen suggested that since all federal offices would be closed over the weekend, their proposal should be sent to Washington through General Short on Monday, December 8. Feeling that they had accomplished something worthwhile, the committee members went home. The next day, December 6, 1941, was an ordinary leisurely Saturday. Islanders shopped, played golf or baseball, spent the day at the beach.

Sunday, December 7, dawned with a cover of low clouds over Oahu. This was not unusual. By midmorning they would dissipate and Honolulu could expect one of its usual balmy winter days. By 7:30 A.M. the first players were already on Honolulu's golf courses when in Moiliili Yoshiaki Fujitani yawned out of bed to hear the radio announce that Pearl Harbor was being attacked. The broadcast did not identify the attacking planes as Japanese, but said that it had been reported that the rising sun insignia had been seen on the wings. Listening to the broadcast, Fujitani was left with the impression that this was just another, more realistic practice maneuver by the United States. The custom of all islanders is to rush to see whatever might be happening in the way of excitement: tidal wave, volcanic eruption, practice attack. This morning was no exception. Yoshiaki Fujitani gathered up his six sisters and kid brother and drove them down to Ala Moana Park, which stretches between Waikiki and Kakaako along Honolulu's water front. There was a modest traffic of others as curious as themselves. The view of the attack was spectacular.

Pillars of smoke were rising from Pearl Harbor. Planes were diving from the sky. Flak was bursting in the air. It was all so real that it seemed unreal. As they drove home, the Fujitanis saw buildings that had been struck by antiaircraft shells burning at the corner of King and McCully streets. Nearby, Lunalilo School had been hit. A shell landed fifty feet short of Queen Liliuokalani's former mansion, Washington Place, now the official residence of territorial governor Poindexter. A short distance away, in front of Shuman Carriage Company's automobile agency showroom, shrapnel had disemboweled a pedestrian.

Abruptly, awareness of the awful reality of the attack gripped Honoluluans. When the Fujitanis reached home, the radio stations had all gone off the air. The news was flashing across the

Pacific, across the American continent, to Washington and the president. The nation from which more than one-third of Hawaii's people had sprung was attacking Pearl Harbor and the island of Oahu in the first assault of a foreign power on American territory since the British attack on Baltimore in 1814.

The Japanese were using precisely the same strategy that had been so successful in their surprise attack upon Russia in 1904, but this time they had the added advantage of air power. The morning's cloud cover had obscured their approach, but the immediate question in every civilian mind on Oahu that morning was why, after a year of civilian preparation for just such an emergency, were American army and navy installations on the island so unprepared? The rows of American naval vessels lined up that Sunday morning in the lochs of Pearl Harbor were easy targets. Air force planes had been parked in similar invitation to destruction on the ground.

Yoshiaki Fujitani's first reaction that the attack was a practice maneuver was shared by early golfers near Fort Shafter, who complained about the distraction of the low-flying planes until they looked up and saw the red ball of Japan's rising sun on the wings of the strafing fighters. Plantation *haoles* in one foursome were not about to believe, even then, that the attack was real until, dodging fiery spurts of live ammunition, an American sergeant ordered them off the course.

Near the Fujitani home in Moiliili, flying shrapnel decapitated two pedestrians. The kitchen corner of the Kondo home suffered a direct hit, and Fujitani's friend, Edwin Kondo, was killed as he sat eating breakfast. His sister, at the table with him, had her arm ripped off. That morning on Oahu 2,403 American lives were lost—2,008 navy fatalities, 218 from the army, 109 marines, and 68 civilians.

At 11:00 A.M., with battleships still burning in Pearl Harbor and business blocks in flaming ruin along King and McCully streets in Honolulu, Governor Poindexter assumed the emergency powers given him in October by the Hawaii Emergency Defense Act. During the next four and a half hours, General Walter C. Short was able to persuade Poindexter that the emergency called for more than civilian control. Thus at

3:30 P.M., in an unprecedented declaration that initiated army rule and suspended all civil rights (including the writ of habeas corpus), the governor placed the territory under martial law. For his authority, he cited Section 67 of the Organic Act that had established the Territory of Hawaii in 1900. Section 67 provided that a governor could declare martial law "until communication can be had with the President and his decision thereon made known." Later, Poindexter justified his action by claiming that General Short had assured him military rule would be brief. If the morning's attack was not the prelude to enemy landing, Short told Poindexter, martial law could be lifted within a few days or weeks.

At 4:25 P.M. radio stations throughout the territory returned to the air to give General Short's announcement:

> I have this day assumed the position of military governor of Hawaii and have taken charge of the government of the territory . . . Good citizens will cheerfully obey this proclamation and the ordinances to be published; others will be required to do so. Offenders will be severely punished by military tribunals or will be held in custody until such time as the civil courts are able to function.[1]

That afternoon, newspaper extras hit the streets with headlines that did little to reassure the populace. Above the *Advertiser*'s front-page details of the morning's attack were the completely unfounded headlines:

SABOTEURS HAVE LANDED!

Suspicion of residents of Japanese ancestry was already high. Were they to be trusted when planes bearing the emblem of Imperial Japan had attacked Honolulu this morning? The non-Japanese community fed each other's apprehensions. Remember the Fukunaga case? Remember the 1920 strike? Remember the Supreme Court decision negating the *haole* community's efforts to close Japanese Language Schools?

In a fear-ridden, hurriedly blacked-out Honolulu that Sunday evening, soldiers began knocking on the doors of civilians

---

1. J. Garner Anthony, *Hawaii Under Army Rule* (Honolulu: The University Press of Hawaii, 1975), pp. 5–6.

whom military intelligence had long before identified as having
served in some capacity with the Japanese government. Those
suspected of strong loyalties to Japan were the first to be arrested. Buddhism itself became immediately suspect this Sunday. Buddhist priests had acted as registrars for the Japanese
consulate, performing as a public service the paper work con-
nected with the dual citizenship held by most *nisei,* particularly
the draft-deferment requests local *nisei* had to file when they
received orders to report for active duty in the army of Imperial
Japan. For similar quasi-official activities, all Japanese Language School teachers and principals, all judo, aikido, and
kendo instructors, Shinto priests, and editors of Japanese-
language papers were picked up, questioned, and, over the next
few days in most cases, interned.

As the first round of arrests began on the afternoon of December 7, Yoshiaki Fujitani and 150 *nisei* classmates responded
to the radio call for all University of Hawaii ROTC students to
report to the National Guard Armory. In that building (later torn
down to make way for the present state capitol), they were
sworn in as members of the newly constituted Hawaii Territorial
Guard. More than 1,300 *nisei* were already in uniform as
members of Hawaii National Guard units. Supply sergeants had
no time that night to issue uniforms to the ROTC students. Each
was given a helmet, a rifle, and five rounds of ammunition and
sent out to his assigned position in the casual shorts, sweat-
shirts, slippers, or bare feet that were islanders' customary
week-end leisure attire.

From midnight until 7:00 A.M. December 8, Yoshiaki Fujitani's guard station was the area between Iolani Palace, which
then housed the offices of the territorial governor and the legislature, and the adjacent King Street main branch of the public
library. It was a long, uneasy night. Throughout the territory all
visible navigational aids along the coasts of every island were
deactivated—lighthouses, channel markers, harbor buoys—all
turned off along with all the lights in every house, hospital, and
civilian and military building. In Honolulu, nervous soldiers
roamed the streets, shooting out illuminated signs and heaving
rocks through any window where a crack of light showed.

In Kamuela, the Big Island's cool upland village (better known by its ancient Hawaiian name, Waimea, changed at the request of the United States Postal Service), *haoles* and Hawaiians from Parker Ranch and small ranches in that South Kohala district had been deputized. The area had a large population of Japanese farmers, independent men and women who long ago had turned their backs on plantation life. Many of the Japanese in the Waimea-Kamuela community also worked as cowboys or supervisors for Parker Ranch. On the evening of December 7, the new deputies knocked at the door of Japanese Language School principal Kiyoto Izumi, a small, cheerful man who had been the adviser, translator, and community leader for Japanese residents of the area for many years. Izumi was told by men who he had assumed were his friends that he was being arrested as an enemy alien and a potential threat to the safety of Hawaii. He was in his pajamas. He begged that they not arouse his sleeping children. Mrs. Izumi ran to get her husband a heavy sweater. Then the deputies rushed him out of his house and into the open back of a truck.

Next the deputies knocked on the door of Izumi's neighbor, Herbert Ishizu, a Parker Ranch employee who was informed he was suspect because he had a short-wave radio that the ranch had asked him to use in communicating with outlying cattle and sheep stations under his supervision. Ishizu was summarily hauled out of bed by deputies who entered the room where he and his wife lay sleeping. He, too, was ordered into the truck. No time for farewells. No chance to change clothes. The two men, with others picked up in the same way in that vicinity, rode more than a hundred miles that night—up over the saddle between Mauna Loa and Mauna Kea, through the cold air of that road's six-thousand-foot summit, then down into the humid heat of Hilo and up again into the chill mists of the volcano district and the army's rest camp at Kilauea, four thousand feet above sea level.

In Honolulu, in addition to those residents of Japanese ancestry and citizenship who were arrested, German aliens, Austrians, and Italians were picked up and taken to Sand Island on the Pearl Harbor end of Honolulu harbor. Only a relatively few were arrested that first frantic night. Invasion was the uppermost fear in the minds of the military and civilian population and manpower was primarily directed to setting up hasty barricades along beaches where it was feared the Japanese forces might attempt to land. Rumors sped through the city—none of them ever substantiated. One story insisted that Japanese pilots shot down in the morning's attack had worn class rings from Honolulu's McKinley High School. Another story had it that arrows pointing to Pearl Harbor had been cut by saboteurs in the canefields at nearby Ewa.

Prejudice flared. Suspicions escalated. The Big Five, plantation management, Honolulu's conservative civilian and military *haoles,* immediately renewed their talk of changing Hawaii's political status to a commission form of government. There was genuine relief in many of those *haole* households that the military had taken command of the territory.

On the docks of San Francisco, University of Hawaii graduate Koji Ariyoshi from Kona carried in his wallet the piece of paper certifying he was born in Hawaii. It was the only "passport" an Asian-American from the territory was given in those days. Even so, Ariyoshi was prohibited from handling restricted cargo on the San Francisco docks, although German and Italian aliens were trusted to do so. At the docks in Honolulu, island longshoremen worked under military guard, loading only essential freight into ships designated to take home the tourists evacuated from Waikiki and the few military and island families fleeing in panic to the mainland.

All of Waikiki's hotels had been immediately taken over by the military. On the morning of December 8, as General Short's aide, Lieutenant Colonel Thomas H. Green moved into Iolani Palace and took over the office of the territory's attorney general for military government headquarters. That same morning, Sergeant Mike Foster of the Thirty-fourth Engineers moved into the Royal Hawaiian Hotel to supervise its transfer from civilian to military control. In solitary luxury that evening Sergeant Foster, a drafted art student from Ohio, dined alone in the splendid Monarch Room and had the entire hotel to himself until on the morning of December 9 the luxurious pink hotel began to fill with military brass, and Foster returned to his outfit. The Thirty-fourth Engineers assignment that day was to participate in a chaotic "scorched earth" program, carrying out destruction of all food supplies in the islands to prevent their falling into invading enemy hands. The top level decision on this was made in haste and fear. Foster and a company of men spent all of December 9 at Castle and Cooke's Dole Pineapple cannery in Iwilei, wiring canned pineapple into bundles that they tried—without success—to blow up with sticks of dynamite.

Not until December 9 was the presidential radiogram approving military rule received. Neither Governor Poindexter's proclamation nor the text of General Short's announcement of military rule was as yet in the president's hands. He had made his decision in an atmosphere that could not wait for the usual bureaucratic procedures of paperwork and legal red tape. Fortunately for the territory, the "scorched earth" program was rescinded in the same haste with which it had been ordered. However, in the area of food supplies, the impact of army rule on the everyday life of the territory's civilians was immediate and drastic. All grocery stores were closed and ordered to make an inventory for military authorities. Until December 10, only milk and *poi* were available for purchase, and those sold only to families with babies.

No sector of civilian life was exempt from the onslaught of military takeover. Bars; liquor stores; the arcades, dance halls, and brothels of Hotel Street; the red-light district of Iwilei and Kalihi; were closed. No such moral stricture as that from the bygone missionary days of Hiram Bingham was contemplated. The army simply needed time to devise regulations by which it intended to control entertainment and vice. Gasoline rationing was imposed at once. No one except doctors and drivers of military vehicles was permitted to have more than half a tankful at any time.

After December 8, the daily papers printed the successive orders of the commanding general, with the admonition that citizens read them and obey. Because so many *kibei* (island-born children educated in Japan) and so many older *issei* could read only Japanese, special permission was given to some Japanese-

language newspapers to continue publication in order to print
military orders. All other Japanese-language publications were
seized and closed, their editors sent to Sand Island to wait transport to mainland internment camps.

The efficient Colonel Green set up the machinery of military
government, immediately transferring all civilian court calen-
dars, offices, and clerk's facilities to army provost personnel. It
was only a few days before defense worker Fred Spurlock received notice that the hearing on the drunk-and-disorderly
charge against him was postponed until a date in January. It was
to be a totally different kind of courtroom in which he would
appear. No civil court now existed. For the next three years,
criminal law would be dispensed and civilian rights weighed by
army officers who often were without any legal training and,
trained or untrained, totally without regard for Hawaii's statutes
or the nation's laws. These provosts were empowered to fine,
imprison, even to impose the death penalty if they so chose. Of-
fenders appealing through the circuit courts ran into the arbitrary
judicial ruling that military justice was necessary to public security in an overwhelmingly Oriental population such as that of
the Territory of Hawaii.

In the islands' legal fraternity, a number of clear-sighted, liberal men and women were appalled at the suspension of the writ
of habeas corpus and at the harsh, archaic punishments meted
out by military officers for the most trivial offenses. Among
those appalled by the application of such undemocratic measures in an American territory were former Hilo magistrate Delbert Metzger, who in 1941 was a federal judge in Honolulu; attorney J. Garner Anthony; and federal circuit court judge Frank
McLaughlin. A change of personnel at the head of military government did nothing whatever to alter the situation.

During the first ten days after the Pearl Harbor attack, the
American press, the public, and the president had decided to
hold General Walter Short personally responsible for Hawaii's
disastrous lack of readiness. On December 17, 1941, Short was
relieved of his command as was Pearl Harbor's Admiral Husband E. Kimmel. Lieutenant General Delos C. Emmons was
named commanding general and military governor of the terri-

tory. Admiral Chester W. Nimitz was the new commander based at Pearl Harbor. The change of commands neither disturbed nor disrupted the extraordinary administrative efficiency of Colonel Green, who continued as General Emmons's aide.

During these first weeks of the war, anti-Japanese sentiment swept the American mainland. On the San Francisco docks, Koji Ariyoshi was searched and questioned by military guards each day as he reported for work. Lieutenant General John DeWitt, military commander of the western region, voicing his sentiment, "Once a Jap always a Jap," enthusiastically began carrying out President Roosevelt's order to intern the 110,000 Americans of Japanese ancestry residing on the West Coast. Among those interned were Mexicans with a Japanese surname inherited from a single Japanese grandparent. In San Francisco, apprehensive Chinese began to wear badges proclaiming "I am Chinese" as a defense against personal attacks from whites who emotionally endorsed General DeWitt's sentiments.

These were difficult weeks for Hawaii's residents of Japanese ancestry, who never knew when the soldiers might knock on their door, or whether the presidential order might expand to send all of them to mainland internment camps. The rumors that persisted contributed to their uneasiness, but no instance of spying or sabotage was ever confirmed. The single case of defection by a local Japanese was that of a storekeeper on Niihau, one of two Japanese in the population of three hundred Hawaiians on the Robinsons' private island. On December 7, one of the Japanese planes leaving the attack on Oahu had been forced to land on Niihau where the pilot persuaded storekeeper Harada to help him. In an effort to deter Niihau men from sending a boat to Kauai with news of the landing, the pilot and Harada took Mr. and Mrs. Benjamin Kanahele as hostages. In the tense hours that followed, Harada became despondent, realized what he had done, and committed suicide. That so upset the pilot that he opened fire on Kanahele, wounding the big Hawaiian in the shoulder, the ribs, and the groin. Roaring in anger, Kanahele picked up the pilot and smashed him against a rock wall. Mrs. Kanahele finished off the pilot by crushing his skull with a rock. By the time a police boat arrived from Kauai, the war on Niihau was ended. The pilot lay dead. Kanahele had his wounds dressed and was soon recovered.

Any question of how long martial law might last in the territory was not worth asking after December 30, when the Japanese attacked Hawaii a second time. On that brilliantly moonlit night, plantation workers assigned as coast watchers in the Big Island's Kohala district saw a Japanese submarine cruising offshore. They made no mention to anyone of what they had seen. The submarine slipped on along the cliffs of the Hamakua Coast, and at midnight, residents of Hilo awoke to the sound of their harbor installations being shelled. The submarine's target was oil storage tanks near the water front. Luckily, most of its shells landed in the pandanus forest beyond the harbor road.

Japanese submarines that night also attacked the neighbor island ports of Kahului, Maui, and Nawiliwili, Kauai. When the Kohala coastwatchers were questioned next morning, they acknowledged having seen the Hilo-bound submarine and having recognized it as Japanese. Years later, one of the former coastwatchers recounted that incident. "Why say anything? Those days, if the Japanese rule us or the *haoles,* all the same hard times for us." That spokesman was Hawaiian.

On December 31, after this second attack, fear of a Japanese invasion redoubled. There was talk of interning all Hawaii's Japanese, but the economic consequences to plantations where Japanese were key members of the workforce and the impact on the territory's heavily Japanese defense and construction industries would have been disastrous. The idea was abandoned, but the suspicion directed toward local Americans of Japanese ancestry—AJAs as *Star-Bulletin* editor Riley Allen began to call them—became increasingly ugly. Police brought no warrants to search Japanese homes. Buddhist temples were ransacked. *Issei* hurriedly burned precious Japanese antiques, scrolls, books, and art objects before the soldiers came. As military governor, General Emmons ordered that workers of Japanese ancestry employed on federal or defense projects must wear a black badge at all times.

The new year of 1942 looked bleak to *nisei* like Yoshiaki Fujitani. The Territorial Guard, to which he and his *nisei* classmates belonged, was "inactivated" in January. After an indecently brief interval it was "reactivated" with non-Japanese only as members. No branch of the armed forces would accept enlistment by a *nisei*. The ROTC program on the university campus shut down.

How, asked the *nisei,* were they to prove their loyalty as Americans? The 150 students banded together under the leadership and encouragement of older men in the community: Ralph Yempuku, Hung Wai Ching, and Dr. Katsumi Kometani. Organizing themselves as the "Varsity Victory Volunteers," the students drafted a letter to the military governor and commanding general Emmons: "Hawaii is our home, the United States is our country. We know but one loyalty and that is to the stars and stripes. We wish to do our part as loyal Americans in every way possible and we hereby offer ourselves for whatever service you may see fit to use us." [2]

The army's answer to them was assignment to the Corps of Engineers where as a civilian volunteer group they went to work digging ditches, building barracks, making roads, and erecting fences. It was not the glorious chance that Fujitani and his fellow volunteers had envisioned, but it would have to do until they were allowed to enlist to fight for their country in the army, navy, air force, or marines. Those *nisei* soldiers already on active duty since December 7 in the 298th and 299th Regiments of the Hawaii National Guard were, at the same time the campus ROTC was disbanded, ordered to return to Schofield Barracks from their guard posts on Oahu's shores. Their rifles and ammunition were taken from them. How to prove their courage, how to fight for their country with only a helmet, a gas mask, and a field pack? The distrust of the army's high command was a heavy burden for these *nisei* soldiers who by birth and commitment felt themselves American.

General Emmons was totally unsympathetic to their plight. He informed Washington he was not taking any chances with *nisei* in uniform and requested General George C. Marshall, the

---

2. Edward Joesting, *Hawaii: An Uncommon History* (New York: W. W. Norton & Company, Inc., 1972), pp. 319–320.

nation's chief of staff, to remove them from Hawaii. Without being told their destination, the men were loaded on transports and taken to the West Coast. Many among them were convinced they were being taken to one of the ten barbed-wire enclosed compounds that the American press euphemistically referred to as relocation centers. Koji Ariyoshi, along with many other islanders caught on the mainland by the war, was now an internee at one of these camps. However, to their immense relief, the former Hawaii National Guard units arrived at Camp McCoy, Wisconsin, combat training center for the Second Division, of which they now became the 100th Battalion.

Those who excelled in the Japanese language and were potential interpreters were sent to army intelligence training at Camp Savage, Minnesota. At both places they had to settle the problem of being called "Japs" in the traditional American way—by bashing a few hard heads. Neither during training nor in their long, valiant combat in Europe could the dog tags of Buddhist *nisei* carry the letter *B* as a sign of their religion. In a nation that prided itself on the religious freedom accorded its citizens, the armed forces recognized as valid religious identifications only Catholic, Protestant, and Jewish. It was much later before the Buddhist soldiers of the 100th Battalion who gave their lives in the fierce fighting in Europe could have their graves marked with the *dhammacakra,* the Buddhist symbol of the wheel of life.

In 1942 as the men of the 100th Battalion made records for achievements in training, the population back home in Hawaii nearly doubled with an influx of soldiers, sailors, marines, air force personnel, Seabees, and defense workers. From its peacetime level of approximately 200,000 residents, the population of Oahu swelled to half a million. A similar impact was experienced on the Big Island, where 40,000 marines set up camp on the lush green slopes of the Kohala Mountains and quiet Hilo was filled with men in uniform.

Enterprising islanders made the best of this sudden opportunity. Independent bus operators, vegetable farmers, suppliers of fresh produce to the troops, bar and theater owners, all had an unprecedented chance to make money and to see a population of *haoles* who were for the most part working people like themselves or young men with eager dreams of an education, just as many of their own sons. Fraternization was the service term for the aloha extended by Hawaii's people—even on Niihau where a Coast Guard detachment forgot the stern warnings to keep to themselves and quietly mingled with the Hawaiians there. For many, despite the humbug of military governance and the arrogance of military government personnel, these war years in the territory were a time of prosperity, of making new *haole* friends, of learning new ideas—especially about how to unionize an industry from GIs who were labor activists in their own home states.

For many who listened with intent interest to union men in bars, at the beach, in casual encounters on the street, the war had brought personal financial hardship. These were the laborers "frozen" in low-paying jobs by army General Order No. 91. Their wages rapidly diminished in purchasing power as prices soared in territorial stores. At the beginning, in December 1941, labor had made a nonstrike pledge, which it honored for the duration of the war, but the substandard wages and working conditions on Hawaii's docks and plantations presaged postwar troubles far beyond those of the 1920 and 1924 strikes.

The hundreds of thousands of service personnel and support and defense workers flooding into the islands included large numbers of mainland prostitutes, imported by the army. They came to staff army-approved brothels opened in rented houses in traditionally quiet residential districts of Honolulu. Neighbors were appalled but powerless to complain about being confined to their homes by the rigid eight o'clock civilian curfew while the "houses" were busy with traffic in and out all hours of the night. The military government felt its new policy was more fair and provided more pleasant conditions to prostitutes than the longtime practice of the Honolulu Police Department limiting establishments of vice to Iwilei, Hotel Street, and a small section of Kalihi.

Vice control was only one aspect of the vast scope of the army's rule over Hawaiian communities and jobs. Everything—taxi cabs, rents, garbage disposal, house numbers, all police work, traffic regulations, public health, insane asylums, hospitals, waterworks, and all transport including space and scheduling on interisland airplanes—was governed by the military. Price control, liquor control, food production, gasoline rations, and control of all materials and supplies, including the critical supplies of newsprint, were also under General Emmons and his indefatigable aide, Colonel Green. They tolerated no criticism and circumvented any possible adverse public comment on their rule by imposing complete censorship upon the territory's press. Riley Allen, who printed a mildly critical editorial in 1942, was informed that if he allowed any further criticism of army rule to appear in the *Star-Bulletin,* the paper's allocation of newsprint would be withdrawn.

In March 1942, the case of Fred Spurlock, the defense worker whose hearing on a drunk-and-disorderly charge had been postponed as the war began, was heard at last by one of the provost officers assigned to conduct the business of civilians in courts that bore no relationship whatever to the pre–December 7 administration of civil justice in Hawaii. To Spurlock's dismay, the provost officer hearing his case pronounced a sentence of five years at hard labor in Oahu prison! Appeals were rarely permitted in such a court, but Spurlock was permitted to appeal that harsh sentence, with the result that he was released on probation.

His experience was not unusual. During that same month of March 1942, military justice on Oahu alone sentenced 943 persons to terms in the county jail and 719 to sentences in Oahu prison. Since the army refused to pay costs of bed and board for such prisoners, the burden of sustaining them fell upon county and territorial government whose usual income was severely curtailed by the military takeover.

All too often during these years of army rule, the criteria for meting out justice in the courts of the territory were incredibly fascistic and severe. In minor traffic cases, the provost courts equated a two-dollar fine with the enforced "donation" of a pint of blood to the blood bank. Civilian officials who directed the blood bank at Queen's Hospital protested the mandatory giving of gallons of unwanted blood drawn from drunks and people affected with syphilis, tuberculosis, and similar transmittable diseases, but all protest was ignored by the military governor.

Another punishment levied by provost courts was the compulsory purchase of war bonds—this in a territory that was among the nation's leaders in voluntary bond purchases. It was not difficult to see the prejudices with which the military courts operated if one knew, as did Lieutenant George Lehleitner, USN, about the kinds of sentences handed down by provost officers as a result of their decision on who was accused of what. A group of Lehleitner's sailors were picked up for disorderly conduct one night after they got drunk in a *mama-san* bar. In court, which Lehleitner attended as commanding officer of the men involved, the provost marshal made the astonishing pronouncement that the bar owner herself was the guilty one in this case. Her crime? Selling too much beer to the sailors. Her punishment? The enforced purchase of six thousand dollars' worth of war bonds, which the provost officer personally stamped "Not Redeemable until V-J Day." Lehleitner, a white industrialist from Louisiana, was shocked. How could this happen in an American territory? Statehood impressed him as being an absolute necessity for Hawaii, and then and there he resolved that once the war ended, he would make it a personal priority to help the territory achieve the full political status he felt that it, and all its citizens, deserved.

That other area of military arrests, internment of residents of Japanese birth or ancestry, slowed in intensity by April 1942, when one of the last of the Buddhist priests to be picked up and taken off for internment on the mainland was the father of Yoshiaki Fujitani. Like a number of *issei* and Japanese aliens in the territory, the elder Fujitani had been shielded as long as possible by *nisei* in the police and military intelligence who knew of his loyalty and integrity. In 1942, as the anti-Japanese hysteria peaked, they were no longer able to prolong his freedom. Yoshiaki Fujitani left the Varsity Victory Volunteers at this point to care for his mother, his six sisters and brother, and Moiliili Hongwanji temple. The same friends who had delayed his father's arrest assured young Fujitani that very soon now he would be permitted to carry out his desire of enlisting in the armed services.

Prominent among those who were not afraid to risk censure or their own careers by helping Hawaii's Japanese was Jack Burns, then a captain in the Honolulu Police Department. Burns also vouched to military intelligence for the dependability and loyalty of Jack Hall, the ILWU organizer, who spent the war years seeing how management—"the other side"—worked.

Not until February 1945 did United States Secretary of the Interior Harold Ickes and territorial attorney general J. Garner Anthony accomplish the first civilian victory of the war. The partial emancipation of the Territory of Hawaii from army rule was achieved by a presidential directive that went into effect on March 10, 1943. Since there had been no free press in Hawaii since December 7, 1941, no report of what had really transpired under martial law could be documented in print, but the battle for Hawaii's freedom was waged in a heated internal federal conflict between Ickes and his Department of Interior and the War Department, with Attorney General Anthony leading the fray in the territory by ousting General Emmons and Colonel Green from his office. The new military government headquarters, a building on the Iolani Palace grounds, was called by newsmen "the Little White House."

No vanquished confederate state at the end of the Civil War was subjected to such total military authority as was Hawaii between December 7, 1941, and March 10, 1943. No public debate of the inequities of army control over an American civilian population was ever held. One example of such inequity was General Order No. 91, the military governor's negation of the Fair Labor Standards Act of 1938. All workers in the territory were ordered to a forty-four-hour workweek—four hours more than the permissible federal standard. All union contracts were suspended. Wages were frozen. Occupational mobility was denied. The clamp upon their freedom that the Chinese had protested when they spoke against the proposed licensing law of 1894 was, in 1943, placed by army rule upon every worker in the territory.

A man who left his job without permission of the military authorities was subject to fine and imprisonment. Thus after forty-three years of freedom from the bondage of contract labor, a majority of Hawaii's workforce were put into wartime bondage under General Order No. 91. Grievances mounted, and along with them the determination to settle scores as soon as the war should end. Labor intended to honor its no-strike pledge, but it would not forget the army's impositions or the meekness with which plantation managers and leaders of Hawaii's Republican party acquiesced to conditions placed on their employees by the military.

Labor used these war years to organize for postwar activity. Mainland labor organizations were now keenly interested in Hawaii's potential union membership. John L. Lewis appointed Harry Bridges his West Coast lieutenant in the CIO. Bridges saw his scope as unionization of West Coast and island docks and of the sugar and pine workers of the Territory of Hawaii where his colleague, Jack Hall, was a brilliant, highly verbal, well-educated, and well-read union leader. On the Big Island, the workers of Waiakea Mill, a large Hilo processor of raw sugar, organized as a unit of the AFL. A group of grass-roots, dedicated men whose commitment to unionization was "all for one and one for all" came to the Big Island in 1943 to go from plantation to plantation and urge organization of units of the CIO, which they described as not discriminating between those who used chopsticks and those who used spoons. The reputation of the AFL was that it was a craft union with a tradition like the early trade unions of this century in the territory, that of a racial bias against minorities, and particularly against Orientals. Jack Kawano, a Kapoho boy, a Big Islander himself; Fred Kamahoahoa, a Hawaiian; and Johnny Elias, a Portuguese, along with *nisei* James Tanaka swung labor sentiment on the Big Island, and across the territory, to the CIO, of which ILWU was the territorial affiliate.

For the young *nisei* of the Varsity Victory Volunteers, and for *nisei* frozen in plantation jobs, 1943 brought the long-awaited opportunity to prove their loyalty to their country. The nearly fourteen hundred *nisei* in the 100th Battalion, in military intelligence, and in engineers' outfits were already proving their loyalty with their lives. In the spring of 1943, as President Roosevelt gave the territory a partial and most welcome release from army rule, the armed forces announced they would accept 2,500 volunteers for a new *nisei* combat unit, the 442nd Regiment. Nearly ten thousand *nisei* applied, among them Yoshiaki Fujitani. He was sent to Fort Snelling, Minnesota, to train as an interpreter for army intelligence.

As a sergeant in the United States Army, Fujitani had the unique experience of having to enter an internment camp barricaded with barbed wire and guarded by soldiers in order to visit his father at Albuquerque, New Mexico. A guard with raised rifle tried to prevent Sergeant Fujitani's spontaneous embrace of the parent he had not seen for two years. At Manzanar Internment Camp, another islander, Koji Ariyoshi, said farewell to his wife and to their baby daughter born in the camp to also volunteer for service in army intelligence. Ariyoshi's assignment was to Yenan, China, where he served as a member of the American liasion team at the north Shensi province headquarters of Mao Tse-tung.

The paradox of being imprisoned unjustly in this land of the brave and home of the free fell not only on *nisei* soldiers' families. In Hawaii two American citizens of German birth, Glockner and Seifert, were held without charge by military authorities on Sand Island from December 1941. In 1943 they were about to become one of the legal cases whereby district court judge Frank McLaughlin and Judge Delbert Metzger forced reinstatement of civil rights and the just practices of democracy through action that eventually went to the United States Supreme Court. Glockner and Seifert were languishing in illegal custody on Sand Island in Honolulu harbor when the black defense worker, Fred Spurlock, drunk again, got into a fight with some civilians. Military police picked him up and held him for four days without charge or bail before he was sent to Oahu prison in the spring of 1943 to serve the original sentence of his first drunk-and-disorderly conviction—five years at hard labor.

The reaction of Hawaii's conservative Republican establishment to such arbitrary action on the part of military courts was tacit approval. Their reaction to the first news that President Roosevelt might be thinking of lifting martial law in Hawaii, in December 1942, at the height of the assault on army power by Harold Ickes and J. Garner Anthony, was alarmed dismay. The executive committee of the Honolulu Chamber of Commerce sent a radiogram to the White House in Washington: "We recognize the dangers still confronting us and do not believe that martial law should be suspended at this time." [3] To older citizens of the territory, there were in this statement familiar echoes of the voices of the old "reform" party who had thrust the Bayonet Constitution on Kalakaua in 1887 and who had chosen to take matters into their own hands to end the Hawaiian monarchy in 1893.

3. Anthony, p. 29.

15

Victory: Overseas and at Home

EN W. Thoron, director of the Department of the Interior's Division of Territorial and Island Possessions, wrote a scathing comment from Washington in January 1943.

> I was somewhat disturbed by the telegram from the Chamber of Commerce to the President which gave the impression that a large and responsible group of American businessmen had so far departed from normal American thinking as to prefer military control of all activities of civilian life and to be accorded access to courts as an act of grace rather than a right in the normal process of American government.[1]

Conditions of war emergency were far graver on the islands of Malta and Ceylon than those of Hawaii, Thoron pointed out, and yet, in those two places, civil government had been maintained.

The presidential proclamation of March 1943 came as the 100th Battalion was shipped overseas to North Africa. In the view of federal judge Delbert Metzger of Honolulu, the president's proclamation had restored the writ of habeas corpus, which had been suspended since December 7, 1941. Metzger, the courageous Hilo lawyer who had averted the "Filipino Massacre" in 1924, now presided over one of the few civil courts

1. J. Garner Anthony, *Hawaii Under Army Rule* (Honolulu, The University Press of Hawaii, 1975), p. 30.

176

left in the territory. He had been awaiting the chance that he felt was given to him by the president's proclamation of March 10, 1943. As did Garner Anthony and Judge Frank McLaughlin, Judge Metzger interpreted the president's abridging of complete martial law as meaning an end to military tribunals for civil cases in Hawaii. The army's detention of the Germans Glockner and Seifert, two naturalized American citizens, gave Metzger the vehicle for defying the continuing authority of the military government in the islands.

On June 1, 1943, General Delos Emmons was replaced by a new commanding general and military governor of the territory, Lieutenant General Robert C. Richardson, Jr. On July 30, 1943, Judge Metzger issued a writ of habeas corpus and directed United States Marshal Otto F. Heine to serve a subpoena upon General Richardson. This procedure meant that Richardson must either release Glockner and Seifert or else appear in Metzger's court to show cause for his refusal to grant the basic constitutional right of habeas corpus to American citizens.

Metzger's confrontation of General Richardson and army rule hit the headlines from Hawaii to Maine. General Richardson continued to give the mainland press front-page material when on August 14, upon his orders, the United States deputy marshal attempting to serve him with the subpoena was manhandled and thrown over a veranda railing. On August 25, Judge Metzger found General Richardson in contempt of district court and fined him five thousand dollars. The general's counterattack typified the arrogance of army rule in the territory and the disdain for constitutional guarantees the military leaders displayed. Richardson issued General Order No. 31, which provided punishment by fine or imprisonment for any person filing or entertaining petitions for the writ of habeas corpus. Richardson was evidently not aware of the slow, but inexorable, processes of a federal Supreme Court. As the battles in which the 100th Battalion was engaged began to be waged overseas and as the 442nd reported for training at Camp Shelby, Mississippi, the biggest legal battle of World War II—the one with the most profound implications for citizens in all United States possessions and territories—began in Hawaii.

On October 21, 1943, Richardson won the first round by moving Glockner and Seifert to San Francisco and releasing them from custody. Metzger's case was now moot. However, the fine against Richardson remained on the books of the court and General Order No. 31 continued in force as a directive from General Richardson that no further legal challenge would be tolerated by the military. Six weeks before Richardson's release of Glockner and Seifert, the *Washington Post* commented in a September 2, 1943, editorial that Richardson's proclamation of a military order suspending the traditional liberties of American citizens set a dangerous precedent. "It would be difficult to show that the President himself has any such power which he could delegate to the general," the *Post* concluded.

While the war on both European and Pacific fronts was being won, the battle for due process and the liberation of Hawaii's citizens seemed at a temporary stalemate. Then, on February 24, 1944, a civilian shipfitter named Duncan (like Glockner and Seifert he never achieved the dignity of a first name in the legal battles fought for his rights) reported to work at Pearl Harbor and for no recorded reason quarreled with two marine sentries at the gate. Duncan was arrested, held overnight by military police, and released. One week later, however, he was called before a provost court and sentenced to six months in Honolulu's county jail for assault and battery against military personnel.

Duncan was not about to allow himself to be railroaded, as Fred Spurlock had been. The shipfitter petitioned the United States District Court on March 14 for a writ of habeas corpus, charging that his conviction and imprisonment were unlawful and unconstitutional, that martial law did not legally exist in the territory, and that even though Hawaii was temporarily under illegal military government, there was no military need for civilians to be tried by military tribunal. His petition for the writ, an illegal act under General Order No. 31, was served upon Honolulu's sheriff, the famous Olympic swimming champion and surfer, Duke Kahanamoku. With this case, Duncan *vs.* Kahanamoku, Judge Metzger reopened his legal arguments, and on April 13 the United States District Court declared that martial law in Hawaii was illegal.

Less than a month later, General Order No. 57 relaxed the curfew, extending civilians' evening hours to 10:00 P.M. This was one of Richardson's last official acts. On June 30, he relinquished the title of military governor, but as commanding general spent the next three weeks preparing for President Roosevelt's second visit to Hawaii, July 21 to July 29, 1944. Ostensibly, the visit was for the purpose of military conferences. In actuality, it was also employed to plan concessions to the legal forces condemning the continuance of martial law in the territory. During the presidential visit, General Order No. 63 changed the title "Office of Military Governor" to "Office of Internal Security." Three months later, on October 24, 1944, in Washington, President Roosevelt issued a proclamation terminating martial law in Hawaii and restoring civil rights— including the writ of habeas corpus—to all citizens in the territory.

This result did not please a number of prominent islanders who testified before the Army–Pearl Harbor Board brought to Honolulu in 1944 by Hawaii's delegate to Congress, Joseph Rider Farrington, publisher of the *Honolulu Star-Bulletin* and son of former governor Wallace Rider Farrington. In the Army–Pearl Harbor Board hearings, Walter F. Dillingham, son of the Dillingham who was stranded in Honolulu in 1863, testified that in 1944, under army rule, "it was the teeth in military control that made people feel comfortable here." [2] He neglected to define just whom he meant by "people." He referred to the concern for civil rights and equal justice expressed by Metzger's court decisions and in Farrington's request for the investigation as "hooey that nobody cared a damn about." [3]

In their support of military rule, *kamaaina* like Dillingham and his colleagues, some descendants of Hiram Bingham's puritan mission, had strange allies. When the army reluctantly returned control of vice to the Honolulu Police Department, and the old strict local regulations governing prostitution were again in force, Honolulu's prostitutes—among them the large numbers of new professionals imported by the army—joined the *haole*

2. Anthony, p. 107.
3. Anthony, p. 107.

establishment clamor to continue army rule of Hawaii. The prostitutes picketed the police station and the office of the military governor for three weeks in a futile attempt to win a return to the more liberal control of the military. Theirs was a lost cause. With a throttled press, this single wartime strike in the territory was never reported.

Only after Metzger's successful challenge of General Order No. 31 did organized labor in the territory make any formal protest against General Order No. 91, which had been imposed by military governor General Emmons early in the war. Early in 1944, when martial law was declared illegal by the district court, a local of the AFL Teamsters Union questioned ''any fancied need for this arbitrary subjugation of a free people that might once have existed when the military situation was critical, but has long since moved over the western horizon with our powerful Pacific offensive.'' [4] The local complained that ''patience has ceased to be a virtue. Competent and constitutional controls on labor must be established in Hawaii. American free men are entitled to no less.'' [5] Their rhetoric was earnest but colored by the desire to woo Hawaii labor away from the CIO.

By now the bitter test of World War II was almost over for the men of the 100th Battalion and the 442nd Regiment who had fought their way up the bloody boot of Italy. The civilian population of Hawaii could begin to relax, although they must still turn off their lights and be off the streets at 10:00 P.M. A complete blackout was enforced every night everywhere in Hawaii except on Honolulu's docks, at Pearl Harbor, and at military posts and airfields. When asked why every military target in Hawaii could be ablaze with lights while the ordinary citizen must observe a rigid blackout from 10:00 P.M. until dawn, the answer of the military authorities was that in an emergency they could be trusted to turn off all their lights quickly.

Not until July 11, 1945, two months after V-E Day and less than one month before the capitulation of Japan, did curfew and blackout end for civilians in the Territory of Hawaii. Fred Spur-

4. Anthony, p. 44.
5. Anthony, p. 45.

lock, freed by Judge Frank McLaughlin in a petition for a writ of habeas corpus in June 1944, was one of those celebrating victory on V-J Day in Hawaii. Captain Alexander Kahopea, a Hawaiian, was the most-decorated island soldier of the war. The men of the 100th Battalion and the 442nd Regiment returned home with the highest honors ever won in combat by an American army unit. They had passed the test, and their hard-won *esprit de corps* was to endure for the rest of their lives, providing a new focus for political unity in the islands and, after nearly half a century, the emergence of a viable two-party system in Hawaii.

Shipfitter Duncan's case was still going through the courts. It was eventually to be remembered as the one legal battle whose purpose, an insurance against future repetitions of Hawaii's experience of martial law, was not clearly established until the Supreme Court's decision of December 7, 1945. Justice Hugo Black, author of that decision, wrote that "the people of Hawaii . . . are entitled to constitutional protection to the same extent as the inhabitants of the 48 states," and that "the phrase martial law, as employed in that Act (Organic Act, Section 67) while intended to authorize the military to act vigorously for the defense of the islands against actual or threatened rebellion or invasion was not intended to authorize the supplanting of courts by military tribunals." [6]

Quietly, while that decision was being made, former military government aide Colonel Thomas Green accepted his new promotion to lieutenant general.

Not until 1946 were the internment camps emptied. In August 1946, Yoshiaki Fujitani's father returned to Honolulu. By then, Sergeant Fujitani had spent his first winter in Japan as an armed forces interpreter, rejoicing in the victory of his country and the coming of peace but moved with compassion and sadness for the defeated Japanese whose starvation and suffering were acute these first postwar months. Like many of his old ROTC classmates and many of the men of the 100th and the 442nd, Fujitani returned briefly to Hawaii after his postwar discharge and then

6. Anthony, pp. 83–84.

went on to the mainland to complete his education under the GI bill. Among the veterans crowding mainland university campuses in these first postwar years were many *nisei* from Hawaii preparing themselves at last for the fulfillment of their longtime dreams, becoming teachers, lawyers, doctors, dentists, engineers, experts in almost every field. Many decided to stay on the mainland for their careers. Many were eager to go home, to take their hard-earned place under the bright Hawaiian sun.

In 1946, while veterans like Daniel K. Inouye were off acquiring an education, a growing cadre of men and women under the leadership of ex-policeman Jack Burns began to build the Democratic party of Hawaii into a strong, goal-oriented political organization. They met each week in Honolulu—*kamaaina* (old-timers) like Burns; Hawaii-born liberal *haoles* like Thomas P. Gill; *malihini* (newcomers) like Frank Fasi, a second-generation Italian-American from Connecticut who decided to stay on in the islands after his wartime service as a sergeant in the marines; Chuck Mau, island-born Chinese.

An editorial in the *Honolulu Advertiser* in March 1946 spurred these new party members and a few of the old-time Democrats in the territory into political expression that would set the tone for the job Democrats felt they had to do in the next decade here. The editorial, looking back upon the years of military government in Hawaii, declared, "They did it—and we liked it!"

Judge Frank McLaughlin, United States district judge, wrote the rebuttal expressing the sentiments of Judge Metzger and Attorney General Anthony, of the liberal members of the legal profession, of labor's rank and file, of union organizers like Jack Hall (now back at the ILWU), of Jack Burns's growing nucleus of Democrats, of the majority of the men and women in the plantation fields, the town offices, and businesses, and of the ordinary people of Honolulu and the territory, the people who were still going to have more battles to fight before they won the final victory of statehood.

"Yes, 'they did it,' " wrote Judge McLaughlin, "They did it intentionally. They did it in knowing disregard of the Constitution. They did it because Hawaii is not a state. They did it because they did not have faith that Americanism transcends race, class, and creed." [7]

Neither war nor peace was a magic wand transforming the basic confrontations between the Big Five Republican economic and political monopoly in the territory and the generation of territorial public school graduates whose expectations and aspirations were that old American dream of "getting there." The paradox of peacetime postwar Hawaii was that this long-postponed major confrontation, with battles to be fought both in the labor and political sectors, could now begin.

The war's accumulation of such inequities as General Order No. 91 against labor was compounded, as after World War I, by the sharp rise in living costs in the territory. In 1946, Honolulu had the dubious distinction of being second only to Anchorage, Alaska, in its high cost of living as expressed in the index that was a new economic barometer of conditions in the cities and towns of America. The wages frozen by the military government's General Order No. 91 had been ten cents an hour lower than those earned in comparable mainland jobs in 1940, when federal Bureau of Labor investigator James Shoemaker labeled territorial labor's condition as "serfdom." In 1940, a dime at least bought six eggs or half a pound of hamburger. In 1946, under the military freeze, Hawaii's wages had dropped nearly fifty cents an hour behind comparable mainland jobs, but the price of eggs and hamburger had more than doubled.

Islanders who served in the armed forces and trained at mainland camps saw a life they envied: independent small businessmen, workers protected by federal legislation and strong unions, ordinary people like themselves owning their own homes, public schools where "standard" English was not a measure for segregation. Beginning in 1946 many families of these veterans and island families who had heard of the very different economic opportunities on the mainland from the GIs moving through Hawaii to the Pacific theater of war began an exodus to the mainland with Los Angeles, the Bay area of San Francisco, and Chicago the major destinations for relocation.

7. Anthony, p. 118.

The war had opened the eyes of islanders to the fact that not all *haoles* were rich, employed in management, or in the military. Veterans of the 100th Battalion and 442nd Regiment still recall their wartime shock at seeing *haoles* doing menial labor in mainland towns near their training camps. A jolt also remembered was the status of blacks on the mainland. In Hawaii the few blacks residing in the islands before the war had been men like Nolle R. Smith, a political leader and holder of high appointive territorial government offices, and Wendell Crockett, a prominent lawyer on Maui. Those islanders who fought the war on the home front in defense or plantation jobs had become friends with GIs who were union members back in Ohio or New Jersey and freely gave advice on how, after the war, island labor should organize and strike for its rights. The lifting of General Order No. 91 saw an exodus of plantation labor from the plantations to towns and, particularly, from the neighbor islands to Honolulu. Those who moved were too impatient to wait out another struggle. In these first postwar years, neighbor island districts like Kohala on the Big Island emptied from 10,000 plantation employees and their families to 3,500. Mechanization was replacing human labor as fast as management could arrange to do so. The total number of jobs in sugar thus diminished, but the exodus to Honolulu and the mainland left the old familiar need for importation of foreign labor.

Few of the boys and girls brought up in plantation camps saw themselves repeating the hard lives of their parents in the double bind of economy and tradition. For them, the social process of the war years expedited the possibility of becoming teachers, physicians, lawyers, executives, legislators. Politics and government jobs had never been open to *nisei*. In 1940, less than 2 percent of those holding government jobs in the territory were of Japanese ancestry. A few Japanese politicians ran and were elected to public office, but during the war years they made a tacit agreement to neither run for nor hold such positions. The sole exception was Sakuichi Sakai, brother of the Kohala *nisei* who became the first American of Japanese ancestry to become a commissioned officer in the United States Army during World

War I. Sakuichi Sakai, also a resident of the Big Island's Kohala district, was elected to the Hawaii County Board of Supervisors and served there all during the war years. For him, as for the young *nisei* on the threshold of new careers, not what you were but what your abilities and education were was the only difference that ought to count.

Politics was going to be the key to a new Hawaii. The cadre of Democrats meeting weekly in Honolulu with Jack Burns kept expanding. Island veteran Dan Inouye, attending law school on the mainland, wrote home to ask Burns to count him in and asked further how he could help. The union thrust through political clout also resumed in 1946, but while Jack Burns had vouched for Jack Hall during the war, he made a strong effort to keep the ILWU an ally and not the dominant force in the revitalized Democratic party, which like the unions of the territory was multiracial in membership and leadership.

In 1946 the ILWU seemed close to being "the One Big Union" George Wright had talked about in 1922 at Aala Park. Equally politically oriented and similarly multiracial were the other primary unions of the territory in these postwar years: Art Rutledge's teamsters, restaurant, beverage, and hotel workers union (which became AFL-CIO after merger of those two organizations in 1955); Henry Epstein's United Public Workers (UPW); and Charles R. Kendall's still comparatively small Hawaii Government Employees Association (HGEA). The slogan of the 442nd Regiment in its training and combat had been "Go for Broke!" With V-E Day, V-J Day, and military government and martial law behind them, labor forces in Hawaii adopted a "Go for Broke!" mood.

In 1946 the market for sugar and pineapple was stable. GIs had poured millions of dollars into the territory's economy. The war ended with full employment. Management, hoping to stave off trouble with the unions, began to recognize and deal with them. Even before the end of the war, in May 1945, the Hawaii Employment Relations Act passed. Management's hope was to try to live with that act with as little attrition to their profit margin and the least cost in prerogatives as might be possible through conversion to mechanization and importation of cheap immigrant labor from the war-torn Ilocano villages of the Philippines.

By the middle of that year, the ILWU was ready for industry-wide labor-management negotiations over wages, working conditions, and such employee benefits as social security, pension plans, maternity and sick leave, industrial accident compensation, seniority rights, and paid vacations.

This third-act climax of the successful organization of Hawaii's plantation and dock workers was not a one-man show. Jack Hall played a major lead, but notable supporting actors were Jack Kawano, the Big Islander who organized Honolulu's docks; former navy diver Dwight "Jim" Freeman; the Big Island's fiery Olaa union leader, Yasuki Arakaki; and countless others. Schoolteachers Aiko and John Reinecke were among the union sympathizers who spent vacations on the neighbor islands working with people in plantation housing camps. Under the aegis of the NLRB, more than a hundred petitions for union locals were granted in Hawaii during the first eighteen months after V-J Day.

Rather than negotiate and see what might happen in collective bargaining, management chose in late 1946 to refuse the ILWU's demand for an 18½-cent hourly wage increase for dockworkers and plantation employees throughout the territory. Management also refused an accompanying demand for the forty-hour work week that was standard in most mainland industries. On September 1, 1946, the ILWU called for its membership to go out on strike. This they did, with full fervor, picketing every sugar mill, plantation shop, and company office for the next seventy-nine days. Strikers carried signs warning planters that the paternalism of the past would no longer suffice. "The Manager Lives in a Castle. We Live in a Chicken Coop!" read one sign carried by Kohala strikers.

Strikers at Olaa, where the "Bloody Monday" battle on Hilo docks eight years earlier was well remembered, courageously faced a menacing line of sheriff's officers and policemen. No shot was fired. No blood was shed. No insult was forgotten, however. On the eightieth day, with the help of a federal mediator at the negotiating table, the strike was settled with a wage increase of twenty cents an hour. Harry Bridges, West Coast director of the ILWU, sent a congratulatory telegram to union headquarters in Honolulu, applauding the settlement, which he described as meaning—at last—that Hawaii was no longer a feudal colony.

The union's victory at the bargaining table that November was matched by victory for fourteen of their fifteen union-endorsed candidates at the polls. These were not all Democrats, for the union had made its own determination of political independence. Among those supported by the ILWU was Republican Joseph R. Farrington, who won re-election as Hawaii's delegate to Congress. Farrington's opponent, Democrat Bill Borthwick, a Honolulu mortician, had been favored by Governor Ingram Stainback, a former Tennessean and a southern Democrat who did not expect to see the 1946 campaign wind up like "rice and roses" for the union. Stainback's bitterness was soon fed with fuel to enable him to "go after" the ILWU.

At about this time, the commanding general of the United States Army in Hawaii, Lieutenant General John E. Hull, and his chief intelligence officer visited Governor Stainback in Iolani Palace. Their purpose has never been documented but was alleged to be to show the governor their top-secret list of the new enemy: Communists in Hawaii. The names of those identified as either Communist or Communist sympathizer were most familiar to Stainback. Jack Hall, whom the governor had appointed to the Territorial Police Commission in 1945, headed the list. Schoolteachers John and Aiko Reinecke were among the names the governor remembered in the fall of 1947. In an Armistice Day speech he split Democrats into liberal versus conservatives like himself when he charged that the Communist party had infiltrated the Democratic party of the territory. Stainback, who had originally intended to press for land reform in Hawaii, proceeded to make anticommunism a crusade that the old "reform" party legatees, Hawaii's antiunion, conservative Republican power clique, could and did join. He and Chuck Mau also persuaded labor leader Jack Kawano that he had been "shelved" by ILWU "reds."

It was a new battle in the old war between the *haole* power structure and a multiracial population educated to expect the guarantees of the Declaration of Independence and the Constitution to be sincere affirmations that race, creed, and color did not deny an American citizen the freedoms of democracy. Stainback accused Democratic National Committeeman Charles Kauhane of being "completely subservient to Hall and his Communist gang," pointing out, as if to substantiate this charge, that "practically no white men were elected to any position" in the elections of 1946. Stainback's crusade paralleled the red-baiting on the mainland, a witch hunt fueled in both places by hatred engendered during four years of war. Americans were not adjusting easily to peace.

Ichiro Izuka, a disgruntled union leader on Kauai, broke with the ILWU and in a widely distributed pamphlet said he was going to tell "The Truth about Communism in Hawaii." Several years later, Izuka retracted all that he had claimed in that pamphlet, but in 1947 his allegations were accepted as fact by those who wished to believe all that he wrote condemning the leaders of the ILWU. Izuka contended that the ILWU had supported Joe Farrington's candidacy only because Farrington had agreed to keep his newspaper, the *Honolulu Star-Bulletin,* neutral in the union-management contest. He charged that Jack Hall and Jack Kawano had spread lies that defeated Borthwick, lies declaring that Borthwick was anti-Japanese and against statehood. It was after the distribution of Izuka's pamphlet that the *Honolulu Advertiser* revived its old editorial opinion that unionism was un-American and that Orientals were the backbone of the Communist party in the territory.

The first victims of Stainback's vicious crusade were John and Aiko Reinecke. In a closed meeting of the territory's appointed Board of Education, a meeting from which the superintendent of education was barred and at which no minutes were taken, John Reinecke was summarily dismissed from his job as a public school teacher on the single bit of "evidence" that Izuka's pamphlet had labeled him a "parlor pink." No one openly mentioned the school board's punitive action against Reinecke as having some connection with his own book, *The*

Truth about the Massie-Kahahawai Case, based upon the official Pinkerton report that lay buried and unpublished in the territorial archives. The board's only charge against Aiko Reinecke
was that she was John's wife. Due process was not granted the
couple. They were fired and denied further employment in the
public schools.

Their dismissal was hailed by Imua, an anti-Communist organization committed to driving "reds" out of the islands. Imua's
flurry of propaganda leaflets and radio programs supporting the
Stainback crusade and condemning the Reineckes was, John A.
Burns recalled years later, funded with "some pretty good support from the old missionary families." During this period, an
abortive five-day strike by pineapple workers was used to persuade popular sentiment to identify antiunionism with anticommunism.

Democratic party chairman Jack Burns walked a narrow path
in those difficult years, trying to keep union support behind
party candidates and programs without relinquishing control of
the party to union leadership. In the red-baiting witch hunts, he
stood by his friends, all of them, as he had during the war
years. He also supported the ILWU in 1949 when it called a
dock strike that kept Hawaii's ports closed from May to October. In the islands, a dock strike means no supplies of such es-
sentials as toilet paper, canned milk, salt, or rice are likely to
remain on store shelves for purchase. Sundry other necessities
are in short supply or unavailable. Small businesses founder.
Employees of larger firms are laid off. During the 179-day dock
strike of 1949, one-fifth of Hawaii's businesses cut employees'
wages in an effort to avoid bankruptcy. The number of jobless
in the territory rose to twenty thousand—twice that suffered during the Great Depression in Hawaii.

Indignant Republican housewives formed a "Broom Bri-
gade," to "sweep the union off the docks." Alarmed that Congress's Un-American Activities Committee investigations might
come to Hawaii during this strike, Jack Burns went to the mainland to enlist support for the union cause, with which Hawaii's
Democrats were strongly identified. From Congressman Francis Walters, chairman of the powerful House Un-American Af-

fairs Committee, Burns received a promise that no investigation of Communists or possible communism in Hawaii would be made until the dock strike was ended. Walters was elected from a Pennsylvania labor constituency and he was not eager to appear in any way antiunion.

For management, the dock strike was an all-out effort to halt ILWU's moves to achieve parity with mainland labor-benefit standards. According to rumors, $100 million was put up by the Big Five corporations and their allies in the 1949 attempt to crush the union. In October, as the strike ended with neither side really winning, union members took their two-step raise of twenty-one cents an hour with the slogan, "Let the Boss Save His Face and We'll Take Home the Dough!"

Walter's congressional committee kept its promise to Jack Burns. Not until April 1950, six months after the end of the dock strike, did he bring his Un-American Affairs Committee to Hawaii for hearings. The congressional investigation was at the request of the territory's Subversive Activities Board, a group whose sympathies were with Stainback, Imua, the *haole* Republican power group, and management. For Jack Burns, Jack Hall, and all the men and women of the territory who remembered what democracy was supposed to be all about, there was one last battle to face before they could stage the political revolution that would make possible a new Hawaii—the goal of those who proved themselves in war and in the peacetime conflicts of this first postwar decade.

16

Statehood

N an emotionally charged atmosphere of anticommunism and antiunionism, citizens of Hawaii went to the polls in 1950 to elect delegates to a convention at which a constitution would be framed in preparation for statehood. Voter turnout in this election was an unprecedented 85 percent. By November the constitution drafted by that convention was completed, and voters were given the chance to accept or reject the constitution for what they hoped would be America's forty-ninth state. The results were a clear and unmistakable message to the United States Congress: 82,788 for the constitution; 27,109 against it.

Historians Charles and Mary Beard record that after reviewing this proposed constitution and visiting the territory to judge its qualifications for statehood, the Senate Interior and Insular Affairs Committee concluded that Hawaii had

> unequivocally met every test applied to 29 other territorial applications for admittance into the union. It is a paradox that the United States should still permit so vital a part of itself to remain in the inferior status of a territory when that part fulfills each and every one of the historic qualifications for statehood and is eager to assume the burdens and responsibilities of full equality as well as to enjoy its privileges . . . It is submitted that if the ultimate test of loyalty and patriotism is willingness to fight and die for one's country, then Hawaii has nobly met this test . . . on the battlefields of Europe and, more recently, in Korea.

The war in Korea had spurred another wholehearted commitment of manpower, womanpower, and idealism from islanders. *Nisei* who had been too young to volunteer in 1943 enlisted for combat in the Korean War, troubled by the fact that the names of many of their older friends and relatives were on the list of suspects that Governor Stainback had been furnished; a list that focused in 1951 on seven persons whom former ILWU leader Jack Kawano claimed were Communists. At 6:30 one August morning in 1951, these "Hawaii Seven" were arrested by the FBI's dramatic foray into each of the suspect's homes.

The seven, charged under the Smith Act with conspiring to overthrow the government of the United States by force and violence, were Charles Fujimoto, head of the Communist party in Hawaii, and his wife Eileen Kee Fujimoto; Dwight James "Jim" Freeman, a professional diver who had worked with the navy in search-and-salvage operations on the sunken battleships at Pearl Harbor; Dr. John Reinecke; Jack Hall; Koji Ariyoshi, long home from his army service in China and editor and publisher of a liberal newspaper, *The Honolulu Record*; and his employee Jack D. Kimoto. A United States commissioner set their bail at $75,000 apiece. Before the morning was over, federal judge Delbert Metzger had intervened and lowered bail for the seven to $5,000 apiece. Each was able to put up that amount, and they were freed to await trial.

On the afternoon of his arrest, back at the *Honolulu Record,* Koji Ariyoshi sat down at his typewriter and with the frustration of those dedicated to a practical application of the ideals of democracy wrote "My Thoughts for Which I Stand Indicted" for publication in the next issue of his paper.

> One of these days I will appear in court to answer the Justice Department's fantastic charges that I, and six others here, advocate and teach the overthrow of the government by force and violence. The court will ask me whether I will plead guilty or not guilty. How else can I answer in honesty but to say firmly I am not guilty. The shoe which the Justice Department is trying to make me wear does not fit . . . the architects of our nation wrote in the Declaration of Independence: "whenever any form of government becomes destructive of these ends (securing of life, liberty, and the pursuit of

happiness) it is the right of the people to alter or to abolish it, and to institute a new government, laying its foundations on such principles and organizing its powers in such form, as to them shall seem most likely to effect their safety and happiness.''

The language here is very clear. I have not said as much in the editorial columns of the Honolulu *Record,* the medium of my communication with the reading public. But I am charged with advocating the violent overthrow of our government. Since my arrest and indictment I have carefully gone over . . . my thinking and activities up to this day. And I find I am innocent of the charges directed against me. In my step by step review of my life, I constantly come up with this question: Is the fight against discrimination because of color, religion, or belief, abuses of laborers, colonialism and subjugation of hundreds of millions, the struggle for civil liberties and for a sane or peaceful world destructive of our government? The ideas which I possess and for which I stand now indicted under the Smith Act, became a part of me as a result of my observations and experiences here in this country. I am not charged with an overt act of crime, but for my ideas, which Attorney-General McGrath seeks to lock behind bars.

The trial of the Hawaii Seven lasted 457 days and ended in a verdict of guilty. Delbert Metzger, denied reappointment to his federal judgeship both because of his stand against the army in World War II and his support of the Hawaii Seven in 1951, testified as a character witness for the accused. So did Honolulu's popular mayor, part-Tahitian John Wilson, the Stanford student who had helped smuggle arms from Maui to help in the abortive counterrevolution to restore Queen Liliuokalani (whom his father had served as police marshal). Sharp internal lines of dissent among Democrats, lines to last through the 1970s, were drawn between those who stood fast during this final time of tribulation and those who refused to speak out in support. Democratic National Committeeman Frank Fasi, later a perennial candidate for Honolulu's Council and during the 1970s Honolulu's mayor and twice loser in the gubernatorial primary, refused to swear to Jack Hall's good reputation. The process of appeal of the guilty verdict was lengthy. Koji Ariyoshi, during those years, saw old friends cross the street to avoid having to speak to him. In 1952, Delbert Metzger's forthright stand for the Hawaii Seven was used to defeat him in his bid as Democratic candidate for Hawaii's congressional delegate.

The ideas that Koji Ariyoshi had refused to acknowledge as undemocratic or un-American were the basic ideas upon which, in 1839, Boaz Mahune had drafted the Hawaiian Bill of Rights. They were the ideas that stirred the Chinese in Hawaii to protest curtailment of their civil liberties under the proposed licensing act of 1894; the ideas that had furnished the American dream for Japanese contract laborers who protested against feudalistic conditions of plantation labor. They were the ideas that all who were Hawaiian by birth or had become Hawaiian by allegiance and American in their commitment to liberty, equality, and justice had been taught in the free public schools of the territory—schools that in the 1950s were no longer segregated by "standard" English. These ideas were fundamental concepts of the new Democrats of Hawaii, not just in theory or the paper of a party platform, but in a practice they sought to apply to conditions of everyday life.

The red-baiting, the trial of the Hawaii Seven, the accusation of another group of suspects ("The Reluctant Thirty-Nine"), expressed a far different philosophy of government, that of the era of Senator Joseph McCarthy on the American mainland, a prejudicial conservatism that seemed an animus too frequently lurking beneath the democratic ideals Americans expressed with such eloquence. In many respects in the 1950s it was Hawaii whose people were willing to stage a revolution back to the democratic practices of those ideals on which the United States had originally been founded. In the elections of 1954, Hawaii's Democrats carried out such a revolution, with statehood as one of the major issues, when by an overwhelming majority they were elected to the territorial Senate and House.

Traditionally, a string tied to the pencil with which a voter marked his ballot had belied the privacy of the voting booth. Observers in plantation precincts had been able to tell who voted for the management's Republican candidate and who dared vote differently by watching the direction in which the string moved as a ballot was marked. The war and the success of union battles had given islanders a new sense of personal freedom. Most of the strings in ballot boxes throughout the territory on election day, 1954, moved in one direction: Democrat. Those election results were revolutionary. Twenty years later, as Jack Burns taped his memoirs during the last years of his life, he quoted the *New York Times* headline reporting that election:

WHEN COCONUTS FELL ON THE GOP IN HAWAII

"That's just about the idea that coconuts fell on their heads," Burns reminisced, with his famous rare smile. "It was almost an eruption of Mauna Kea or Mauna Loa. Totally unexpected by the newspapers or anyone else." Ironically, the year of his party's stunning victory was the year of Jack Burns's first political defeat. During the 1954 campaign he traveled from island to island with an old suitcase whose broken handle was mended with a piece of string. Campaign funds for him were short, as they were for all other Democrats running that year. Tadao Beppu, a Maui veteran home from graduate work at the University of Chicago and a political apprenticeship with Illinois's Adlai Stevenson, recollects that two dollars represented a big outlay in the Burns campaign, of which he was treasurer. Labor, which he had done his utmost to support, cost Burns that election by a mere 870 votes. Art Rutledge's Unity House labor group was pledged to Joe Farrington to repay Rutledge's debt of gratitude for having been saved from deportation. In the Democratic revolution of 1954, Hawaii had a congressional delegate who was Republican. Since Dwight D. Eisenhower won that year's presidential race, a Republican occupied the White House for the first time since the days of Herbert Hoover and thus by political paradox this newly Democratic territory was given a Republican appointee, Samuel Wilder King, as governor.

Statehood was, for the moment, beyond their reach, but the Democratic majority in the legislature were young tigers (whom twenty-five years later old Art Rutledge scorned as "fat pussy-cats"). They were determined to legislate their basic ability policy, to end the discrimination against racial minorities in government jobs and private industry, to open up the territory to independent small business, and above all to improve the quality of public education, to extend the range and opportunities for higher education. Jack Burns called this revolution that he had helped to bring about a "quickened, legislatively hastened change." Two years later, in the 1956 elections, he was at the leading edge of that change in his successful election as Hawaii's congressional delegate. His campaign treasurer, Tadao Beppu, won a seat in the territorial House in 1958.

In the University of Hawaii's journal, *Social Process in Hawaii,* the 1950 annual issue had carried an article by sociologist Bernhard Hormann entitled "The Caucasian Minority." His sociopolitical prophecy was that

> the maturation of the middle class in Honolulu and its increasing influence over the whole society means that the colonial or frontier or plantation era in Hawaii is about to pass into history. Hawaii's admission to the union as the 49th or 50th state will be the symbol that Hawaii's social structure has attained the characteristics of American Society. It will augur the disappearance of minorities, Oriental, Hawaiian, and *Haole.*

To Professor Hormann, as to most residents of the territory, there was something magical about statehood: it would be an alchemy transmuting all the racial distrusts, the union-management strife, the short circuit of democratic privilege, to a new society in which the ancient Hawaiian values of aloha, *kokua, aloha aina,* the Christian emphasis on brotherhood and love for one's fellow man, and the Buddhist ethic of compassion would meld. All the old distinctions and discrimination would then be erased. Many of the young Democrats elected to office in 1954, and their idealistic supporters, shared Hormann's view of statehood.

In 1958, with Burns's second term as delegate, probability was the wisest word to use concerning Hawaii's chances for admission. The issue of whether Hawaii would precede or follow Alaska was decided in congressional cloakrooms and offices by Delegate Burns and his congressional friends, Lyndon Baines Johnson and Speaker of the House Sam Rayburn. Their circles of influence in the Congress were considerable. Their advice was Alaska first, and against bitter, adverse comment from home and many of his Hawaii supporters, Jack Burns made that choice his political strategy. Foes of statehood for Hawaii were still numerous, both in Congress and in the territory itself. A small Republican minority still spoke wistfully about the advantage of Hawaii's becoming a commonwealth, like Puerto Rico. The vast majority of islanders, Democrats and many Republicans, disagreed. In Honolulu in 1954, people waited in line to sign a block-long petition for statehood laid out along Bishop Street, and in 1958 that sentiment was equally strong. The Junior Chamber of Commerce sponsored an annual "Forty-ninth State Fair" in Honolulu. What could now prevent a territory that had so proved itself, and waited so long, and been so patiently studied by congressional committees, from gaining full partnership in the Union?

To the average American in 1958, Hawaii no longer seemed a vague, remote place where natives dozed away long lazy days under palm trees. The dual realities of sunny beaches, magnificent surf, Hawaiian music, friendly *wahines*, ideal year-round climate, and of labor strife, interracial jealousies, economic monopoly, and the curtailment of democratic privilege to territorial citizens of Oriental ancestry were now appreciated by more than a million GIs who had passed through or served in Hawaii during the war. Even when Hawaii's beaches were girded in barbed wire and its citizens lived under curfew, blackout, and military despotism, the charm and beauty of the islands, the friendly sincerity of their people, enchanted mainlanders experiencing the warmth of aloha for the first time. Just as millions of mainlanders had discarded the grass-shack myth of Hawaii by the 1950s, so had islanders had their illusion of *haole* stereotypes, and of mainland blacks and Hispanic-Americans, stripped to a reality that often presented as much of a paradox as their own problem-ridden paradise.

In 1958, under the new political developments begun in the Democratic political revolution, the middle class that Hormann had predicted in 1950 had begun to mature. It was not a middle class typical of white Anglo-Saxon Protestant America. The Chinese, who had long since reached the top in business and the professions and moved out of Chinatown, were solid *alii* and upper-middle-class citizens like Chinn Ho and Hiram Fong, both of whom had grown up poor and become wealthy. Hiram

Fong's Finance Factors was one of the leading lending institutions in Hawaii in the 1970s, with large real property holdings and diversified investments. Chinn Ho's family empire of hotels, office buildings, and businesses reached out from holdings in Honolulu to Hong Kong and Guam.

As there had always been, there were wealthy Hawaiian *alii* plus a large core of middle-class Hawaiians, but their numbers were less than those of the new middle-class *nisei* who had come home from the wars to earn college degrees that prepared them to fill government jobs as lawyers, engineers, social workers, accountants, teachers, analysts, and to move into the top rank of the professions of medicine, dentistry, and law. The established professional societies of the territory that stood on the threshold of statehood did not extend their welcome and begrudged their membership. The struggle to "get there" seemed never-ending to many *nisei*. Their struggle, and the fact that there were so many of them—so able, so well qualified, and ambitious in a very American way—was later to seem a threat to many Hawaiians and conservative old and new *haoles*. Numbers pose a problem in the context of economic competition and political power. It would not be long before anti-Japanese sentiments would again grumble through the island community.

In the unskilled workforce of the territory there were also still large numbers of Japanese and increasing numbers of *haoles*, but in 1958 the majority of the *makaainana* doing field labor on plantations and unskilled labor in construction and private industry, loading and unloading freight on the docks, were Hawaiians, Puerto Ricans, newcomer Samoans, and Filipinos. Those in the latter group were looking toward their own future with the same aspirations that the Japanese had had in the early days of the territory. As had the Japanese, they became ardent Americans with aspirations toward economic advancement and their own voices in the territorial legislature. No longer, in the 1950s, were Filipinos a group of predominantly single men. The shift to families, to pride in their cultural heritage, to a new and upwardly mobile status in jobs and professions would mark the next twenty years in which new Filipino immigrants were often to find their own ethnic group as difficult as strangers. The major social change in the 1950s was the flowering of a multiracial middle class and the postwar exodus from the neighbor islands to Oahu. The City and County of Honolulu now had 80 percent of the population of the territory. The neighbor islands had become the rural regions of Hawaii. Oahu had fulfilled its ancient name. It was, indeed, the gathering place. It was also, in the vernacular of servicemen in Honolulu, the "Rock."

Walter Kolarz of the British Broadcasting Company, visiting Hawaii in 1954, had noted that one out of every three marriages in Hawaii was racially mixed. Kolarz came to attend a Honolulu conference on race relations and was much impressed by what seemed to him the amicability of Hawaii's several ethnic groups. The paradox seems always to have existed that the visitor, the outsider, tends to see harmony. The resident, the insider, tends to see disharmony—but then to protest that it's not really that bad, that the aloha spirit is still here. In 1954 Walter Kolarz recognized that Hawaii's social and cultural diversity held a potential for misunderstandings and tension between various subgroups and cliques. He felt, however, that such tensions need not be characterized by racial antagonism. He did not anticipate the disruption of Hawaii's dynamic racial relationships by internal factions or friction. What he did correctly foresee was disruption caused by the transients coming to the islands in increasing numbers. Whether these were tourists from wealthy international high society, budget vacationers from America, bonus vacationers from Japan, the vanguard of the hippies who were to flood into the islands in the sixties, or sailors from the Pacific Fleet, Kolarz sensed they presented a danger to the attitudes and aloha of island society. That danger lay in the transient visitors' irresponsible, pleasure-bent moods, and from both locals and visitors in the escalation of the prejudice that had long been a factor in the islands' social scene.

In 1958, when congressional delegate Burns repacked his bags for Washington, nearly 200,000 tourists were expected to visit Waikiki during that year, the great majority of them not venturing on to any neighbor island resort destination. Kauai had a few attractive hotels such as Coco Palms. Kaanapali,

Maui, was still a developer's dream. In Hilo, the Hilo Hotel and the stately old Naniloa, a wooden, wide-verandaed structure, enjoyed a modest tourist business, as did Kailua-Kona, whose Kona Inn was the same old-fashioned rambling wooden structure as the Naniloa and the old Pioneer Inn at Lahaina, Maui. Lawrence Rockefeller had not yet thought about leasing acreage on the South Kohala coast to build Mauna Kea Beach Hotel. The personal safety of visitors and the easy atmosphere that Charles Nordhoff remarked in 1872 remained in effect only on the neighbor islands. In 1958, in Honolulu, people had begun to lock their doors when they left home, and rumors floated that the Mafia was about to move in on the local syndicate that controlled gambling and vice. Probably more than any other populace in the United States, Hawaii's people are eager gamblers, good customers in Las Vegas, and at home, aficionados of mahjongg, poker, craps, the numbers games, football and basketball pools, cockfighting, and whatever else they can find to bet on, including the outcome of political elections. In the new Hawaii, bars were as popular as nineteenth-century grog shops had been, but unlike grog shops, the new bars—in a wide range of location, décor, and clientele—became an accepted and important part of daily social life for both women and men.

Members of the constituency Jack Burns represented in the Congress were in every way as American in their attitudes, commitment, and personal identity as those of any congressional district in mainland America. To the Midwest tourist, they only looked different. One third of the population was Oriental, heavily Japanese; one third was part-Hawaiian, Filipino, and Puerto Rican; and about one third was *haole*. The Big Five had lost political power but retained a hold on the economy. Not until after the tenth anniversary of statehood would they open their executive ranks to nonwhites. Plantations were the fulcrum of the economy in the rural areas of the territory. Federal defense spending was the fulcrum of the economy in Honolulu and the number three source of income for the territory. Sugar and pine still held first and second place. Tourism, in the 1950s, was climbing up from fourth in the amount of dollars pumped into Hawaii's economy.

In Washington, spokesmen for the Big Five no longer had the

political power they had once wielded over delegates like Prince Kuhio. In 1958, Jack Burns could be his own man and view the obstacles that lay between Hawaii and statehood with clear eyes. Palmyra Island, legally part of the City and County of Honolulu since 1912, had been one such obstacle to previous statehood bills introduced by previous congressional delegates from the territory. The federal government had been understandably reluctant to accept as part of a state an island 1,100 miles distant from that state's boundaries. Burns removed that obstacle by removing Palmyra Island from the provisions of the statehood bill. Another change that he considered critical was his language change from "to enable admission" to the more specific, "to admit."

Louisiana industrialist George Lehleitner, the former navy lieutenant who had been a shocked observer of Hawaii's wartime military justice, had not forgotten his resolve to help the islands achieve statehood. Lehleitner did help, both morally and financially, even when Speaker Sam Rayburn and Lyndon Baines Johnson advised Burns to let Alaska's request for statehood be pursued separately from Hawaii's. Violent opposition came from many supporters at this, but Lehleitner stuck with Burns.

On January 3, 1959, Burns helped to make Alaska America's forty-ninth state. As he worked that spring gathering votes in Washington for Hawaii's statehood, his opponents worked with equal vigor at home and in the nation's capital. Walter Dillingham, former governor Lawrence Judd, and former governor Ingram Stainback had been appalled by the successful appeal of the Hawaii Seven and their vindication in the courts in January 1958. They and Hawaii's other conservatives joined forces with Senators Strom Thurmond of Georgia and James Eastland of Mississippi to try to keep Hawaii a territory. They failed. Alaska's friends came through, as they had promised, to aid Jack Burns with votes. His strategy brought success. On March 12, 1959, newspaper extras in Honolulu and front-page headlines from coast to coast on the mainland announced passage of Hawaii's statehood bill in the House. One last step remained: the approval of the president.

Historians Charles and Mary Beard summed up the signifi-

cance of that spring of 1959 in one short paragraph: "Turning to
matters of civil rights, Congress and the President brought an
end to the historically inferior position of both Alaska and Hawaii by admitting both areas to statehood in 1959, thus giving
their inhabitants greater voice in government and stronger constitutional guarantees of liberty." The Beards' calm assessment
gives no hint as to what statehood meant to the people of the
new fiftieth state of Hawaii. That afternoon, University of Hawaii classrooms emptied and public schools were dismissed for
two days so students and teachers could join in the celebration.
Government offices closed. Retail stores locked their doors and
let their employees off to celebrate. All ships in Honolulu harbor blew their whistles. In towns and villages throughout the
islands, air-raid sirens sounded statehood's victory. In Honolulu, that night, thousands turned out to dance in the streets and
on the lawns of Iolani Palace. On Sand Island, a statehood bon-
fire burned with wood from every state in the union sent for that
special purpose.

Once the formalities of presidential approval, a plebiscite,
and elections of state officials were observed, Admissions Day
was set for August 21, 1959. The ceremony came sixty-one
years and nine days after Hawaii's annexation to the United
States. Like that 1898 Annexation Day, the statehood admissions ceremony was held at Iolani Palace. No longer were there
gates to be opened to admit the crowds who came by bus along
King Street or parked their cars in nearby municipal lots. Neighbor islanders flew over on one of the frequent interisland flights
of Hawaiian Air or Aloha Airlines. It was a far more enthusiastic, casual, and cosmopolitan crowd than that of 1898—and it
was far larger. Only the people of Niihau and a few thousand
diehards who wanted continuance of territorial status, commission government, commonwealth status, or a return to the Hawaiian monarchy voted against statehood in the 1959 plebiscite.
Everyone who could manage to get to the August 21 ceremony
in Honolulu came. But the one man who had done the most to
make this day happen was not invited by the Republican governor, presidential appointee William Quinn. John Anthony
Burns was not among the dignitaries at Iolani Palace that day.

17

Aloha Aina: A Love for the Land

S͟TATEHOOD was indeed the magic wand islanders had dreamed would transform Hawaii. The economy, government services, the population and population patterns, the very appearance of the islands themselves, changed drastically everywhere except on privately owned Niihau during the first two decades of Hawaii's full partnership in the American Union. The problem and the paradox were that this change occurred during the period when the venerable American ideal of "progress is better, more progress is best" began to be questioned by those who translated the ancient Hawaiian value of *aloha aina* into such technical terms as ecology, environmental protection, and conservation.

In the 1960s, the sound of the new state was the daily rhythm of pile drivers working to keep up with the pace of the construction boom. The popular joke was that Hawaii's new state bird was the Dillingham crane. The long steel necks of the cranes bobbled from high rise to high rise, in activity local construction companies had never before known. In less than twenty years, a phalanx of steel, glass, and concrete towers marched from downtown Honolulu to Pearl City and Salt Lake, thrust up from the slopes of Punchbowl and Tantalus, lined the beach at Waikiki and pushed out along the freeway in a Koko Head direction toward Henry Kaiser's residential development, Hawaii Kai. Across the island, over the Pali whose mountain barricades were

203

pierced by two freeway tunnels, high rises loomed in a resort hotel at Kahuku (where the nineteenth century labor protestors had started their forty-five mile march to Honolulu), and high-rise buildings began to give the suburban community of Kailua, Oahu, an urban flavor.

In 1979, as planes came in for a landing at Honolulu's International Airport, with its new reef runway extending out over the channels where the old Pan Am clippers had made their water landings in the 1930s, the view of the city was framed and contained by the cloud-hung jagged profile of the Koolau Mountains. Along the shore and up the valleys was the urban sprawl that local residents lamented, but Honolulu, 1979, was still a small and lovely city by most mainland standards. Golf courses and parks were green oases along the water front and behind Waikiki, where drainage canals had reclaimed former swamp acreage. Thomas Square, where the admiral had returned his nation to Kamehameha III in 1843, was graced by great banyan trees and surrounded by condominiums and medical centers. Toward Ewa, the sun slanted silvery lights on cane fields pierced by freeways.

Honolulu had not adopted the recommendations made by a mainland planner in 1938 for a boulevard-and-park-studded city, but despite the statehood-boom urge to convert acreage into income-producing real estate and the pressure of 85 percent of the state's population needing housing and office and work space on Oahu, Honolulu became a city where joggers could run through almost any neighborhood and find green peace and shade.

Iwilei, the old red-light district, was now the Dole pineapple cannery and the Salvation Army depot, an industrial zone. Massage parlors abounded on Hotel Street and along the fringes of Waikiki. Prostitutes roamed the tourist tráffic of Kalakaua Avenue. Bars, particularly Korean bars, offered accommodating girls who would sit with patrons while they enjoyed a few drinks. The onetime elegance of the Royal Hawaiian Hotel was due for possible demolition as statehood's twentieth birthday was celebrated. Airspace in Waikiki had become as valuable as the square footage on which a hotel sat. The only way to go was up in this pleasantly palm-shaded "concrete jungle" along the famous surfing beach whose fabled white sand was now brought in by the bargeload from Molokai.

Aloha Tower, the landmark at the old Matson Terminal where a more leisured generation of tourists had steamed in to watch island boys dive for coins tossed into the harbor, was dwarfed by the new construction surrounding it. Few steamers called at Honolulu in these days of fast jet travel that brought nearly four million tourists a year from the mainland states, from Canada and Mexico, from Europe, Japan, all the world. From the West Coast cities of San Francisco and Los Angeles, the one-time five days by Matson liner was now less than five hours' flying time. Fares were low enough so that the average Mr. and Mrs. and Ms. America, older tourists who had dreamed of this trip as they listened to "Hawaii Calls" on their radios in the thirties and forties, and younger ones who knew the islands from the popular television series "Hawaii Five-O" could and did afford the trip. As many as thirty thousand Japanese tourists spent their year-end bonus and celebrated the New Year with a five-day jaunt to Hawaii from Tokyo.

Weddings were a popular feature of these New Year excursions from Japan, and Buddhist temples like Bishop Yoshiaki Fujitani's gracious Taj Mahal–inspired Honpa Hongwanji Mission on Pali Highway performed numerous ceremonies for Buddhist visitors. The Japanese Language Schools attached to many temples were no longer so well attended. Third and fourth generation Americans of Japanese ancestry, *sansei* and *yonsei*, were curious about their cultural roots but they were Hawaiian and American in their interests and feelings. As was the case in much of America and across Europe, church attendance in the islands dropped. Membership tended to be a diffident affair for many Buddhists and Christians. Ecumenical services were held each Thanksgiving, with Catholic, Protestant, Buddhist, and Unitarian ministers and congregations participating. Mormons were numerous, especially among Hawaiians and Samoans, with a large, beautiful Mormon temple on Beretania Street, near Punahou, and the Mormon Zion of Hawaii flourishing on the windward side of Oahu at Laie, where the Mormon's Polyne-

sian Cultural Center was a major tourist attraction. Father Bachelot's original kiawe was long gone, but its descendants had
spread throughout the islands, and Niihau's dry, sandy low
areas, the hot, dry South Kohala coast of the Big Island, Molokai, and Maui had forests of these thorny mesquites. In downtown Honolulu, on the very land where the original Catholic
Mission settled in 1829, Our Lady of Peace Cathedral stands at
the end of Fort Street Shopping Mall. Out King Street, Kawaiahao Church, that venerable coral stone edifice built by Hiram
Bingham as the largest building in the islands, is still a part of
island history and of contemporary island life. It is the nucleus
of Hawaiian Congregationalists, and in the 1970s its pastor, the
Reverend Abraham Akaka, whose brother is U.S. Congressman
Daniel K. Akaka, was a Hawaiian who counted among his ancestors some of the Amoy men from Fukien province who had
arrived in 1852–1853 with Captain Cass on the *Thetis*.

By 1959, Honolulu's former duckponds between Kakaako
and Waikiki had been filled and were the foundation for what is
advertised as the world's largest shopping center: Ala Moana,
with 164 stores on three levels, cooled by the natural flow of the
tradewinds, embellished with outdoor art, landscaping, sun-
screens, and fishponds, and girdled with expansive parking lots.
No longer, with statehood, were island consumers locked in to
island retail stores. Sears, Kress, Woolworth, Ben Franklin, and
J.C. Penney were among the mainland retail chains established in
Hawaii. Shirokiya of Tokyo was the first of the Japanese department stores to open, in Ala Moana Center. Liberty House, that
pre–World War I German-owned firm, was an AmFac subsidiary far more profitable than most plantations. Its fashionable
department store branches opened on Kauai, Maui, and the Big
Island's Kona Coast. Like Dillingham, Castle and Cooke, C.
Brewer, and other prestigious island corporations, Liberty
House ventured into merchandising outside Hawaii in the
1970s, taking over the old City of Paris department store in
downtown San Francisco and opening a number of California
branches.

The World War II position assumed by Hawaii as second
only to Alaska in cost of living and consumer prices was not

lost with statehood. Water and air freight rates continued to push island prices higher than almost anywhere else. New residents gasped at the cost of eggs, dairy products, and fresh produce, but were relieved to have been freed of the mainland burdens of fuel cost to heat houses and clothing costs for a seasonal wardrobe. In general, incomes had risen along with prices. During the first ten years of statehood, personal incomes for the average citizen in Hawaii increased by 76.8 percent and the state led the nation in the number of women workers. The second ten years continued the pattern of rising incomes that still bought less as inflation made the once high prices of each of the world wars seem very low by comparison with the attrition of the peacetime dollar.

In 1969, union lobbyists walking from office to office in the party atmosphere of opening day at the state legislature, spoke of the gains Hawaii labor had won since World War II. A forty-hour week had been established by state law. The minimum wage had climbed from $0.40 an hour to $1.40. Unemployment compensation, now extended to all workers, had risen from $25 to $86 a week. Maximum weekly disability payments had similarly been increased from $25 a week to $112.50. Maternity-leave benefits were guaranteed to women workers. Sick leave benefits and group medical coverage were secured. Many plantations, such as Kohala Sugar Company, Father Bond's old missionary firm that was now a Castle and Cooke subsidiary, were dismantling housing camps in 1969 and offering employees one-third-acre house lots for one dollar. Industrial compensation cases were reviewed by a board where labor was well represented. Temporary disability insurance paid 55 percent of an average weekly wage. Employee pension plans supplemented social security retirement income, and for those Filipino workers who wished to retire back in their home *barrio* in the Philippines, repatriation and a retirement settlement were provided.

Plantation labor and dockworkers were no longer the majority voice in union concerns. The most powerful union and during the decade of the 1970s the major political force in Hawaii was HGEA (Hawaii Government Employees Association) and its blue-collar friend, UPW (United Public Workers). In 1958, there had been 21,000 territorial and county employees. By 1968, state government employees and those at the county levels totaled 34,000. By 1979, HGEA claimed a membership of 21,000. More than 9,000 teachers in the public schools of the state exercised their collective bargaining rights (provided in the Public Employees Collective Bargaining Law, the nation's first) through HSTA, Hawaii State Teachers Association, which co-operated in political action with the government employees union.

After the war, *nisei* veterans returning home with a GI bill education had been willing to take low-paid government positions—sometimes because of the security offered by civil service, sometimes because not that many private firms were yet willing to hire non-*haole* professional employees. With union pressure and political clout and with the advent of public employees' collective bargaining early in the 1970s, the salaries of such government workers climbed to a scale higher than that offered by private industry. Affirmative action was called for in loud voices by newcomers to the state and by those who either no longer held or never had held government jobs. New *haoles,* some *kamaaina haoles,* Hawaiians, and Filipinos led the affirmative action protests of the late 1970s against the visibly *nisei* majority of those holding white-collar and professional jobs in public employment. Paradox: Americans of Japanese ancestry had just accomplished their own affirmative action, a process that took twenty years of statehood to accomplish. Their increase was from a prewar level of 1.7 percent representation in government jobs by a then 40 percent level of their ethnic group in the islands' population.

In the first two decades of statehood, with the out-migration of second and third generation AJAs, and a net in-migration of 4,500 new residents a year from the mainland, from Canada, from the Philippines, Samoa, and southeast Asia, the population balance of the state was still such that no one ethnic group was a majority. The 1970 census showed a total population gain of 28.1 percent for Hawaii, and the floodtide of in-migration continued at increasing rates with new people from Canada, Alaska, the mainland states, Korea, Hong Kong, the Philip-

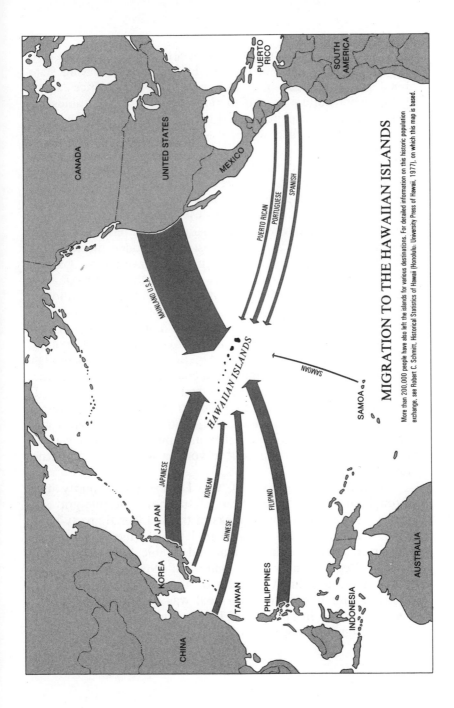

MIGRATION TO THE HAWAIIAN ISLANDS

More than 200,000 people have also left the islands for various destinations. For detailed information on this historic population exchange, see Robert C. Schmitt, Historical Statistics of Hawaii (Honolulu: University Press of Hawaii, 1977), on which this map is based.

pines, Samoa, and increasing numbers of Southeast Asian refugees. The 165.3 percent increase in construction during statehood's first decade provided new housing, office space, government buildings, and tourist facilities. Voice cables and communication satellites linked the fiftieth state with the East-West worlds between which it was a bridge in transport, finance, investment, education, tourism, and cultural interchange.

Those who cried out that Hawaii—and particularly Honolulu—was ruined had never seen or smelled Honolulu in 1846, never choked on the dust from its narrow streets in 1820, never lived in a plantation camp in the early nineteenth century, never known the restrictiveness and tensions of the territorial regime for many of Hawaii's people. Nostalgia clouded the reality of how things had been in 1916 when Charmian London observed that Hawaii was a paradise—but only for the well-to-do. The basic ability policy of the Democratic political revolution of 1954 had been implemented. With statehood, doors were opened to new ideas, new dreams, new industries, as well as to new people. The removal of barriers to Asian immigration and the naturalization of Asian-born Americans in the 1960s brought Hawaii's *nisei* Gold Star mothers a chance to become citizens of the country for which their sons had sacrificed their lives. In 1968, the constitutional convention that the law mandates be held every ten years in the islands proposed lowering the voting age in the state to eighteen, a measure approved by an electorate no longer so eager to turn out to vote as when that had been a rare privilege.

Politically, the power of the Democratic majority held throughout the first twenty years of statehood, despite grave internal dissension within the ranks of the Democratic party in the state. The first elected governor in 1959 was the territory's last appointed governor, the popular and affable Castle and Cooke lawyer, Republican William Quinn. In 1962, former congressional delegate John A. Burns won the governorship, and was re-elected for three terms. His goal was a new Hawaii, a concept elaborated in all three of his inaugural speeches—a statehood design that under him led to profound changes in structure, personnel, and philosophy of Hawaii's government. Environmental protection, consumer protection, a pioneer land-use commission, zoning of the state's lands into categories of industrial, agricultural, urban, resort, and conservation, were instituted, often over the loud protests of large landowners who lamented the freewheeling days of territoriality.

Governor Burns made *kokua* the basis for a new, surprisingly co-operative relationship among a Big Five who did not relish the political power of labor, labor who did not want any return to the economic stranglehold of the big corporations before statehood, and government who enlisted both labor and management to participate in building the new Hawaii. His critics condemned him as "Stone Face." His supporters, with affection, called him "the Old Man." Nonpartisan onlookers acknowledged him as a statesman. During his twelve years in office, new and improved airports, roads, schools, a statewide community college system, a satellite four-year campus of the University of Hawaii in Hilo, vast expansion to the university's Manoa campus, flowed out of the capital improvements budget appropriated by a Democratic legislature whose aspirations were identical with those of Burns. Unlike the previous territorial government, the Burns administration emphasized public participation—from a public that seldom had that chance before. Citizens who served on public boards and commissions were, by law, reimbursed for their public service time by their employers. The voter turnout dropped each election, not so much from apathy but from a lack of interest in doing things any differently from statehood's status quo. Yet, there were more elective offices—51 seats in the state House, 25 in the state Senate, the membership of each of the four county councils, the mayors of each county, the governor and lieutenant governor, two United States congressmen, and two U.S. senators. In 1966 the Board of Education, which since 1846 had supervised the unique centralized public school system of the islands, became elective. In 1974 the State Board of Education was the target of a judicial one man–one vote ruling so that it became the only political entity to accurately reflect the population patterns of the state: seven members elected at large from the island of Oahu and two elected at large to represent all six populated neighbor islands.

In 1965, as Governor Burns walked with a *Honolulu Advertiser* reporter from the governor's mansion to a downtown barbershop, he pointed with pride at what to him, and to many of the state's residents was the most important project of statehood's building boom. A huge excavation gaped where once the royal barracks and nearby the National Guard Armory had stood. This was the site of the new state capitol. In the groundbreaking ceremony, Burns had used an authentic *oo*, an ancient Hawaiian digging stick, borrowed for the occasion from the Bernice P. Bishop Museum. Burns told the reporter, in a voice choked with an emotion this taciturn man did not usually display, that for him the new capitol symbolized a new Hawaii that would be the financial, trade, cultural, and educational hub of the Pacific—one of the scientific research centers of the world in cloud physics, astronomy, geothermal energy, volcanology, and oceanography. By 1969, the new capitol was in use: a handsome five-story concrete structure that seemed to float on the reflecting pools mirroring the slim pillars that soared like the trunks of royal palms to support the overhanging roof. Its architects had known and felt Hawaii. The heart of the building was a great open court, its ceiling the cloud-studded blue sky by day, the star-studded heavens by night.

House and Senate chambers were volcano shaped, one on either side of the courtyard whose center was paved with a handsome mosaic, "Hawaiian sea and sky," the creation of island artist Tadashi Sato. At each of the open entrances to the central court, the bronze seal of the state hung, with the motto proclaimed by Kamehameha III in his July 31, 1843, thanksgiving service at Kawaiahao: *Ua mau ke ia o ka aina i ka pono,* "The life of the land is preserved in righteousness." On the Beretania Street entrance to the capitol stands a statue of Father Damien, who died serving the lepers at Kalaupapa, Molokai. Inside the capitol, handsome art—the 1 percent of construction allocated by Hawaiian statute—embellishes the offices of the governor and lieutenant governor. Their koa-paneled executive suites are on opposite sides of the capitol's upper story. On the second, third, and fourth floors, balconies look down on the central courtyard and up at the open sky. The one lack is that nowhere in this most stunning capitol building of any state in the Union is there a tribute to the Hawaiians whose lands these islands once were. A fifty-thousand-dollar appropriation to fund a statue of Queen Liliuokalani was in the limbo of "funds not yet released" as the state that was once the Kingdom of Hawaii celebrated its twentieth birthday in 1979.

To the tourists who have become the state's number one industry, and to the local population who still pride themselves on the family-style, first-name basis of their government, it is fitting that the new capitol is here in the historic heart of Hawaii's past. *Mauka,* across Beretania Street, is Washington Place, former residence of Hawaii's last queen, now the mansion of Hawaii's governors. *Makai,* toward King Street, screened from the new capitol by an enormous banyan tree, is Iolani Palace, handsomely restored as a museum. On its grounds, the bandstand where King Kalakaua was crowned is still used for the inauguration of Hawaii's governors. In 1974, George R. Ariyoshi fulfilled Charmian London's 1916 prediction, becoming the first governor of Japanese ancestry. He and his cabinet, a multiracial balance of Hawaiian, Portuguese, Chinese, Filipino, Japanese, and *haole,* walked between maile leis on the palace grounds for the 1974 inaugural, and did so again after his re-election in 1978. Each Friday noon, the bandstand is in regular use—a public free concert given to all who care to sit on the grass and listen, by the Royal Hawaiian Band. Within sight of the palace grounds is Kawaiahao Church, where the Hawaiian women keened their lament on Annexation Day, 1898. Adjacent to it is the original mission compound where the Reverend Hiram Bingham and his colleagues took their meals in the cool basement and carried their water from distant Punahou Spring. The entire compound and the printing press on which the first Hawaiian spelling sheet was run off in 1822 are now part of the Hawaiian Mission Houses Museum. On King Street, a block toward the old Spanish-style federal building and post office, the replica of a statue commissioned by King Kalakaua stands in front of Aliiolani Hale, the state's judiciary building, which has undergone a history-conscious renovation. The statue is of King Kamehameha I, uniter of the Hawaiian Kingdom. The original, salvaged from a wreck in the Falkland Islands, is on the courthouse lawn in Kapaau, Kohala, the heart of the district of Kamehameha's birthplace. Within a four-block area around Honolulu's replica of Kamehameha the Great one can stroll through the history of this kingdom and, having done so, be better ready to appreciate the major phenomenon of statehood: the Hawaiian renaissance.

Within the first two decades of statehood, the Hawaiians (by modern definition, those with any Hawaiian ancestor) had not only survived but revived in numbers and spirit. Theirs was the most pleasant paradox of island history: the cultural, political, and demographic resurgence of a people whose extinction had been so long predicted that in 1898 they had come close to accepting the future certainty of their own demise. By 1979, and the bicentennial of their ancestors' first western contact, their culture had made its impact on each of the foreign immigrant groups who came to make the Hawaiian Islands their home.

Hawaiian music, the rhythm of the hula, the moving cadence of ancient chants, are again eagerly learned, practiced, and performed—not as tourist entertainment, but in a genuine return to the dance and chant as one of the ritual celebrations of life. Hawaiian canoes, slender outriggers, glide again on island waters in a renewal of canoe paddling and canoe racing as a popular sport. In 1976, the *Hokulea* (Star of Gladness), a great twin-hulled, mat-sailed outrigger lovingly fashioned as authentically as was possible, was taken by a Hawaiian crew, using Hawaiian navigation techniques, on the long voyage of their ancestors— back and forth to Tahiti. The ancient technology, abandoned by the Hawaiians themselves, was being rediscovered in this last quarter of the twentieth century by young Hawaiians and those who felt Hawaiian by emotional allegiance as a symbol of the rediscovery of pride in the culture so denigrated by Bingham and his fellow missionaries after 1820.

The Hawaiian language, still spoken on the island of Niihau, permeates the English and pidgin vocabularies of modern islanders. Place, street, and building names are predominantly Hawaiian. Island directions are still Hawaiian: not east, west, south, or north, but *mauka* (toward the mountains) or *makai* (toward the sea). Hawaiian studies has been accepted as an academic discipline on the University of Hawaii campus. Hawaiiana is a required course in island public schools. Above all, the ancient Hawaiian values of aloha, *kokua,* and *aloha aina* have during the course of two centuries become dominant values in Hawaii nei. Paradoxically, at the same time that their own culture was universally recognized as the unifying culture of the fiftieth state, as Hawaiians shucked off that old missionary burden of a "dark past," contemporary Hawaiians were banding together to petition that the 1980 census count them in the "native Americans" category!

As statehood brought change to the Hawaiian psyche and change to every area of the islands and island life, there began a divisive feeling between those who were "local"—island born, long-time residents—and newcomers. It was, as with that old missionary prejudice against socializing with Hawaiians, a subtle, elusive feeling, and yet it was there. The family-style "local" society politely lives with newcomers and tourists but has been increasingly reluctant to let them become "insiders." Part of the schism has been the tendency of many new residents to cloister themselves in expensive, tight-security condominiums, frequent private clubs for recreation, lead the kind of exclusively *haole* social life observed by Charmian London in the Honolulu of 1916, and join the ranks of the nearly defunct Republican party. Many mainland newcomers are told that *haole* children will not be happy in public schools, to choose Punahou or one of the numerous private schools that abound throughout the state. And the long-haired "hippie" type young *haole* is likewise an "outsider." The old myth of separatism that was a fact of plantation Hawaii dies hard with statehood. Neither political party claims to woo membership from any particular ethnic group, but the impression often given newcomers is that in Hawaii, most *haoles* are Republican. Those who give this impression never knew, or have forgotten, about Lincoln McCandless, Delbert Metzger, federal judge Martin Pence,

former Senate president David McClung, former U.S. congressman Tom Gill, present U.S. congressman Cecil Heftel, and
above all they have forgotten about John A. Burns. By the same
token, the Republican party is also multiracial, with active
members like state senators Pat Saiki and Wadsworth Yee, Representatives Donna Ikeda, Ralph Ajifu, and former U.S. senator
Hiram L. Fong.

To those who have had little or no contact with Hawaiian history, aloha in 1979 seemed a superficial, commercially oriented
veneer. "Hawaii Five-O," the popular television series by
which much of the world has become familiar with the climate,
the scenery, the people, and the crime in the Aloha State, was
all too evocative of an island (including neighbor islands) society where everyone now locks doors, where car thefts are all too
common, where rapes, mugging, and vandalism approached the
rate of mainland American communities, and where, in the first
seven months of 1979, there were thirty-three bank robberies on
Oahu alone. The newest, most profitable agricultural crop in the
state's economy was illegal. On the Big Island, rumor was that
marijuana was more profitable in the 1970s than had been sugar
in its best boom years. Islanders differed little from their fellow
Americans of the continental United States in that, while deplor-
ing crime, graft, and corruption, many shrugged and went after
the fast, illegal dollar themselves. Paradoxically it was the Hawaiians, who formed the majority in Oahu's prison population,
who were leading the movement for finding solutions to the
islands' problems: too much crime, seemingly too many people,
apparently too little aloha. What emerged from the statehood
construction boom appeared as a threat to the beauty and tran-
quility that has always balanced the negative aspects of life in
this Aloha State.

In the 1970s, the Hawaiian-ness of Hawaii suddenly became
precious to most who live here, and with a tenacity and aggres-
siveness that surprised their critics, islanders of Hawaiian ancestry actively staked their political claims and announced their
goals. They were again to be, as they had been in 1779, at the
vanguard of the real change, the change in psychological climate of these islands that had since statehood experienced

marked environmental, population, economic, and social trans-
formation.

In 1971, at a Governor's Conference on New Communities
held in Honolulu at the Ilikai Hotel, state planning and economic development director Shelley Mark outlined three alter-
natives that were options for the state's future. He labeled this
triad of choices: "Hawaii Unleashed," "Hawaii Primaeval,"
and "Balance Is Beautiful." "Hawaii Unleashed" was what
developers and real estate speculators urged under the guise of
letting free enterprise take its natural course. "Hawaii Primaeval" was the antidote, the far swing of the development pendulum urged by conservationists like the extremely active organization, Life of the Land. "Hawaii Unleashed" could, Dr. Mark
proposed, result in islands that were shore-line ranks of high
rises, the loss of prime agricultural lands that were also a scenic
treasure to assure the continuance of the tourist industry, and a
society where there might be little room for the local, middle-
class family to survive.

"Hawaii Primaeval" ignored the need of the state's people to
use land and its other resources, to continue prosperity, and to
attract island youngsters to return home. "Balance Is Beautiful"
was the state government's choice under Burns, with vast tracts
of land taxed at an extremely low rate to keep them undeveloped and other areas given state assistance in zoning
change, building roads, and providing water to stimulate hotel,
resort, or subdivision developments. On Maui, with a supportive county government and the stimulus of so many Canadian
investors and residents that the island gained the nickname "Little Canada," the once lonely beaches of Kihei and Kaanapali
became tenanted in one decade with strips of resort and con-
dominium development. On the Big Island, where Parker Ranch
owned more land than was in the entire Hawaiian Homes Commission (200,000 acres), and where Bishop Estate held title to
vast acreages as did the Liliuokalani Trust, an initial subdivision
boom on the lava slopes of Puna and south Kona in the 1960s
stung the county government into caution. Their planner, Ray-
mond Suefuji, later director of Oahu's Kakaako Redevelopment
plans, was a "Balance Is Beautiful" advocate. The continuance

of open space and wide vistas, of few high rises on that island, continued to hold the "Balance Is Beautiful" option open for Hawaii County as the twentieth anniversary of statehood was celebrated with a week end of festivities in Kamehameha's ancient capital, the pleasant modern resort village of Kailua-Kona.

As Hawaii entered her third century of modern history, the "new wave" of philosophic leadership was the Hawaiians—whom Congress had sought to rehabilitate in 1919 with the passage of the Hawaiian Homes Act, dedicating 200,000 acres of island lands for award as farmsites and house lots to those with at least one half Hawaiian ancestry. The problem was that although the idea originated with congressional delegate Prince Jonah Kuhio, and although his intentions were of the best for his people, the Hawaiian Homes project was a paternalistic method of rehabilitation that did nothing to restore the cultural identity or cultural confidence of the Hawaiians. Throughout the territorial era they kept being confronted, as they had since 1820, by the seeming superiority of *haole* religion, lifestyle, and sexual mores. They lived, worked, worshipped, studied, and survived under a *haole* dominance whose emphasis on material success and competition was in no way compatible with their own innate cultural emphasis on co-operation and day-to-day living.

In the angry words of a Hawaiian scholar who administered the program in the early years of statehood, lands set aside for the Hawaiian Homes Commission were, in general, more suitable for the rehabilitation of goats than of Hawaiians. Yet, poor as much of the land was, the waiting list for homesteads was so long that a lottery method was used to award them. Ninety-nine-year leases were given for only one dollar a year, but the improvement costs were so high that many Hawaiian families became heavily mortgaged in the development of sites not worth their initial investment. Others, like homesteaders on Molokai, could only manage by leasing their lands to the pineapple company and thus the livelihood and return to the soil envisioned for them, and by them, was circumvented by the large-scale agricultural development to which the island economy was geared.

The paradox was that all these years while their "rehabilitation'' was being discussed, the Hawaiians had quietly chosen to rehabilitate themselves, to abandon the attempt to adopt the foreign culture of the *haole*, and simply, openly to be themselves. Their rallying cry was *aloha aina*, a Hawaiian phrase seldom heard until the late 1970s, and never before one of the Hawaiian terms that had become natural to island vocabularies. Those other natural adaptations of Hawaiian gave the islands a unique flavor which continues to charm tourist visitors. For example, *kane* and *wahine* are on public toilet doors, rather than "men" and "women." An islander does not say he is "finished" with a meal or task. He (she) is *pau*—pronounced "pow." *Pau hana* time is when the working day ends. *Holoholo* is just going around for relaxation and recreation. A child is a *keiki*. Delicious food (*kau kau*) is *ono*. A stranger is a *malihini*. An oldtimer is a *kamaaina*. But with the exception of "aloha," the value words of Hawaiian were rarely heard by visitors. Locals used and understood *kokua*. Their use and understanding of "aloha" differed subjectively—and in depth and range—from the casual commercial use of that word as a greeting in the tourist industry or as a television commercial from the legislatively funded Hawaii Visitors Bureau pleading with local people to keep "aloha" alive. "Aloha," protested islanders like Lois Fukuda Yoon, (a *sansei* married to a Korean, but equally *haole* and Hawaiian in her cultural outlook), "is part of me. It's my spirit. I was born with it. How can that go away?"

It was this strong subjective value-dimension of aloha that was embraced by the rallying cry of the Hawaiian renaissance: *aloha aina*. In 1979 as it had in 1779, it meant respect for the *mana* of the land of these islands and for the life the land sustains.

The Hawaiian resurgents chose as their first target for Hawaiian achievement the freeing of the single island that after World War II remained the province of the military. Kahoolawe had always been a small, lonely island. Semiarid. Strewed with sites of ancient Hawaiian *heiau* (temples) and settlements that may well have been seasonal. Bingham's exiled adulterers and adulteresses had managed to survive there. In the records of the kingdom, a public school is listed in operation on Kahoolawe during the nineteenth century. Much of its natural vegetation has been denuded by goats, from the period when it was used as a ranch, before World War II. All the postwar years, Maui residents had flinched at the possibility of near misses as bombers flew in from Texas and from a height of forty thousand feet dropped live bombs on the island target, only six miles from Maui's shores. There was a brief furor when a bomb was found in former Maui mayor Elmer Cravalho's cattle pasture. But it remained for the Hawaiians in the 1970s to do something about the situation. They selected Kahoolawe as the symbol of *aloha aina,* and in continuing and effective protest demonstrations demanded the liberation of this Hawaiian island from military use and military jurisdiction.

Daring the combined might of the armed services and the political threats of generals and admirals, young Hawaiians landed on Kahoolawe to protest the continuance of the bombing at the risk of their lives. One Hawaiian, George Helms, died in the rough waters off Kahoolawe. Sometimes overtly, sometimes only emotionally in support of the "Free Kahoolawe" movement were many *sansei* and *yonsei,* many young islanders (and some not so young) of Chinese, Korean, Puerto Rican, Portuguese, Filipino ancestry and many *haole* people. Most of the latter were young, long-haired, and vocal like the Democratic legislator Neil Abercrombie whom the voters support, but the Democratic establishment of the 1970s decried. A mix of such islanders, but predominantly Hawaiians, were in the *ohana,* the group formed to demonstrate, protest, and actively campaign for return of Kahoolawe to state government jurisdiction and public access. It was a new kind of identification for the state's community, a unification around shared values such as Professor Bernhard Hormann had predicted in his *Social Process* article, "The Caucasian Minority," in 1950. That unification had the potential of becoming the focus of political, social, and economic decisions shaping the future of Hawaii and contributing important ideals to revitalize the entire American society.

The Protect Kahoolawe Ohana, like the Coalition of Hawaiian People and A.L.O.H.A.—the association for return or reparation of Hawaiian lands—signaled the Hawaiian shift from political apathy to an activism that involved Hawaiians of every age and economic status. Political affiliation was of minor importance in goals sought by the Congress of the Hawaiian People and Alu Like, the federally funded project designed to encourage, promote, and protect the culture of Hawaiians who in the eyes of the federal government are a disadvantaged minority in their own state. As is characteristic of any movement of this scope, there were and continue to be internal disagreements on method and timing and leadership, but the essential is that the different Hawaiian groups are not competing, but cooperating in a spirit of *aloha aina*.

In their push for land reparation claims, it was the crown lands that were the rightful personal property of Hawaii's last queen that are at issue, as well as the settlement by Congress of that old unsettled issue of 1893 and the petition of Queen Liliuokalani to the United States government: redress for loss of both dominion and sovereignty that was wrested from her by force and again in 1895 on her abdication, which was forced under duress. In its way, this claim too is a focus on *aloha aina* and a reminder to the nation to which Hawaii has belonged throughout this twentieth century that the fundamental ideals on which America is based continue to be viable for all parts of the Union, continental and extracontinental. The right to liberty and justice for all is neither exclusively nor discriminatingly guaranteed in the Constitution of the United States.

One of the foci for protest by Hawaiian activists was the misuse and abuse of some of the 200,000 acres of Hawaiian Homes lands, much of which had never been opened for award although the commission had been in existence for over half a century and the waiting list of Hawaiians petitioning for homesteads and homesites was long. On Labor Day 1978, some 200 Hawaiians, wearing maile leis and waving ceremonial ti leaves, marched onto the runways of Hilo International Airport to protest state use of 95 acres of Hawaiian Homes lands for which no rental had yet been paid the Hawaiian Homes Commission by the state, nor any equivalent land transfer for Hawaiian Homes use arranged. The televised account of that demonstration was reminiscent of the 1938 union-management confrontation on

Hilo's docks. This time, forty years later, a line of National Guardsmen faced the demonstrators with rifles and bayonets. Another line of riot-helmeted guardsmen bore down on the Hawaiians, riot sticks poised against resolute faces and garlands of fragrant maile—a green vine which is the symbol of high rank and special dignity or special occasion.

Some of the guardsmen had no heart for the orders they had been given. These were local men, Hawaiians many of them, and as the demonstrators approached waving their ti leaves, a calm intensity of emotion steadying their lines, one of the guardsmen pulled off his helmet, threw down his riot stick, and joined the demonstrators. No violence occurred, Governor Ariyoshi noted in a news interview on television that night.

For the Hawaiians, for the state as a whole, for *kamaaina* and *malihini*, local and newcomer and visitor, Hawaii's 1979 bicentennial of Cook's first western contact brought a positive sense of cultural renewal. *Aloha aina* was a long-overdue keystone to the development of a new Hawaii where respect and balance, rather than exploitation, might be the framework for political and economic decisions in this island state.

The questions asked by Professor Hart in 1906 as to the set of problems posed to national ideals by the acquisition of Hawaii in 1898 had been answered by time, by the achievement of statehood, by the very fact of the Hawaiian Renaissance and its values unification of a substantial portion of the island community. Islanders had become an integral part of America and the American Dream.

History rarely has the tidiness of fiction. Endings and beginnings are rarely discernible. Solutions to old problems pose new ones. So, as Hawaii began its third century of modern history there were new, perhaps temporary, questions to pose.

The question of local versus newcomers was one of a social process in Hawaii that had been happening with an alternation of tensions and harmony, and often a concurrent experience of tensions and harmony, over the previous 200 years. Could aloha continue its effectiveness here?

The question of personal and public safety could not be answered simply by locking doors and hiring security guards. Might community-wide *kokua* be the answer?

The matter of population controls, of continuing construction boom eating up canelands with subdivisions and clogging beach areas with hotels and condominiums, of the long-range problems of water resource from the limited water tables of the islands and the question of an economy based on air transport of tourists in an energy-crunch future—could state or federal legislative controls here be effective in a climate where investors and developers pushed for laissez faire?

The openness of the Open Society that was the ambition of the Burns administration and the legacy of Governor Ariyoshi's two terms was being questioned by Filipinos and Samoans as well as by Hawaiians, Koreans, refugee Southeast Asians, and—paradoxically—by *haoles* who as a group had once themselves closed political and economic doors.

The dynamics shaping America's fiftieth state were not strange or new: the rights of individuals in a democratic society—life, liberty, and the pursuit of happiness. These were the basic American influence that had molded Hawaii for 200 years as, in turn, the Hawaiian influence of aloha, *kokua,* and *aloha aina* could mold the attitudes of fellow Americans in Hawaii's sister forty-nine states, in the commonwealth of Puerto Rico, and the overseas possessions like American Samoa where local government still struggled through the gap between democratic ideals as taught and as practiced by a federal government.

In 1980, these were, still, Hawaiian islands—as lovely a fleet as ever lay anchored in the sea. They epitomize the cosmopolitan nature of America at its most idealistic, and extend America's own idealism by the Hawaii State Constitution's proclamation of "an open heart toward all the peoples of the world."

In contemporary Hawaii, to be Hawaiian—whether by blood, residence, or cultural allegiance is a highly emotional choice. Disharmony, ardent and occasionally violent protest, the clash of ideals and values, struggle for political and economic advantage, are dominant strands of past history and present experi-

ence. It is, when you understand that history and this experience, no paradox that for most of us who live here, the aloha
spirit continues to be real and deeply felt. It is Hawaiian. It is an
East-West cultural awareness. It is American at America's idealistic best.

Could it be, despite the freeways, the high rises, the exhaust
fumes, the crime rate, the generation gaps, the tensions, and the
contentions, that Hawaii is still—and can continue to be—a paradise?

Suggestions for Further Reading

A Texas friend of mine has every room in his house lined with shelves to hold his collection of books about Hawaii, but even so he has only a portion of the Hawaiiana published in the past 190 years. My personal recommendation to those wishing to read further about our islands, their history, culture, and peoples, is to begin with the following.

Ralph S. Kuykendall's three-volume history, *The Hawaiian Kingdom,* published by the University of Hawaii Press, Honolulu, is by far the most reliable, comprehensive work of its kind, and is both scholarly and well written. Volume 1 is *1778–1854, Foundation and Transformations.* Volume II is *1854–1874, Twenty Critical Years.* The third and final volume, which Kuykendall did not live to complete, himself, is *1874–1893, The Kalakaua Dynasty,* published in 1967. These three volumes were originally copyrighted in 1938, 1953, and 1967 respectively. The University of Hawaii Press brought out a new edition of Volume II in 1966 and of Volume I in 1969. The books were the fruits of a project begun in 1932 under the sponsorship of the Historical Commission of the Territory of Hawaii, to prepare a comprehensive general history, based on a thorough study of original resources available in Honolulu, the national archives of the United States, Great Britain and France, the archives of Belgium and Mexico and a number of libraries and collections in the United States.

Complementing this scholarly work are three books that give the Hawaiian view of the pre-Cook years and the early Kamehameha period. Samuel Kamakau, whose *Ruling Chiefs of Hawaii* was published by the Kamehameha Schools Press in Honolulu in 1961, was a Hawaiian who lived close enough to the old life to write of it with authenticity. His 430 pages of Hawaiian history range from the sixteenth-century ruling chief Umi to the death of Kamehameha III in 1854 and were written during and following the reign of Kamehameha III. A similar first-hand view is *Fragments of Hawaiian History,* recorded by John Papa Ii, translated by Mary Kawena Pukui and edited by Dorothy B. Barrère, a slim memoir of 167 pages published in Honolulu in 1959 by the Bishop Museum Press. *Hawaiian Antiquities* by David Malo details early Hawaiian culture and beliefs, published in 1951 by the Bishop Museum Press. For the most vivid account of Hawaii's first Christian missionaries, I like Albertine Loomis's *Grapes of Canaan, Hawaii 1820* (Honolulu: Hawaiian Mission Childrens Society, 1951). Eleanor Davis's fine biography *Abraham Fornander* (Honolulu: University Press of Hawaii, 1979) is an excellent, beautifully written, and extremely well-researched account of a key person in Hawaii's history during the years 1844 to 1887.

Alfons Korns's *The Victorian Visitors* (Honolulu: University of Hawaii Press, 1958), *Northern California, Oregon and the Sandwich Islands* by Charles Nordhoff, reissued by Ten Speed Press in 1974, and Isabella Bird Bishop's *Six Months in the Sandwich Islands* (Honolulu: University Press of Hawaii, 1964; reprint ed., Rutland, Vt.: C. E. Tuttle, 1973) are charming portraits of the middle years of the Hawaiian Kingdom. *Hawaii's Story by Hawaii's Queen* is Liliuokalani's account of the last days of her kingdom (Rutland, Vt.: C. E. Tuttle, 1964). J. Garner Anthony's *Hawaii Under Army Rule* (Honolulu: The University Press of Hawaii, 1975) and Lawrence Fuchs's *Hawaii Pono: A Social History* (New York: Harcourt, Brace, and World, 1961) are the best glimpses of modern Hawaii.

For sheer pleasure, Kathleen Mellen's *The Lonely Warrior* (1944), *The Magnificent Matriarch* (1952), *The Gods Depart* (1956), *An Island Kingdom Passes* (1958), all published by Hastings House, New York, rank with my favorite bedside Hawaiiana: W. Storrs Lee's *Hawaii* (New York: Funk and Wagnall's 1967) and *A Hawaiian Reader* by A. Grove Day and Carl Stroven (New York: Appleton Century Crofts, 1957). Gavan Daws's *Shoal of Time* (New York: Macmillan, 1968) is also superb.

Index

Act for the Governance of Masters and Servants, 66
Admissions Day, 202
Ala Moana Shopping Center, 11, 75, 206
Alexander and Baldwin Co., 130
Alii (chiefs): representatives of gods, 12–13; in peace sessions, 14–15; and taboo, 18–19, 29–30, 31, 36; and Cook, 21; Great Kahola, 23–24; Kaiana, 25; *haole*, 25–27; Kaumualii, 27, 29–30, 31, 36; great wealth of, 32, 61, 198; uprisings of, 35; and direct hiring, 51–52; and cultural inferiority, 54–55; in legislature, 55; and land titles, 59, 61
Aliiolani Hale, 79, 214
Allen, Anthony (farmer), 32
Allen, Riley H. (editor), 156, 166, 170
Aloha aina: meaning of land and sea, 4, 13; chiefs turned from, 36; in modern terms, 203; in modern Hawaii, 215, 219, 221–222; in 1970s, 219
Aloha spirit: today, 3, 215, 219, 222, 224; and kinship, 12–13; and newcomers, 33, 36
American Board of Foreign Missions, 37
American Factors, 130, 135
American Federation of Labor (AFL): teamsters, 128, 152, 180; attempt to organize, 141; reputation of, 173; CIO merger, 185
American Protestant Mission, 71
Annexation: urged by American residents, 4–6, 63, 83; opposed by Hawaiians, 5, 63, 18; and Pearl Harbor, 6; opposed by Chinese, 7–8, 68; bill in Congress, 63; king's death, 64; and Committee of Safety, 99–102; and Japan, 108; Hawaiians declared to be Caucasian, 115, 120
Annexation Day, 5–10, 109–110

Arakaki, Yashuki (union leader), 186
Ariyoshi, George (governor), 213, 222
Ariyoshi, Koji: as publisher, 142, 192–193; as student, 154; in World War II, 162, 165, 168, 174
Asians. *See* Chinese; Filipinos; Japanese; Koreans; Okinawans; Polynesians; Samoans

Bayonet Constitution, 96, 99, 103
Bernice P. Bishop Museum, 94, 212. *See also* Bishop, Princess Bernice Pauahi
B. F. Ehlers and Co. (Liberty House), 135, 206
Big Five: monopoly of, 130, 200; and strikes, 139, 140; and steamer lines, 147; and Republicans, 148; and labor, 150; and business, 150; and commission government, 162; and service people, 168; and union, 190; in 1950s, 200–201; and *kokua*, 211; today, 217–218
Big Island (Hawaii): largest chiefdom, 15; Cook's visit, 20–21; and Kamehameha I, 23, 24; and taboo, 35; cotton on, 70; as county, 117; and labor, 126, 141, 173; department stores on, 205
Bill of Rights, Hawaiian, 52–53, 194
Bingham, Hiram (missionary leader), 37–38, 39–43, 45–48
Bishop, Princess Bernice Pauahi: suggested as heir to Kamehameha V, 76; founder of Kamehameha Schools, 94, 131; mentioned, 63
Bishop, Charles Reed: Princess Pauahi's husband, 63, 76, 94; as banker, 70; and sugar, 82, 86
Board of Commissioners to Quiet Land Title, 59, 61
British: Hawaii a protectorate of, 7, 26; Hawaii under provisional government

227

British (*Cont.*)
   of, 9, 56–57; and Cook, 16–22; colonial
   ambitions of, 23, 24, 25, 26; attack on
   Hawaii, 55–57; and reciprocity treaty,
   85. *See also* Tripartite Treaty
Buddhism: and Japanese, 123–137; Honpa
   Hongwanji Mission, 132, 205; temples,
   138, 166; Moiliili Hongwanji Mission
   and temple, 156, 171; and World War II,
   160, 168; ethic, 196
Burns, John Anthony: in public school,
   131; as policeman, 149, 153, 172; and
   Democratic party, 182, 185, 189–190,
   195–196; as congressional delegate,
   196–197, 199–202; as governor, 210–
   212, 216

California Feed Company, 141
Castle and Cooke, 70, 130, 144, 148–149,
   163, 206
Catholicism, 45–47, 52–53, 59, 205
Catton Neill Co. (foundry), 141
Caucasians, 3, 13, 115
C. Brewer Co., 130, 206
Chants, 9, 12, 36, 109
Chiefs. *See Alii*
Chinese: and annexation, 7–8; first resi-
   dent, 26, 32; and sugar, 32, 60, 86–88,
   90; and Hawaiians, 36; saved Honolulu,
   53; in 1845, 58; contract labor imported,
   66, 69–70, 75; wedding, 70; and rice, 75;
   fear of, 95; and licensing act, 103–106;
   and plague, 110–111; population in Ter-
   ritory, 115; in government, 118; and
   China politics, 122; as Christians, 137,
   138; as *alii,* 197
Chinese Exclusion laws, 7, 90, 114–115,
   123, 128
Christianity, 37–53, 55, 118
Cleveland, Grover (president), 5, 102–103
"Cognate races," 72, 73
Commission government, 146, 162
Committee of Safety, 99–102
Commoners. *See Makaainana*
Communist scare, 187–194
Congregationalists, 206
Congregation of the Order of the Sacred
   Heart of Jesus and Mary, 45
Congress of Industrial Organizations (CIO),
   173, 185

Constitution: of 1840, 53–54; of 1852, 65,
   71, 80; of 1864, 71, 80; of 1887
   (Bayonet Constitution), 96, 99, 103
Constitutional convention, 191
Contract labor, 7, 66, 69, 73, 120. *See also*
   Hawaii: labor; Plantations
Cook, James (captain), 3, 11, 14–22, 78
Coolies, 28, 69
Cotton 26, 27, 60, 70

Damien, Father. *See* DeVeuster, Damien
Democracy: and Chinese, 7–8; and Ameri-
   cans, 10; taught by Richards, 50, 51; and
   Kamehameha III, 52–53; and mis-
   sionaries, 54
Democrats: in 1900, 115; post-war build-
   ing, 182, 185; political victories, 187;
   communists and, 187, 189; "Hawaii
   Seven" and, 193; elections of 1954,
   194–196, 210; in 1970s, 215-216, 220
DeVeuster, Damian (Father Damien,
   priest), 96, 212
Diamond Head, 39, 109
Dillingham, Benjamin F., 74–75
Dillingham, Walter F., 139, 179, 201
Dole, Sanford Ballard: president of the
   republic, 8, 100, 101, 103–104, 108,
   109; as territorial governor, 114,
   115–116
Dole, Jim, 8, 130, 143, 147
Dole Pineapple Co., 8, 147, 163
Doukhubors, 120
Dutch, 23

Education. *See* Hawaii: education
Emma, Queen, 70, 76–77, 79, 81–84, 94
Emmons, Delos (lt. gen.), 164, 166–167,
   170, 172, 177
Ewa Plantation, 42, 126
Exile colonies, 47–48

Fair Labor Standards Act of 1938, 172
Farrington, Joseph R., 179, 187, 188, 195
Farrington, Wallace R. (governor), 141,
   143
Filipino Higher Wages Association, 141
Filipino Labor Union. *See* Manlapit, Pablo
Filipinos, 120, 136–138, 141–144, 198–
   199, 207
Flags: Kingdom of Hawaii, 6, 8–9, 28, 30,
   101, 104, 109, 114, 116; U.S., 9, 57,
   101, 103; Russian, 10, 28; British, 56

Fornander, Abraham (editor), 67, 68–69, 71, 72, 96

French: early visitors, 23, 32; colonial ambitions of, 26; Catholic mission, 45; insult to, 47; attacks by, 53, 62

Fujimoto, Charles (Communist party), 192

Fujitani, Yoshiaki, 156–158, 160, 166–167, 171–174, 181–182

General Order No. 91, 169, 172–173, 180, 183–184

Germans, 18, 74

Gibson, Walter Murray, 72, 81, 90, 95

Glockner and Seifert (prisoners), 174, 177, 178

Golovnin, Vassily (captain), 29–31

Great Britain. *See* British

Greater East Asia Co-Prosperity Sphere, 154

Great *Mahele,* The, 59–61

Green, Thomas H. (lt. col.), 162, 164–165, 170, 172, 181

Hall, Jack: and union, 149–150, 153, 173, 182, 186; in World War II, 172; and Communists, 187–188, 192, 193

Hamakua district, 35, 79, 136

Hana: district, 15; wharf, 141

Hanapepe (Kauai), 143

Haole: definition, 7, 13, 17, 22; and annexation, 83, 115; and statehood, 115

Hawaii: geography of, 3, 4, 12, 14–15, 39–40; first inhabitants of, 3, 11–15; and early foreigners, 13, 17, 24, 25; as paradise, 22, 33, 37; Chinese name for, 27; state motto, 57, 212. *See also* Cook, James (captain); Kamehameha

—agriculture: crops introduced, 12, 26, 32, 41, 75; livestock introduced, 32; exports, 60

—culture: ancient chants, 9, 12, 36, 109; and Kalakaua, 90; in 1970s, 214. *See also* Hawaiian-ness; Hawaiians; Language

—economy: sugar, 8, 32, 60, 68, 70, 85–86, 130, 146, 200; pineapple, 8, 130, 136, 143, 200; sandalwood, 27–28; whaling, 39, 68; rice, 75, 130; tourism, 75–76, 133, 143, 199–200, 213

—education: mission stations, 42; coeducation, 43, 79; mission press, 44–45; mis-

sion schools, 44, 54; literacy, 45; teaching Catholicism, 47; high school, 50, 53; political economy and chiefs, 51; department of, 58; private schools, 60, 88, 131; dual public school system, 62, 67, 69; Board of, 72, 110, 188; teaching in English and Hawaiian, 72, 96, 153; and Princess Pauahi, 94, 131; American ideals in, 117–118; Catholic high school, 131–132; Japanese Language Schools, 132, 137, 205; Japanese majority in public schools, 132; strikers' children and, 138; higher education, 149–150; GI after World War II, 181–182; in 1950s, 194; and statehood, 202; in 1970s, 211–212, 215

—government: Kingdom of Hawaii, 4–5, 23–56, 57–101; American provisional government (Republic of Hawaii), 4–5, 102–109, 115; British provisional government, 9, 57; chiefdoms, 14–15, 23, 26–27, 84, 116–117; Territory, 110–202; statehood, 203–224

—labor: Japanese and, 125–126; and management, 126–127, 129; strikes, 127, 129–130, 137–140, 141, 142, 149–150, 156–157; wage rates, 130, 136, 138–139, 140; and NLRB, 148–149; political clout of, 150, 185; teamsters' union, 152; Labor Department report on, 152–153; and General Order 91, 172–173; "Go for Broke" mood, 185; and ILWU demands, 186, 187; political victory, 187–188; since World War II, 207–208

—population: Polynesians, 3, 4, 12; in 1970s, 3–4; census, 7 (1896), 42 (1825), 151–152 (1940), 208 (1970), 215 (1980); in 1790s, 26; Hawaiians, 42, 52, 93; statehood requirement, 117, 119; in 1950s, 200

—postal service, 69, 118

—public health: venereal diseases, 18, 21, 42; *mai okuu* (cholera), 27; other foreign diseases, 42; death from trauma, 54; vaccination program, 67; smallpox, 67; leprosy, 69, 96; bubonic plague, 110–111; influenza, 138

—social life: in 1840s, 54–55; in 1850s, 70; in 1907, 133

Hawaii, University of: entrance require-

Hawaii, University of (*Cont.*)
ment, 150–151; student demonstrations, 154; ROTC, 156, 160, 166–167; and statehood, 202; in 1970s, 215
Hawaiian Commercial and Sugar Co. (HCSC), 86, 186
Hawaiian Evangelical Association, 71
Hawaiian Federation of Labor, 140
Hawaiian Homes Act, 116, 218, 221
Hawaiian-ness, 3–4, 216–224
Hawaiians: as "Native Americans," 4, 199, 214, 215; as minority, 5, 68–69, 119; foreign influences on, 21–22, 24–25, 30, 31, 33; work habits, 51–52; guilt of, 54
Hawaii Emergency Defense Act, 155, 158
Hawaii Employment Relations Act, 185
Hawaii Government Employees Association, (HGEA), 128, 185, 207–208
Hawaii Island. *See* Big Island
"Hawaii Seven," 192–194, 201
Hawaii State Teachers Association, 208
Hawaii Sugar Planters Association, 136–137, 139, 142–143
Heiau (temple), 20, 34, 36
H. Hackfeld and Co., 74, 130, 135
Hilo district: early visitors, 15, 17; Naha Stone in, 23–24; life in, 54–55; Hilo Bay, 79, 115, 117; and unions, 147–150, 186; attack on, 166, hotels, 200
Hilo Docks, Battle of, 150
Hispanic, 3, 26, 32
Home Rule party, 115–116
Honolulu: today, 4, 203–205, 206, 212–214; in 1898, 5–9, 109–110; in 1778, 14; as capital, 25–26, 38, 58, 111, 116–117; and Golovnin, 30; and Bingham, 39–41, 42, 45; capital moved, 51; foreign threats to, 53–54, 55–57, 62; in 1845, 57–58; waterfront, 68, 69, 180; in 1866, 75–76; in 1873, 78, 79; Chinatown in, 87, 110–111; in 1889, 97; in 1894, 104–107; and labor, 141, 149–150; attack, 154–163; statehood and, 197, 201; population of, 199; Admissions Day, 202. *See also* Big Island; Oahu; Pearl Harbor; Prostitution
Honolulu Federation of Trades, 128
Honolulu Rifles, 94–97, 101

Inter-Island Steamship Co., 141, 149

International Longshoremen's and Warehousemen's Union (ILWU), 128, 149, 152, 173, 185–190
International Workers of the World, 139–140
Iolani Palace: on Annexation Day, 5–8; building of, 90; as prison, 106–107; as governor's office, 146, 160; as military government headquarters, 162, 172; after World War II, 187, 202, 213
Iolani School, 88, 131
Issei, 122, 161
Italians, 32
Iwilei, 163, 169, 204

Japanese: on Annexation Day, 7; as "cognate" race, 73; as contract laborers, 74, 119–120, 125–127, 136–140; immigration of, 91, 115; prejudice, 122, 128, 129, 151–152; in World War II, 159–166, 181. *See also Issei; Kibei; Nisei; Yonsei*
Japanese Federation of Labor, 136–140
Japanese Higher Wage Association, 129
Judd, Gerret P. (missionary), 54, 59, 61–63, 67
Judd, Lawrence (governor), 146, 149

Kaahumanu (chiefess), 32, 34–35, 41–43, 45–46, 49–54
Kaanapali (Maui), 199–200, 217
Kahoolawe, 14, 47–48, 61, 117, 219–220
Kahunas (priests), 12–14, 18, 21, 36, 72
Kailua-Kona: capital, 26, 29, 32, 34; capital moved, 38, 117; resort village, 200, 218
Kaiulani, Princess, 116
Kakaako, 91, 123, 157
Kalakaua, David (king), 80–85, 88–98, 175, 213
Kalaniopuu (chief), 15, 20–21, 24
Kalaupapa (leper colony), 96, 117, 212
Kalihi: valley, 32; district, 131, 163, 169
Kamaaina, 153, 182, 219, 222
Kamehameha the Great; and his kingdom, 8, 23–24, 26–27, 32–33; as a youth, 19; and foreigners, 25–26, 28, 29–31; death of, 34; mentioned, 113, 214
Kamehameha II (Liholiho): son of Keopuolani, 29–30, 34; ended taboo, 35–

Kamehameha II (Liholiho) (*Cont.*) 37; and missionaries, 38; death of, 41; mentioned, 49, 113, 214

Kamehameha III (Kauikeaouli): and Nahienaena, 37, 41–42, 49–51; and Bingham, 45–47; and democracy, 51–54, 55, 57; and liquor laws, 53; and tripartite treaty, 53, 55; and foreigners, 54, 58; and attacks, 55–58, 62–64; and *mahele*, 59–61; death of, 61, 64–65; mentioned, 149, 212

Kamehameha IV (Alexander Liholiho), 46–47, 63–64, 66–71

Kamehameha V (Lot), 63, 68, 71–77, 90

Kamehameha Rifles, 96–97

Kamehameha Schools, 131. *See also* Bishop, Princess Bernice Pauahi

Kamuela (Waimea), 161

Kanaka (men), 24, 219

Kapiolani, Queen, 84, 115

Kapiolani Park, 96, 97

Ka poe kahiko, 12–13, 14, 32, 36, 84

Kapu. See Taboo

Kauai: and Captain Cook, 11, 16–19, 21; and Polynesians, 12; as chiefdom, 14, 26–27, 28, 35; and missionaries, 39; population, 42; and legislature, 55; and plantations, 69, 87, 121, 136; as county, 116; and organized labor, 141, 142–143, 150, 188; and tourism, 199; and stores, 206

Kauikeaouli. *See* Kamehameha III

Kaumualii (chief), 27, 28, 41

Kaumualii, George. *See* Sandwich, George

Kawaiahao Church: on Annexation Day, 7, 9, 110, 213; and Bingham, 48, 206; service of thanksgiving in, 57, 212

Kawano, Jack, 149, 186, 187, 192

Keapuolani (chiefess), 30, 34, 37, 41, 49

Keoni Ana (John Young II), 59

Kiawe (algarola tree), 45, 57, 206

Kibei, 151, 163–164

Kinau, 46–47, 63, 68

Kohala district: south coast, 15, 20, 206; king's home, 19, 214; in World War II, 161, 166; plantations on, 184; tourism on, 200

Kohala Sugar Co., 67, 207

Kokua: help freely given, 12–13, 215, 219; to foreigners, 36; to government, 53; to factions, 141, 211; future safety, 223

Koloa Plantation lease of 1835, 59

Kona district, 15, 20, 35, 142, 217

Koreans, 120, 122, 137, 208

Kuhina nui: Kaahumanu as, 34–35, 41–45; Kinau as, 46–47

Kuhio, Prince, 116, 135, 218

Labor. *See* Hawaii: labor

Ladd & Co., 51–52

Lahaina (Maui), 44, 50–51, 67, 127, 200

Lanai: in third chiefdom, 14, 24, 26; and sugar, 32; death toll on, 42; as exile colony, 47–48; and Mormons, 69, 71; in Maui County, 117; and pineapple, 143; mentioned, 17, 19

Land title. *See* Board of Commissioners to Quiet Land Title

Language (Hawaiian): words, 6–7, 12–14, 17, 219; spelling, 17, 44–45; pronunciation, 19, 29. *See also* Pidgin, Hawaiian

Liberty House, 135, 206

Liholiho. *See* Kamehameha II

Liholiho, Alexander. *See* Kamehameha IV

Liliuokalani: deposed as queen, 4, 6–7, 101, 102; and redress, 5, 108, 221; and counterrevolution, 97; reign of, 99–101; fight for restoration, 103–107; mentioned, 116, 213

Liquor laws, 47, 53

Lot Kamehameha (Kamehameha V), 63, 68, 71–77, 90

Lunalilo, William Charles: elected king, 80–81

Magna Charta of Hawaii, 52

Maheli, the Great, 59, 60–61, 68, 107, 221

Makaainana (commoners): tax from, 12, 43; serfdom of, 14; and sandalwood, 27–28; taboo and, 32–33, 35, 36; and Ladd & Co., 51–52; oppose constitution, 53–54; oppose foreigners in government, 58; and land, 59, 61; and Kamehameha V, 72; Battle of Hilo Docks, 149–150; in 1958, 198

Makahiki (time of peace), 14, 19, 20

Malihini (newcomers), 182, 219, 222

Mana (basic spiritual essence), 12, 27, 36–37, 49, 219

Manlapit, Pablo (union leader), 136–138, 140, 141–143

Marin, Don Francisco Paulo de, 26, 31, 41

Maui: today, 4, 217, 220; government of, 14, 15, 23–26, 55, 117; and Captain Cook, 19; and Chinese, 25; death toll on, 42; beaches of, 54; ranches and plantations, 60, 70, 86, 136; and labor, 127

McCandless, Lincoln (Democrat), 115, 215

Metzger, Delbert: war veteran, 109; and Democrats, 115; and labor, 143; as federal judge, 164, 174, 176–180, 182, 192–194; mentioned, 215

Missionaries, 37–48, 50–51, 53, 66–68, 80

Molokai: and planters, 7; government of, 14, 24, 26, 55, 117; death rate, 42; lepers on, 96; today, 205, 206, 218

Molokans, 120

Mormons, 69, 71, 205–206

Nahienaena, 37, 42, 49–51, 88

National Guard, 139, 143, 160, 167–168, 221–222

Niihau: geography of, 14; and British, 21; and education, 44, 72, 214; purchase of, 74; and World War II, 165, 169; and statehood, 202–203; in 1970s, 214, 215

Nisei: citizenship of, 122, 152–153; and democratic ideals, 132; and World War II, 153, 154, 160–162, 166–168, 173–174; in Korean war, 192; and politics, 184–185; new middle class, 198. *See also* Japanese

Oahu: today, 4; and British, 11, 19, 21; geography, 14, 25–26, 39–40, 54, 79–80, 136; government of, 23–24, 26, 30, 55, 84, 116–117; death toll on, 42, 67, 138; plantations on, 70; railroads on, 75; and war, 109, 158, 170; Korean school, 122; and labor, 126, 129, 137; and military, 130, 139; changes to, 199, 200, 203–204. *See also* Honolulu

Okinawans, 122

One Hundredth Battalion, 168, 173–174, 176–177, 180, 181

Organic Act of 1845, 112, 127, 159, 181

Orthography, standard, 44–45

Our Lady of Peace Cathedral, 45, 206

Palmyra Island, 116–117, 201

Parker Ranch, 60, 61, 161, 217

Pauahi, Princess Bernice. *See* Bishop, Princess Bernice Pauahi; Bernice P. Bishop Museum

Paulet, Lord George, 55–57

Pearl Harbor: U.S. use of, 6, 81, 109; report on, 82; and reciprocity treaty, 84–85, 96, 98; prime target, 154, 158–160

Pidgin, Hawaiian, 69. *See also* Language

Plantations: conditions on, 16, 67, 86–87, 120–121, 124, 126, 151–153; sugar, 82; rice, 84; plantation colonialism, 89, 120; pineapple, 136, 163; exodus from, 184

Polynesian Cultural Center, 205–206

Polynesians, 3–4, 11–22, 36

Portuguese, 32, 79, 92–93, 118, 213

Prostitution: city-controlled, 131, 142; in World War II, 163, 169, 179–180; after World War II, 183, 204

Puerto Ricans, 120, 136, 198

Punchou School, 60, 131, 215

Reciprocity Treaty, 82, 84, 85–86

Reform party, 4–7, 94–96, 99, 103, 115

Republicans: in 1900, 115; and Big Five, 148; in World War II, 173–175; ILWU backing, 187; and Communists, 187, 189; in 1954, 195; in 1970s, 215–216

Rice. *See* Hawaii: economy

Richards, William: and Nahienaena, 50; teachings of, 50, 51, 66, 67, 88, 149; in government, 54–55, 57, 59; death of, 62

Rooke, Emma. *See* Emma, Queen

Roosevelt, Franklin D. (president), 146–147, 165, 175–176, 179

Russians, 10, 23, 28, 29–30, 120

Rutledge, Art (organizer), 152, 185, 195

St. Andrew's Priory (school), 131

St. Louis College, 131

Samoa, 44, 134

Samoans, 198, 205, 209

Sandalwood, 27–28, 37–39, 43

Sand Island, 161, 164, 174, 202

Sandwich, George, 31, 37, 39

Sandwich Islands, 19, 26, 29, 30, 33

Sansei, 205, 220

Scheffer, Georg Anton, 28

Scotch, 18, 32

Seifert. *See* Glockner and Seifert

Shoemaker, James (labor investigator), 152–153, 183
Short, Walter C. (general), 156–157, 159, 183
Spanish, 23, 26, 111, 120
Spanish-American War, 6, 108–109
Spreckels, Claus (merchant), 86, 90–91
Stainback, Ingram (governor), 187–189, 201
Sun Yat-sen: and China, 8, 109, 122; Hawaiian influence on, 88, 104, 107

Taboo: and gods, 12, 17–18, 20–21, 24; and animals, 17, 32; dietary, 18–19, 30, 31, 32; and chiefs, 29–30; still intact, 31, 32–33; ended, 35–36; of missionaries, 41–42, 46–47, 49, 54
Tan Heung Shan (Fragrant Mountains), 27
Taro (kalo), 12
Theo Davies and Co., 130
Thurston, Lorrin, 100, 101–102
Tripartite treaty, 53, 55, 62, 64
Tsutsumi, Takashu, 137, 138

Unitarians, 205

United Public Workers Union (UPW), 128, 185, 207

Varsity Victory Volunteers, 167, 171, 173

Wahine, 18, 22, 24–25, 219
Waikiki, 99, 133, 144, 204–205. *See also* Honolulu
Waimea. *See* Kamuela
Waimea Bay, 11, 16, 21
Washington Place, 6–7, 103, 107, 157, 213
Whaling, 39, 68
Wilcox, Robert, 96–97, 115–116
Wilson, John, 106, 193
Women, status of: taboos, 9–10; chiefesses, 16, 17, 43; taxes, 24; in government, 30, 207; church membership, 43
World War I, 135, 136
World War II, 153–156, 159–179
Wyllie, Robert Crichton, 58–59, 63, 64, 70, 73

Yonsei, 205, 220
Young, John (hoale chief), 25, 28, 31, 70
Young, John II, 59